W9-CND-938

THE SURPRISING DESIGN OF MARKET ECONOMIES

CONSTRUCTS

The Constructs Series examines the ways in which the things we make change both our world and how we understand it. Authors in the series explore the constructive nature of the human artifact and the imagination and reflection that bring it into being.

SERIES EDITORS
H. Randolph Swearer
Vivian Sobchack
Robert Mugerauer

THE SURPRISING DESIGN
OF MARKET ECONOMIES

BY ALEX MARSHALL

UNIVERSITY OF TEXAS PRESS *Austin*

Requests for permission to reproduce material from this work
should be sent to:
    Permissions
    University of Texas Press
    P.O. Box 7819
    Austin, TX 78713-7819
    www.utexas.edu/utpress/about/bpermission.html

⊗ The paper used in this book meets the minimum requirements of
ANSI/NISO Z39.48-1992 (R1997) (Permanence of Paper).

LIBRARY OF CONGRESS CATALOGING-IN-PUBLICATION DATA

Marshall, Alex, 1959–
The surprising design of market economies / by Alex Marshall. — 1st ed.
        p.   cm. — (Constructs)
Includes bibliographical references and index.
ISBN 978-0-292-71777-0 (cloth : alk. paper) — ISBN 978-0-292-73918-5 (e-book)
1. Economics.   2. Capitalism.   3. Free trade.   4. Markets.   I. Title.
HB171.M333   2012
330.12′2—dc23   2012007467

TO KRISTIN BARLOW, FOR HER ENCOURAGEMENT,
SUPPORT, AND EDITING; AND TO BOB, FOR HIS CONVERSATION

CONTENTS

THE DESIGNER DISAPPEARS:
MARKETS AND THEIR MAKERS

When any great design thou dost intend,
Think on the means, the manner, and the end.
SIR JOHN DENHAM, "OF PRUDENCE," 1688

When you're building your own creation,
Nothing's better than real than a real imitation.
AIMEE MANN, "FRANKENSTEIN," 1996

NOT FAR FROM MY APARTMENT here in Brooklyn lies the lovely Prospect Park, almost six hundred acres of spacious meadows surrounded by rolling, forested hills and lakes and ponds. Just steps away from the busy, crowded streets of the city, you enter via one of two curving, arched tunnels at Grand Army Plaza. Walking toward the light at the end of either tunnel, you exit to find yourself in an enormous meadow surrounded by rolling hills carpeted with thick trees. As you wander around this veritable Eden, with waterfalls and winding lakes and hopping squirrels and twitting birds, you think how wise it was of the city fathers way back when to leave this piece of unspoiled nature as a beating, primal heart in the middle of this dense city of millions of people.

And then, if you have some knowledge of urban history, you realize that this story you've told yourself is completely false. What's hard to accept about this beautiful landscape, even after one learns its history, is that it is completely human-made and -maintained. City fathers didn't just leave nature as is, they constructed it. They hired Frederick Law Olmsted and Calvert Vaux, who designed Prospect Park in the 1860s a few years after they designed the similarly naturalistic Central Park. Crews following Olmsted and Vaux's plans pushed hills into place, cleared trees, and even brought lakes and ponds into being where none existed. For the lakes they scooped out earth and then painted the bottom with blue clay, brought in by barge from upstate New York, so the water would not just drain into the ground.

Once in place, the grand park then had to be maintained, as it does now. The trees need trimming, the grass cutting, and the waterways kept clear of debris—and supplied with water. The placid lakes and burbling streams are linked up to the city's water system, the same one that supplies the city with drinking water. One of those beautiful waterfalls you gaze at actually is fed by a pipe and is the water source for all the lakes and streams in the park. This beautiful park is actually "one gigantic potted plant,"[1] completely dependent on care and feeding by humans.

I'm beginning this book with Prospect Park because it's a wonderful analogy for economic markets.[2] Parks constructed in the naturalistic style pioneered by Olmsted and Vaux *appear* natural. If Prospect and Central Parks, as well as the Emerald Necklace around Boston and the dozens of other naturalistic parks designed by Olmsted around this country, had instead been created in the geometric, formal style favored by the French, on display in the Luxembourg Gardens in Paris, then there would be no doubt who created these works. But the great strength of Olmsted and Vaux's craft is its tomfoolery.

Similarly, markets, well-designed ones, *appear* natural. They *appear* as if they run themselves. They *appear* as if they just are. But in actuality, markets are human creations, some of our best and most important ones, but creations all the same. But if we forget that we are the creators, we risk seeing these worlds become corroded and corrupted. That's what happened to Prospect Park in the 1970s and 1980s as the city stopped maintaining it. Streams silted up, waterfalls stopped running, and weeds choked meadows. Without care, Prospect Park stopped functioning.

I would like to start a new conversation, a public conversation. Typically in public discourse, we talk about markets as if the only choices are to submit to them, to regulate them, or to run from them. But we have forgotten that markets *are* designed, by us! We shape them as much as we do a presidential race, or any important public choice.

Most of us don't know this, and even if we do, we forget. "It's not just laypeople who don't get this," said Gerald Frug, a Harvard law professor who studies local government, cities, and corporations. "A lot of people in a lot of disciplines, you have to tell them and then retell them. You tell them in the morning and by the evening they've forgotten."[3]

THE WALLS WE BUILD

My background as a journalist who has written a lot about urban planning and architecture explains why I find it empowering to think about "designing" markets. The word calls to mind a human hand and rids us of the idea that markets simply are. The term also can prompt humility, because we realize what a debt we owe to our forefathers who have labored to create the complex markets we take for granted. Whether this book is primarily liberal or conservative in its political outlook is debatable. What is true is that writing it has given me even deeper respect for what came before, for the work of our ancestors.

If we follow this metaphor of design, then we can come to its components, which are structures. For some time I've been concerned with structures, the walls we build that both constrain us and shape us, as societies. I see markets that way, as human-made structures that in turn shape and make possible human behavior. We shape our markets, and our markets shape us, to adapt Winston Churchill's remark about buildings. This of course contrasts with the view of "free," or "open," markets, which sees markets as defined by a lack of restraints. This view of markets is incorrect. Without structures, there are no markets. In this book, I look at types of structures that build markets, as well as the consequences and effects of those structures. Here are the types of structures I look at.

I look at legal structures, that is, the laws we pass as cities, states, and nations. The most basic of these are laws creating the opportunity to own something, or property "rights," to use the common, if misleading, term. Laws allow us to create patents, corporations, cooperatives, and a range of types of markets that I will examine. These are the most basic foundation of markets.

I look at physical structures, including roads, bridges, train lines, water systems, and power lines. The current term for such things is "infrastructure." Infrastructure systems support and establish markets. Because they come, in a sense, before a market, actions by government are usually necessary to establish infrastructure systems. It was the study of infrastructure, in particular transportation systems, that first led me into thinking about markets. The subject of infrastructure still fascinates me, because it relates to something dear to my heart, community. Infrastructure is a sterile label for the things we do in common, as communities of towns, cities, states, nations, and even the globe. In this book, I'll look at some of the infrastructure systems we have built and how they relate to markets.

I look at the mental, or cultural, structures, the ones we have inside our heads, and the role government has in building them. These are a fascinating arena. Nations cultivate and create common languages and bodies of knowledge, which in turn make the functioning of markets, among other things, easier. The cultural realm is destabilizing to a person's preconceptions, because as one studies it one realizes that government has long been an actor in the most intimate terrain one has, one's mind. This is a vast subject, and I only touch the surface of it in a chapter on the creation of a national language and educational system.

I look at the international structures, those we build between and among nations, which make possible global trade. These international structures encompass all three of the domains I have just named, legal, physical, and cultural. As is obvious when one looks into it, government-made legal and physical infrastructure in particular— from international law itself, to undersea communication cables, to satellites over our heads—makes possible the torrents of goods, services, cash, and bits and bytes that stream around the world now. The flat earth depicted by *New York Times* columnist Thomas Friedman is no force of nature, but one we have constructed.

Throughout these discussions, I look at the effects of markets and some of the overarching themes that can be drawn from their design. I look at the role of the state, the phenomenon of "path dependence," and other things. I look at the history of markets, including how it came to pass that serious thinkers made the error of conceiving of markets as akin to natural systems that operate by themselves. And I look to the future.

Some might counter that I am talking about more than markets. The language that we learn, the education we receive, and laws against hitting your neighbor in the head are not just about constructing *Homo economicus*, able to go out and buy and sell things, and to receive a wage for his labor. Which is, of course, true. Most of the structures I talk about in this book are not only about markets. But they are vital to them, and I believe often would not be put into place without their contributions to markets. And it's always "markets," plural, by the way. There is no such thing as "the market."

Another false construct relates to competition. We think of markets and capitalism as embodying competition, but markets depend more fundamentally on cooperation. In essence, we cooperate to compete. We agree on some underlying premises, such as not using violence; respecting contracts, patents, or whatever legal agreement has been made; and competing in a more limited sphere.

THE GREAT RECESSION

Starting with the bankruptcy of the Lehman Brothers financial services firm in September 2008, the United States and then Western Europe entered what some are now calling "The Great Recession." Based on a financial bubble around housing prices and the mortgages associated with them, which included various and extreme sub-bubbles around financial devices such as "credit default swaps" and other esoteric tools, this Great Recession led to, most concretely, the loss of jobs for millions of people. It also led to the evaporation of billions, if not trillions, of dollars in wealth, and the bankruptcy of banks and other entities, including at least one entire country, Iceland.

These events underscore the constructed nature of markets, as well as their vulnerabilities to corruption from faulty ideology and venal selfishness. The faulty construct that government could "get out of the way" and that markets could then expand in an unencumbered way helped create the Great Bubble that preceded the Great Recession. Markets operate within frameworks created by government. They are not something that government "gets out of the way of."

One improbable result of the Great Recession, which has not really ended at the time of this writing, is that it appears to have strengthened populist movements to let "the market" operate on its own, unchecked. Serious academics who backed the existence and merits of a "free market," such as those freshwater Chicago school economists around Lake Michigan, found their position seriously weakened. Many admitted they needed to rethink their views. Judge Richard Posner, who although not an economist had been a spokesman for this school of thought, essentially admitted he was wrong.[4] But populist movements that advocate less government regulation and the power of the free market seem stronger than ever. This is evidence of how contagious the belief system of the natural free market is, where all events become evidence of it, even ones that contradict its very existence.

WHAT THIS BOOK IS NOT ABOUT

This book is not about regulating markets, or the "regulatory sphere," as it is commonly called. I have nothing against the Federal Trade Commission, the Food and Drug Administration, the Occupational Safety and Health Administration, the Federal Communications Commission, the Securities and Exchange Commission, the Environmental Protection Agency, and so on. They for the most part do good and important work. But they get in the way of the conversation I'm trying to have. I'm talking about *designing* markets, not regulating them. The metaphor, or model, of regulating markets presupposes that the market being regulated is somehow there already, waiting to be regulated. I'm saying and showing how this is not so. We designed the markets, before we started regulating them.

Corporations are a good example of this. The political Right and Left debate endlessly how much to regulate corporations, or whether to "let them go," to unleash them, without noticing or talking about the fact that the corporation is a government creation. Governments create corporations. If we really wanted to alter corporations, we should tinker with their essential DNA, the laws that make it possible to create corporations and grant them a specific set of expansive powers. We could create, for example, a National Companies Act, rather than leave it to states, mostly the state of Delaware, to define how corporations act. More about this later.

This book is not about the establishment of a cap-and-trade system to control the output of carbon, even though almost no better example exists of the invention and creation of a market, one being born as you read this.

This book's mission is to provide a broad overview of how a market economy is constructed, of the various components and how they came to be. My hope is that this book, rather than prompting any specific reform, will stimulate a conversation about the design of markets, so we can create ones that are fairer, more prosperous, more creative, and more beautiful.

ON THE BOOKS: THE MARKETS WE MAKE BY LAW

CHAPTER I

COMING INTO BEING: IN PRAISE OF MARKETS

Their wanderings through the almost limitless building were interminable; they would set off as if for some unknown land, and unknown indeed it was because in many of those apartments and corners not even Don Fabrizio had ever set foot (a cause of great satisfaction to him, for he used to say that a palace of which one knew every room wasn't worth living in).
GIUSEPPE TOMASI DI LAMPEDUSA, *THE LEOPARD*, 1958

MARKETS ARE A WONDERFUL THING, I thought, as I cruised the aisles of this supermarket on Sharon Amity Road in Charlotte, North Carolina. One aisle had probably ten different kinds of tortillas. Compare Foods, which was the name of the large supermarket, had different kinds of dried beans in big bins that people could go through with their hands, and numerous bins of different types of dried chili peppers, all arrayed in their various colors and sizes. This was in addition to all the usual supermarket stuff, like Rice Krispies and Pampers.

Charlotte, formerly one of the whitest of white-bread cities, has had its Latino population swell from insignificant to more than 10 percent of the population in just a decade or so. These immigrants were brought in by the city's burgeoning economy, including its enormous banking sector, which had fueled the city's rise to prominence. Charlotte was home, as of this writing, to the corporate headquarters of Bank of America, one of the largest banks in the country. (The financial crisis of 2008 weakened Charlotte as a banking center. One of its twin powerhouses, Wachovia, was facing bankruptcy in 2008 and was acquired by Wells Fargo with government assistance. Charlotte's other big bank, Bank of America, kept in the game but was viewed by many as seriously weakened because of its exposure in home mortgages.) The immigrants weren't brought in to work in the banks, for the most part, but bankers need computer programmers and computer programmers need houses built for them and construction crews like cheap, skilled labor—you get the idea.

The presence of these brown-skinned immigrants, many of whom did not speak English well and were here illegally, had not gone down easy in this city traditionally dominated by white Protestants. While employers liked the cheap labor, the city's African American population saw competitors that brought down wages. Many people, particularly conservative Republicans, disliked the presence of tens of thousands of people openly flouting the law, and the law openly ignoring them, essentially. All big and serious issues.

All this meant nothing to "the market." If you were working on a construction crew in Charlotte, and wanted a particular kind of tortilla and bean and chili pepper, there was a good chance you could find it at Compare Foods, which was not a specialized Latino market, but just a regular supermarket in an area that happened to have a lot of Latinos. As if by magic, the goods materialized. Suppliers found a way to deliver them to this supermarket, which found a way to find the suppliers. It was amazing, I thought to myself. Supply and demand did its job.

There are various analogies for "the market," or "markets," as I prefer. In the Introduction to this book, I compared markets to great parks that are so well designed the designer disappears. Bruce Scott, a professor at Harvard Business School, compares markets to professional sports, where official bodies decide where the lines are on a field or court, what the official ball size is, and what the rules are, and then stand back and let the players compete, while penalizing those that break the invented rules.[1] In common language, we talk about "the market" for dating in a particular city, or for playing bridge. This is fine. It's when the market entails buying and selling for a price that the designer, usually government, enters.

The kind of market I'm seeing here in Charlotte is your classic open market that appears to operate free of controls or supports. But of course that's not true at all. This market did not build the roads outside Compare Foods that allow its customers to travel there. It did not hire the police who arrest people who steal some of those tortillas or the cash from the register. It did not create the various laws that make it possible for people to "own" things, even a stack of tortillas. The plant grows, but only in the container we provide. And I don't want to even get into the regulatory apparatus that creates things like the Food and Drug Administration, which keeps the food safe or requires sellers to disclose the ingredients in something. (In a different chapter I discuss the difference between designing markets and regulating them.)

Accepting all this, we can also accept that it does its job very well, this market for Latin foods inside this formerly white, Protestant city. But it should be seen for what it is. My point here is that there is no abstract "market" that will solve all our problems for us, and work without the help of human hands. Markets, even the most open ones, are tools, designed by human hands. Conventional "open" markets are great and have their uses. But they also have their limitations, and they should be recognized as the constructed things they are. It is this open, or free, market that so many people have fallen in love with, and which does not exist. In this chapter, I rip the tissue paper off this surface appearance of markets and reveal the hardware underneath. I also look at how this appealing but misguided notion of a self-operating market developed within the emerging discipline of economics in the nineteenth and twentieth centuries. In the end, I want us to acknowledge that there is not just one market, but many, countless really, beyond the ability to number, yet all constructed by human hands and minds.

A HISTORY OF MARKETS

Markets, in the sense of both a place for buying and selling and the activity itself of buying and selling, began about five thousand years ago, said Keith Roberts in his *The Origins of Business, Money and Markets*. Initially, trading was slight. Goods were exchanged through barter, through "gift economies," or by edict of powerful central states, as under the masters of the Persian empire, who had great wealth, but there was little trade in conventional terms. Developing true markets involved mastering a series of conceptual challenges over centuries.[2]

As with so much of our society's heritage, it was in ancient Athens that modern markets began to emerge, under the leadership of the state. Among the most significant developments was coinage. This was as much a conceptual challenge as a feat of production, because money as an idea and tool is not immediately obvious. People had often traded things for gold or silver, but that is different than accepting a piece of gold or silver, eventually a coin, when making a trade, regardless of whether one personally needed gold or silver. Money is such a convenient tool because it can be used to buy anything. The Athenians grasped this quickly. Using silver from mines it controlled, the Athenian state began producing the famous four-drachma piece, often called "the owl" because one side of the silver coin was stamped with that large-eyed bird, which was the symbol of the goddess Athena, the patron saint of Athens. It became the coinage of the ancient realm, accepted all over the Greek world and beyond.[3]

After Athens lost leadership of the ancient world, markets and the development of business practices moved to ancient Rome, which, along with its empire, developed what could rightfully be called a global economy, insofar as the term refers to the portion of the globe Rome controlled. This global economy would wax and wane with the Roman empire, and it would eventually collapse with Rome. What's important to understand for my purposes is that trade only happens within the framework of a state. As nations collapsed into feudal fiefdoms, most trade did as well, and markets in a contemporary sense vanished. As nations and states emerged in the Renaissance and Enlightenment periods, so again did markets, with their specifics put in place by the controlling powers.

THE CITY MARKET: FROM THE RIALTO TO PIKE PLACE

Whether markets were global or merely local, a key question was where they would take place, because exchanges needed to take place in a physical location. This location was usually chosen and operated by the state.

In medieval times, the Crown usually sponsored and carefully controlled the colorful fairs—highlighted in fairy tales and Arthurian legends—where goods were sold and jousts were held.[4] "In the four principal cities of Champagne six fairs were held, each of which lasted for 50 days, including the business of arranging and opening the fair," said Max Weber in his *General Economic History*. Fairs reached their greatest development in size and importance in the thirteenth and fourteenth centuries, he said.[5] In Venice traders still gather in several ancient public buildings near the Rialto Bridge, where they have been gathering for more than a millennium.

Most cities of any age have had their version of "the city market," cavernous and often physically grand buildings of iron, stone, or wood where sellers of meat, fish, dairy goods, and produce would congregate in stalls and sell their wares. Such markets were usually built by the city and leased out to agricultural producers and other vendors. Cities used to compete to see which had the grandest city market building, the same way cities now compete with football stadiums.

These markets still survive in some cities. In Barcelona vendors sell blood sausage, Manchego cheese, fish, and produce under a huge roof right off Las Ramblas, the grand promenade through the heart of the city. In Seattle, Pike Place Market, a rabbit warren of stalls set into a cliff overlooking the Puget Sound and a brutal elevated freeway, still survives, and not just as a tourist trap. It remains a place for local farmers to sell produce, even though restaurants and other vendors are in the mix, because there is a commission that oversees the market and must approve vendors. The first written goal of the commission is that the market be "A place for farmers to sell their own produce."[6] Rules such as these have been common in city markets, even at their inception.

When you're buying some eggs from a vendor housed in a building constructed and owned by the city you live in, it's clear that government has something to do with markets. But as markets have become less physical, and as the thread between government and markets has become longer, it becomes easier to forget government's involvement in markets.

ECONOMICS AS A SCIENCE: A USEFUL METAPHOR OR BLIND ALLEY?

As trade increased in the seventeenth and eighteenth centuries, the idea of the "free market" emerged as a reaction against the mercantilist economies of the time. It was a useful idea, but it was taken too far, a process that began in the early to mid-nineteenth century. It is worth understanding how this happened. Essentially, leaders in the new field of "economics" attempted, in an act of hubris, to pass off their brainchild as being on par with the great physical sciences that were emerging then as well. Implicit in the comparison was a faulty metaphor, but one that lasted.

In 1969, the Royal Swedish Academy of Science began awarding what is usually referred to as the Nobel Prize in Economics, the first addition to the ones for physics, chemistry, medicine, literature, and peace created by Alfred Nobel in 1895. Although the award was technically placed in a different category than the other prizes, its creation was seen as validation for a century-long quest by economists to have economics considered a science, just like physics and chemistry.

The story of how economics moved from something that was seen as part of political or moral philosophy, which is to say thinking about how the world should work, to a science, which looks at how the world does work, is a tragic one.

Science explains, and explanations provide both light and power. The periodic table of chemical elements enables someone to create both Bakelite and Viagra. The theory of relativity helped produce the atom bomb. What if we could understand human behavior in a similar way? Particularly human behavior as related to wanting stuff, to buying and selling things? Wouldn't such understanding give us tools of unimaginable power, to help us organize and channel human behavior in ways that would correspond with these newly discovered laws?

This is my sense of the thinking of the great eighteenth- and nineteenth-century thinkers who did this work. These great men (and they were largely men) were laboring in the shadow of the revolutions in math, physics, and chemistry of those times. (It is relevant that Sigmund Freud and others would soon attempt to create a similar science of the mind, except dealing more with emotions and desires.) These early economists wanted economics to come up with laws that resembled the laws of gravity or thermodynamics, and had similar explanatory power. Nassim Taleb, author of *The Black Swan*, in speaking about economists a century and a half later, called their ambition "physics envy."[7]

FROM SMITH TO MARSHALL

When Adam Smith in 1776 published *The Wealth of Nations*, a book that is a bible of sorts to economists, he viewed himself as a moral philosopher, not a scientist or an economist. But he could be said to have planted the seeds of viewing economics as a science with his descriptions of the division of labor among factory workers making pins, and derivation of insights from those workings that might be compared to principles or laws.

Smith, at least in the English-speaking world, invented the idea of the modern market, where people enter, buy and sell stuff, and leave everyone better off. Writing in an age of mercantilism, when so many aspects of trade were tightly controlled, this idea had great merit. What Smith didn't see as clearly was that government put into effect the rules that created this place of neutral exchange. He also didn't note that neutral exchange is not always for the best, nor that producers sometimes need the rules stacked in their favor, so they can make quality better and pay better wages. Underdeveloped countries sometimes need the rules stacked in their favor so they can get a head start. But whatever the specifics, Smith certainly did not see economics as a science. And he talked mostly about how things were produced under markets, less about distribution, the part that has so fascinated modern economists.

Leon Walras, a French mathematician, is generally credited with coming up with the general theory of equilibrium in economics, which is that supply and demand tend to balance each other out and come to rest at a point of equilibrium. In the fascinating book *The Origin of Wealth: Evolution, Complexity and the Radical Remaking of Economics*, Eric Beinhocker tells how Walras actually borrowed these concepts wholesale from an 1803 physics textbook to come up with the equations and theories in his seminal work in the 1870s, *Elements of Pure Economics*. Apparently, Walras had an "aha!" moment when he conceived of the idea that human beings and their desires may work in ways similar to falling bodies or other phenomena in physics.

"In building his equilibrium model, Walras put to one side the production half of the economy and focused on trading between consumers," said Beinhocker.

> In his model, he assumed that various goods already exist in the economy and the problem is to determine how prices are set and how the goods would be allocated among the individuals involved. . . . Walras's willingness to make trade-offs in realism for the sake of mathematical predictability would set a pattern followed by economists over the next century.
>
> An important reason for this focus on allocation of finite resources was that mathematical equations of equilibrium imported from physics were ideal for answering the allocation question, but it was more difficult to apply them to growth. Equilibrium systems by definition are in a state of rest, while growth implies change and dynamism.[8]

Walras even lifted the phrasing from one chapter in the physics book that was entitled "On Conditions of Equilibrium Expressed by Means of Equations." While Adam Smith had focused on how goods were produced and best practices associated with that, Walras began a shift toward the distribution of goods and how markets "cleared" that would be continued into the present day.

After Walras, the scientification of what soon would be called economics continued apace. A big step was the publishing in 1890 of *Principles of Economics* by the Cambridge professor of political economy (*emphasis mine*) Alfred Marshall, considered by many to be the father of mainstream economics. Marshall consciously opted to not call his book, which was brilliant in many respects, *Principles of Political Economy*. It was part of his effort to make economics more of a science, and to disassociate it from the messy world of men and their decisions. By dropping the term "political economy," Marshall was leaving behind the governmental and political decisions and acts that produce markets and economies. He wanted to depoliticize economics, which, given that economies are political creations, is kind of like depoliticizing politics. But amazingly, the name change worked. In a generation or two, the term "political economy" would be relegated to the backwaters of universities.[9]

"Marshall clearly understood the stakes in the new terminology," said Michael Perelman, who summed up this evolution of economics in *The End of Economics*. Marshall saw the change in terminology as helping economics become "an objective science, capable of representing the interests of society as a whole." Not only could the new profession of economics claim to practice science, but economists could, like physicists or chemists, claim to be above or outside of politics and its choices.

Like Walras, Marshall continued the shift of economics away from analyzing how production works to how exchange works.

"This new emphasis on the mathematical modeling of exchange had several appeals," said Perelman.

> By stressing the formal mathematics of exchange relationships, economists could take a more scientific posture. Although political economists could hardly pretend to have a monopoly on the analysis of production, no other discipline could claim to be a science of exchange. Moreover, an analysis of the economy from the perspective of exchange was relatively effective in obscuring conflict. Both parties must benefit from voluntary exchange; otherwise the exchanging would never have occurred in the first place.[10]

Here's one way to look at markets that may cut through this science-or-not question. While mating is a specific instinctual act and thus amenable to being described through the science of biology, marriage is a human institution. So with markets. While wanting stuff may be elemental, buying and selling as organized, mostly peaceful transactions take place only through a process and within a framework constructed by government. Any "laws" about how markets operate need to take this into consideration.

AN APPEALING STORY

In the twentieth century this conversion of political economy into the science of economics continued apace, as well as efforts to turn other disciplines into sciences. The twentieth century opened with Sigmund Freud and others working to come up with laws as to the way individual humans worked, which would be called psychology. John Dewey and others were creating other "social sciences" in the fields of education and anthropology. Urban design, which dealt primarily with streets and buildings and water lines, was giving way to urban planning, which dealt with numbers and regulations. There was a sense that science could help humankind leave behind many of its troubles. Economics would not be left out.

Although different schools of thought developed, most focused more on exchange than production and continued this analogy of human beings working similarly to natural systems. John Maynard Keynes in the 1930s helped counter this trend with his *General Theory of Employment, Interest and Money*, which asserted that labor markets do not always stabilize at near zero unemployment, and that government intervention is sometimes necessary to prime the pump of demand. In this, he was arguing against his old teacher, Alfred Marshall. Despite the strength and commanding influence of Keynes's work, neoclassical economists would wage a fifty-year rearguard action against Keynes. Even those who praised Keynes sought to cast his views as part of economics as science. Paul Samuelson, in his influential textbook *Economics: An Introductory Analysis*, helped mathematize Keynes, which would give the illusion of certainty and glow of science to Keynes's work that Keynes himself would have probably rejected. Nassim Taleb in *The Black Swan* said Samuelson is an example of "badly invested intelligence," as he converted Keynes's useful uncertainties into precise but erroneous equations.[11]

I don't want to pretend that economics as a discipline has accomplished nothing in its two centuries or so of existence, despite its misplaced classification as a science. It took a Great Depression and a Second World War, but there is knowledge now that if an economy falters, you lower interest rates and expand the money supply through a central bank.

This knowledge did not come cheap. Often it took rebels like Keynes, or politicians acting on their own, to work out these principles. President Franklin Roosevelt abandoned the gold standard in 1933, something that immensely helped the country, against the advice of virtually every expert. It is revealing to read still-well-regarded economists like Joseph Schumpeter, whose only advice to government during the Great Depression was to do nothing.

As important as these things are, though, economics as a discipline would do well to spend more time and energy thinking about how markets could be constructed, and what purposes they can serve. Economics should be about more than questions of deficit spending, interest rate hikes, money supply, and so forth. Lewis Mumford, the great writer on urbanism, asked, "What is transportation for?"[12] The same question should be posed about production and economics. What is an economy for? What are markets for? To realize that markets are our ongoing creation is then to ask, "Why and for whom?"

We could think of markets, rather than as just a way of creating wealth, as playing fields that we create for varying purposes. We could design a copyright system, for example, to encourage experimentation and creativity, as well as compensate creators. We could design a property rights system in ways that enrich the society, as well as the property "owners." We could design corporations in ways that further business creativity and societal advancement. The possibilities are endless. Often only the free market ideologues concern themselves with the design of markets—although they probably wouldn't use this term—and they use their simplistic theory like a stick, whacking everything in sight to explain how it could be "marketized" further. There are more creative ways to design markets.

A DANGEROUS EUPHEMISM

The insidious thing about this term "the free market" is that nominal opponents of it accept its validity as a concept. Thus a carcinogenic idea is smuggled into the body politic.

If you were to open *The New Yorker* in October of 2008, you might have spotted a fancy ad occupying two pages that asked, "Does the Free Market Corrode Moral Character?" Under this heading, a variety of scholars, including Robert Reich, Bernard-Henri Lévy, Jadish Bhagwati,

Qinglian He, and John Gray, answered this question in various ways: yes, no, it depends, etc. Sponsored by the John Templeton Foundation, this was, I gathered, supposed to be an example of how you can have a civil conversation about a sensitive subject, thus leading to greater enlightenment.[13]

Actually, what it is is an example of how you can advance and solidify a concept by asking a question where the concept is an unexamined assumption. The question "Does the Free Market Corrode Moral Character?" assumes the "free market" as a given. It doesn't ask whether there is such a thing as a free market and, if so, what it is, or hold that concept up for examination. It simply assumes there is such a thing, and that we all know what it is.

If I were answering this question of the John Templeton Foundation, I would respond, "There is no free market. There are only markets, and government creates them. Markets are diverse in character and have different rules and boundaries. Whether a market corrupts or makes the world more moral depends on those rules and boundaries. A market where government establishes a price on Jews' heads obviously corrupts. A market that establishes a place to buy green beans does not. There are no 'free' markets, in any meaning of that word, whether free as in open, or free as in costless."

The term "the free market" is really a slogan masquerading as a neutral description. Neil Postman, in an essay in his book *Conscientious Objections*, suggests that rather than teaching people to be smart, it might be equally effective to teach people ways of not being stupid. He listed ten ways of being stupid. One of them was to use euphemisms, which, in Postman's words, are no problem if used as mild substitutes for unpleasant things. "But when euphemism becomes a dominating mode of expression in our institutional life, it is dangerous and ought not to be tolerated."[14] "Free market" is a euphemism, usually an unconscious one, which makes it more dangerous. But for what?

The word "free" in free market can have two meanings. The first is that a market is open and without rules or conditions. This meaning is demonstrably false, as I'll show over and over. You need rules to have markets. Second, there is the meaning of "free" as in without cost, meaning no one has to pay for it. This is also not true, because our economic system has great costs. Even the freest markets in the modern era depend on government-provided or -paid-for education and infrastructure, as well as functioning courts and so forth. Finally, there is the word "market" in its singular form. The phrase is usually "free market," not "free markets." This suggests that there is only one market, one huge open market, not many, constructed markets.

The financial panic that gripped the world in 2008 and 2009 helped shake the belief in markets as natural, or operating by themselves. Even though these mammoth financial markets were always clearly constructed things, there was still some belief that they could self-correct. John Lanchester wrote in *The New Yorker* in 2009, "This should be an enduring lesson of the crisis—an understanding that the rules governing the operating of markets were not handed down on stone tablets, but are made by men, and in constant need of revision, supervision, and active, imaginative enforcement."[15]

SOME PEOPLE GET IT

Despite the sloganeering and the investment in the concept of the self-operating free market, some people get that this just ain't the way things are.

John McMillan, in his book *Reinventing the Bazaar: A Natural History of Markets*, stated: "Faith is not needed. The 'hand' that guides the market may be invisible, but it is not actually supernatural. The market is not omnipotent, omnipresent, or omniscient. It is a human invention with human imperfections. It does not necessarily work well. It does not work by magic or, for that matter, by voodoo. It works through institutions, procedures, rules, and customs."[16]

While I like McMillan's thoughts above, I prefer to talk about "markets" in the plural, because for one thing, it suggests there are choices. I also like the word "design," because it states even more clearly that markets are our handiwork, and that we have choices in how we sculpt them.

As many have noted, the rise of a belief in the omnipresent, all-powerful market has coincided with the decline in belief in an omnipresent, all-powerful deity. To quote Lewis Mumford:

> The most fundamental of these postulates was a notion that the utilitarians had taken over, in apparent innocence, from the theologians: the belief that a divine providence ruled over economic activity and ensured, so long as man did not presumptuously interfere, the maximum public good through the dispersed and unregulated efforts of every private, self-seeking individual. The non-theological name for this pre-ordained harmony was laissez-faire.[17]

The late scholar and public intellectual Tony Judt, in an essay entitled "Captive Minds" written shortly before his death in 2010, made a similar observation, which is that the homage paid to the market can be similar to the Marxist Left's religion-like faith in Communism and its supposed laws and historical inevitability: "But 'the market'—like 'dialectical materialism'—is just an abstraction, at once ultra-rational (its argument trumps all) and the acme of unreason (it is not open to question)."[18]

Thom Hartmann, an author and commentator, gets it. One of his essays is worth quoting at length:

> The conservative belief in "free markets" is a bit like the Catholic Church's insistence that the Earth was at the center of the solar system in the 12th century. It's widely believed by those in power, those who challenge it are branded heretics and ridiculed, and it is wrong.
>
> In actual fact, there is no such thing as a "free market." Markets are the creation of government.
>
> Governments provide a stable currency to make markets possible. They provide a legal infrastructure and court systems to enforce the contracts that make markets possible. They provide educated workforces through public education, and those workers show up at their places of business after traveling on public roads, rails, or airways provided by government. Businesses that use the "free market" are protected by police and fire departments provided by government, and send their communications—from phone to fax to internet—over lines that follow public rights-of-way maintained and protected by government.
>
> And, most important, the rules of the game of business are defined by government. Any sports fan can tell you that football, baseball, or hockey without rules and referees would be a mess. Similarly, business without rules won't work. . . .
>
> Markets are a creation of government, just as corporations exist only by authorization of government. Governments set the rules of the market. And, since our government is of, by, and for We The People, those rules have historically been set to first maximize the public good resulting from people doing business.[19]

Roberto Unger, the Brazilian-born Harvard law professor and political advisor, gets it. And Jeffrey Sachs, a well-regarded economist, does not, or at least didn't use to. In the fall of 1999, while on a fellowship at Harvard University, I audited their class at the law school "One Way or Many?," which was a weekly debate between Unger and Sachs over the best way or ways for developing nations to progress. Sachs, then perhaps more of a free market purist, defended the "Washington consensus" that there was only "one way" for a developing nation to progress. The Washington consensus was that a country should open its markets, get rid of state controls, and embrace globalism. Unger maintained that there were "many ways" for a nation to progress, and the market itself was open to experimentation and tinkering.

"You can't succeed by imitating," said Unger in the November 8, 1999, class inside the semicircular lecture hall inside Austin Hall, a grand brick and stone building designed by H. H. Richardson as Harvard Law School's home. Unger said that growth and prosperity should be used for the self-expression of a people, both as a group and as individuals. The creative nature of capitalism should be recognized, not just for the individual, but also for the society that constructs the rules capitalism depends on.

During that same class I stood in the big lecture hall and asked a question. The two men had been discussing China, which even then was taking off in prosperity and growth. I asked Sachs: "Doesn't the success of China threaten the market model and the 'Washington consensus,' given that China has developed over the last 20 years without a judicial system, without private property rights, without free currency, and all sorts of stuff? Doesn't this mean there are many ways, rather than just one?"

"No," said Sachs, shaking his head, a well-built man with a head of nicely placed dark hair. The only reason China has been able to rise, he said, is that it started so far below. "When you start at a peasant level, it's easy to lift the hand of the state and see growth. These guys on the coast are making computer CDs and sneakers. It's easy."

"I disagree thoroughly," Unger said. "The questioner is right. With the market project, there is always an exception. Always an exception that proves the rule. In the United States, the US during World War II massively rebuilt the economy with cooperation between state and private enterprise. It lifted the country out of the Depression. But this was supposed to have been impossible. It's not about technology, it's about institutions, political and legal."[20]

This was an important exchange. Time has revealed that Unger was more correct than Sachs.[21] China's growth has not been driven by the lifting of the hand of the Chinese state, as Sachs said. The Chinese state has been directing growth, managing it, even micromanaging it, according to all reports. This management, which included setting exchange rates for the nation's currency and not allowing the free flow of capital, enabled China's leaders to avoid the financial crisis of 2008–2010, something they were quite smug about. Actually, China's state is so embedded into its version of capitalism that it's difficult to summarize.

"China is a seething cauldron of experimentation in the institutional invention of the market," said Unger, who has a mane of white hair and always seems preoccupied, in a later interview in his office in 2008. The United States was like this in the nineteenth century, he said.

What made Unger so good is that he caught the air of creativity and possibilities that can come into the design of markets.

"My driving argument is that the market does not create its own presuppositions," Unger said in 1999. "The world market depends on larger background conditions. We can't achieve stuff by simply 'signing up.' . . . The work of democracy and experimentation remains incomplete. We must apply to the market its own experimentalist medicine."

"A political economy," he said, "is not a perpetual motion machine."

CONCLUSION

Looking in the rearview mirror, it is easy to see that we can build market economies many different ways, using and inventing many different models. On the level of countries, the United States and European nations have built their markets on judicial supervision and private property, with huge variations within that simple principle. Japan, Korea, and other Asian nations have developed variations on those themes, with more overtly state-led components. China is developing its own model, one where the state plays a far more direct role, with the judiciary and private property playing a subordinate role. As we look to the future, what's important is recognizing that we as a democratic society have choices, and that we should talk about those choices. Our hands are on the steering wheel, more than we usually recognize.

CHAPTER 2

ME AND MINE: PROPERTY, THE FIRST MARKET

Private Property is a creature of society, and is subject to the calls of that society whenever its necessities require it, even to the last farthing.
BENJAMIN FRANKLIN, *QUERIES AND REMARKS RESPECTING ALTERATIONS IN THE CONSTITUTION OF PENNSYLVANIA*, 1789[1]

For it would be a direct contradiction for anyone to enter into a society with others for the securing and regulating of property, and yet to suppose his land, whose property is to be regulated by the laws of society, should be exempt from the jurisdiction of that government to which he himself, and the property of the land, is subject. JOHN LOCKE, *SECOND TREATISE ON GOVERNMENT*, 1689

WHEN I WAS A YOUNG NEWSPAPER REPORTER at *The Virginian-Pilot* in Norfolk, I used to walk around the basement of city hall and the circuit court. I would open up the big, dusty deed books, some going back several hundred years, which recorded who owned what. As I looked at these books near the fluted columns that supported the building, I realized I was looking at the literal foundations of capitalism. Those dusty books were its pillars.

Markets concern property, and so it's essential in markets that somebody or something be able to own something. And because you can only own something to the extent that you can prevent others from taking it from you, owning something—that is, property—is an invention and responsibility of the state. You need the state to prove you own something and to stop others from taking what you own. In this chapter, I look at some of the ways we have been able to own stuff, and how that relationship of possessed to possessor developed. In the design of markets, owning something is part of the core architecture, so it behooves us to understand that better.

What does my story about the musty record books in the municipal and circuit court building show? That property rights have political foundations. The only reason I own something, particularly something as conceptual as land (conceptual because you are making invisible lines on the earth and then defining it as "yours"), is because I can point to a public record, examinable by all, that says I do.

"Property is not protected by government because it is property; it is property because it is protected by government," say Nicholas Mercuro and Warren J. Samuels, editors of *The Fundamental Interrelationships between Government and Property*.[2]

But this isn't the usual rhetoric. Conservative politicians, from the most recent President George Bush to Margaret Thatcher in Britain, usually refer to the state as in opposition to property, note Michael Moran and Maurice Wright in the introduction to *The Market and the State*:

> The notion that "the market" and "the state" are two diametrically opposed systems of social organization is embedded in both the rhetoric of political actors and in the thinking of scholars.[3]

Or, as Mercuro and Samuels say:

> Property rights can be defined, mistakenly, as if they existed independently of the regulatory or police, and tax, powers of government, in which case the exercise of its regulatory or police and tax powers by government becomes a fundamental infringement on and loss of property rights. Alternatively, property rights can be defined so as to recognize and encompass the ongoing role of the regulatory or police and tax powers of government, in which case the exercise of those powers is a constituent part of the nature of property itself.[4]

Basically, property is whatever the state says it is. The state has set up systems for people to own land, people (as in slaves), objects, wives, children, and animals. It has sometimes put limitations on those rights. It was illegal in the United States, when slavery was legal, for an owner to kill a slave, even though the slave was "owned." It is illegal to beat your dog. It was sometimes legal, sometimes not, to beat your wife, when a man's relationship to his spouse was more akin to ownership than a contract between equals. It is illegal in many states to buy a historic church and burn it down. What you own, how completely you own it, is set up by the state.

Even a brief survey of "property rights" reveals a fascinating assortment of different ways of attaching a person to a thing in the minds of others. Because that's the important thing, isn't it? For us to own something, other people must think we own it.

"You can't have a market without property rights, and property rights are established by law," said Gerald Frug, a law professor at Harvard.

I'm not going to buy anything of yours if I already own it, and whether I own it or you own it is a matter of law. That laptop you're working on right now, I say I own it. You say you own it? Who does? It's not as simple as it sounds. That's why every law school in the country has a first-year property rights course.

China and other parts of Asia have very different histories of property. We can understand property systems in the United States better by looking at the history of its legal forefather, Great Britain.

THE DOMESDAY BOOK

In 1086, the English king known to history as William the Conqueror, recently arrived from France, sent his soldiers out to the farthest reaches of his kingdom to record every goat, sheep, and household, and every stretch of land. All this was compiled in something called the Domesday Book. And everything in that book, William owned. The king owned everything, he decreed. He would allow the present tenants to use the property if they paid him rent, in the form of taxes and knights, to fight his wars.

This book, with writing in Latin shorthand on pages of parchment, can still be seen at the Public Records Office of the National Archives in London. Updated and added to over the centuries, it became the final arbiter of who owned what. Although it originally had a more formal title, it acquired the lasting nickname of "The Domesday Book" because its verdicts were final and could not be appealed, like the Day of Judgment that some branches of Christianity hold will come at world's end, or on Doomsday. Domesday is a Middle English spelling of "Doomsday."

Those dusty property ledgers in every city hall in America are descended from the Domesday Book, which could settle who owned what, or rather, had use of something. I'll address the distinction in a minute.

"Indeed, during the middle ages it [the Domesday Book] was so respected that it was called simply 'the record,' so great was its authority. The land was described county by county, village by village, the owners and their subtenants were listed and their holdings valued, even the farm stock was recorded, with a view to settling clearly the rights of the Crowd and the taxable resources of the country," said Theodore Plucknett in *A Concise History of the Common Law*.[5]

The Domesday Book was a milestone in the creation of property ownership, "free and clear," particularly of land. This is ironic, because essentially what the Domesday Book did was establish that the king or the Crown owned everything, and anyone else got to use it only with the king's permission. It would take many centuries for even the concept of individual land ownership to emerge. And despite the intention of its creator, the Domesday Book would help, because it began a system of accurate public records, which is one of the prerequisites for property ownership.

As Andro Linklater makes clear in his masterful *Measuring America*, through the Middle Ages and even into the Enlightenment period of the seventeenth and eighteenth centuries in Europe, property possession and use were bound up with a system of obligations and responsibilities akin to feudalism.[6] You did not own land. You had use of it, in return for fulfilling a set of obligations to your king, or your duke or baron, or their vassals.

Because of this—something I'll explore in more detail in a later chapter—the systems of measuring land and of marking boundaries between property users were inexact, because land was not something that was bought and sold like a commodity: "the land was the state, and only the head of state could own it outright."[7] What was important in the feudal system was the relationships among the various possessors of property, not the property itself. Units of measurement, like the "peche," were defined in terms of people, usually the amount of land necessary to support a family, or that a man could till in a day.

It should be noted that the Domesday Book began as part of a conquest. The old anarchist notion that "property is theft" is not completely groundless. Property rights are synonymous with state power, and most states establish themselves through war.

Often the use of property is relatively static until moved by large events that come over the centuries. In the Norman Conquest in the eleventh century, the French newcomers seized the land from the English nobility and took it for themselves, "the lands of over 4,000 English lords passing to less than 200 Norman barons, with much of the land held by just a handful of magnates."[8] Then they established a new system to solidify their holdings and make their tenure legal and practical. King Henry VIII's rejection of the Catholic Church in the early 1500s was in large part a land grab and redistribution. In the Glorious Revolution in England in 1688, nobles, in turn, took property of the king and redistributed it. In the American Revolution in the eighteenth century, the rebels seized land and goods from the king and his supporters, and then formed a new system for holding and using that wealth. The French Revolution in the same time period redistributed land of the Crown and the Church and gave clear title to it. The American conquest of Japan in 1945 resulted in the breaking up of large estates and wealth centers there, and in a redistribution of land from large holdings to new, smaller ones. There are many other examples.

"There are moments in history when societies choose (or are forced) to create particular social institutions and the legal institutions to support them," said Harvey M. Jacobs, editor of *Who Owns America? Social Conflict over Property Rights*, in an interview.

> With regard to private property we can pick a set of these moments and see how radical change can occur. So, for example, in many parts of the world for much of the history property ownership was highly concentrated; a few people owned a lot and most people owned little (if any). And then, things changed. After World War II this happened in Japan under the mandate of the Allies, it also happened in Taiwan under Chiang Kai-shek, after he fled the mainland after losing to Mao Zedong. In both of these cases feudal-style systems of land ownership were broken apart and private property was created.[9]

Historically and counterintuitively, these land grabs by states have led to stronger property rights, because it is important, when taking something, to establish what you took and who gets to use it. A key event was King Henry VIII in the 1530s seizing the land of more than eight hundred monasteries and other religious communities as part of his rejection of the Catholic Church.[10] King Henry VIII then turned around and sold the land, or rather leased it, and accurate records were necessary to show who had the use of what parcel of land and where these parcels were. This process was a big step toward land itself being something that could be bought and sold.

THE MAGNA CARTA: THE KING OWNS
EVERYTHING, BUT NOT COMPLETELY

The conflicted relationship between property and the state here in the United States, in which we forget property's foundation within the state itself, can be explained in part by looking further into the history of our legal father, Great Britain.

A century or so after William the Conqueror compiled the Domesday Book, in the early thirteenth century, his descendants were having a tougher time of things. Struggling with both the nobles and the Catholic Church for power, King John was backed into a corner and forced to sign something called the Magna Carta, the "great charter of freedoms."

The Magna Carta granted the nobles attacking King John certain privileges and limited the king's powers. The great charter prohibited John or any king from acting arbitrarily and without due process, whether taking property or punishing someone. The king had to follow the law. But if the king had to follow the law, was he still king?[11]

A number of good but also schizophrenic things happened that day. King John agreed to give the nobles certain privileges, including use of property, and to not take those privileges away arbitrarily. In return the nobles pledged fealty to him. It's as if parents are being ordered by their children to give them dessert every night, which henceforth becomes "a right." And who makes sure that this "right" is honored? Why, the parents themselves.

In this environment of "rights," pieces of paper showing what those rights were, including property, became even more important. It's important to remember that most property is paper. That is, to prove you own something, you need to refer to a piece of paper, whether a sales receipt or an official court or city hall record. That the paper now can be accessed online doesn't change things much. There is still usually a physical copy somewhere. Property is paper. Eventually that piece of paper winds up in the records room of city hall, where a young reporter could go look at it.

This can result in absurd things, at least absurd by theories that people "naturally" own something. In my hometown of Virginia Beach there existed a scavenger of sorts, nicknamed "the bottom feeder." This individual made a nice living researching old nineteenth-century companies that had once owned beachfront land. He would buy up the shell of a company and everything it once owned. Then he would show up at someone's beachfront hotel or home and say, "Hi, you're occupying my property. Get off." A lawsuit would typically follow, and a settlement. He earned some healthy sums of money, if "earned" is the right word. That he could do this shows how fictional or derivative property rights are. According to John Locke's theory of natural rights, this man had no claim. He had not occupied the land he claimed or improved it. He had not mixed his labor with it. He had simply bought a piece of paper that said a company once owned it a century ago. But that was enough.

PROPERTY: A RIGHT, A PRIVILEGE, OR A BOON?

When you review the literature on property rights, what you find is an amazing assortment of ways that things have been owned, and an amazing assortment of ways that people have justified owning something. And an amazing assortment of ways that things could be owned in the future.

Owning land can be viewed as a privilege. This was the case in England, and to some degree still is. In England "land ownership was tightly concentrated in relatively few hands," and "in theory no person owned land absolutely: All land was held under a tenurial relationship with the Crown. . . . property ownership was conditional and involved continuing obligation to a superior," said James Ely in *Guardian of Every Other Right: The Constitutional History of Property Rights*.[12]

Despite this, it was in England and in Europe, where similar systems prevailed, that the concept of owning something free and clear, at least in practice, evolved. "In much of the rest of the world, especially where land was concerned, the European notion of 'fee simple,' that land ownership could be passed by will to anybody, was foreign."[13]

When the American colonies were founded, the English system of ownership passed to them. Originally the king owned all the land, and he allowed colonists and institutions such as churches and schools to use it at his pleasure. But this system gradually broke down in practice, and eventually in fact.

Although the English system of land tenure nominally prevailed in much of colonial America, it was largely drained of any substance. Outside New England, landowners were responsible for paying a quit-rent [an annual payment to a king or feudal lord] to the Crown or proprietor. But the collection of quitrents was usually lax. Moreover, the colonists intensely disliked the feudal implications of quitrents, regarding them as a distasteful form of tribute. Consequently, they evaded payment.[14]

Nevertheless, at the time of the American Revolution, King George III technically owned all the land under Great Britain's control, about half a continent. A particular issue was that King George had expressly forbidden settlement west of the Allegheny Mountains, including even the surveying of the land. On October 7, 1763, King George proclaimed "that no governor or Commander in Chief in any of our Colonies or Plantations in America do presume for the present, and until our further Pleasure be Known, to grant Warrants of Survey, or pass Patents for any Lands beyond the Heads or Sources of any of the Rivers which fall into the Atlantic Ocean from the West and North West."[15]

Scarcely examined in our high school history books, this dispute over the use of the millions of acres of forests and streams west of the Allegheny Mountains was a cause of the American Revolution. After winning the war, the new country could and did claim this land as its biggest war booty. Selling this land off, something facilitated by Thomas Jefferson's systems of measurement and surveying, helped finance the new government.

This larger history should not obscure that the individual states have different histories. In Virginia, the Carolinas, and other southern colonies, land was generally given by "headright." Each individual got a set amount of land, just for showing up. Fifty acres in Virginia. In the Carolinas in 1689, you got 150 acres. This was meant to encourage immigration, and did.

In New England, by contrast, land was often granted to an entire township or church congregation, which were institutions leading the immigration. They, in turn, distributed land to individuals, but often retained some land for public purposes.[16]

This history endures today. In New England citizens still turn to their local governments to solve problems for them, whether it be cleaning up after a snowstorm or providing for health care. In the South, people whip out their chain saws and help their neighbors clean up after a windstorm has toppled trees. In New England, they are likely to ask why city hall is so slow at doing its job, and to complain about any neighbor whipping out a chain saw as endangering them!

POLITICAL RIGHTS AND PROPERTY RIGHTS

Although we like to think that we own things free and clear, in reality we own most things to a degree. What we can do with our property is defined by law, and through enforcement and arbitration of that law by the state. Our elected representatives pass laws that define the scope of our rights, including property rights. Our courts further define property in the process of arbitrating whose rights get enforced or circumscribed in property rights disputes. Judges and juries often act subjectively, sometimes by necessity, in weighing different privileges and obligations of property ownership. Which individuals or groups get favored in these decisions changes over time, revealing yet another powerful but unacknowledged way in which property rights are far from "natural."

The ability to own something, particularly land, "free and clear" has on balance been a great boon to both societal and individual wealth. But you can see how something like tackling global warming through regulation of the use of property would be easier if it were more widely seen that property ownership is created by society itself. In the words of Benjamin Franklin, who was an entrepreneur and no fan of big government, "private property is a creature of society," and so for property to exist, we must attend to the health of the society that makes it possible.

CHAPTER 3

LEX NON SCRIPTA: THE LAWS WE
DON'T MAKE, OR, THE COMMON LAW

*There are two errors equally to be avoided both by writer and
reader. One is that of supposing, because an idea seems very
familiar and natural to us, that it has always been so. Many things
which we take for granted have had to be laboriously fought out or
thought out in past times. The other mistake is the opposite one
of asking too much of history. We start with the man full grown.
It may be assumed that the earliest barbarians whose practices
are to be considered, had a good many of the same feelings and
passions as ourselves.*
OLIVER WENDELL HOLMES, *THE COMMON LAW*, 1881

IN THIS COUNTRY, teaching civics—basically how our government
works and how one becomes an effective citizen within it—has unfortunately fallen off, and now even the word itself sounds quaint. Still,
eventually somewhere in school a student will come across a paragraph
that says something like: "The legislative branch makes the law, the executive branch carries out the law, and the judiciary interprets the law."

These simple rules sank in deep with me. So I was quite shocked
when I learned, well into adulthood, that there was a substantial body
of law, perhaps the bulk of it, that our legislatures did not make. This
body of law, called "the common law," has been handed down through
the ages like a basket of goods, one where some things can be taken out
and others added, but the whole nearly impossible to change in large
ways.

In this chapter, I look at what common law is and how it relates to
these things that we make, that we design, called markets. I also look
at some aspects of law in general and how they relate to our lives.

Understanding common law is essential to understanding how we make markets, because markets are things of law, and if a substantial body of law is not determined by us, the voters, it means markets themselves are more difficult to shape than one might think. A market needs rules to work, and the entity that makes and enforces the rules is government. But laws are infinite in their potential number. So it's not enough to say that markets (and democracy) depend on laws. Which laws? What laws? It should be seen that what is called common law provides ballast to both the state and markets, giving them great stability, but also interfering with the will of the people and making markets less flexible and supple in their evolving design.

And just what is common law? Matthew Hale said it quite well around 1650 in his book *The History and Analysis of the Common Law of England*:

> The Laws of England may aptly enough be divided into Two Kinds. Lex Scripta, the written Law; and Lex non Scripta, the unwritten Law: for although (as shall be shown hereafter) all the Laws of this Kingdom have some Monuments or Memorials thereof in Writing, yet all of them have not their Original in Writing, for some of those Laws have obtain'd their Force by immemorial Usage or Custom, and such Laws are properly called Leges non Scriptae, or unwritten Laws or Customs.[1]

More contemporary writers basically say the same thing: "Common Law is of course the 'unwritten law' made not by legislatures, but by courts, lawyers, and judges in cases," said Richard Hamm, writing in the introduction to *Essays on English Law and the American Experience*.

> The source of Common Law is presumed to be custom, reason or natural law. . . . In England, the system had its creation when kings issued charters acknowledging the authority of "ancient customs" and created royal courts. These courts and the lawyers who practiced there interpreted the ancient customs, metamorphosing them into Common Law.

Common law is "not rooted in the code of an authority but in ancient customs and general principles."[2]

All of this sounds profoundly undemocratic. So "courts, lawyers, and judges" make the common law? Weren't the legislatures supposed to make law? Wasn't that their job? Indeed, the common law is profoundly undemocratic. It is a body of law that has arisen over the centuries, and in effect removes the great mass of the law from the legislature's—and thus the people's—grasp. It is profoundly difficult, although not impossible, for the legislature to pass laws that overrule common law. Precisely because it is not written down in one place, it is difficult to write anything that overrules one specific part of it. It is like trying to squash a jellyfish. In addition, the courts are defining and establishing new law through the evolution of common law all the time.

Both the political Right and the political Left engage in a tacit conspiracy to hide this undemocratic aspect of the courts from the public. It leads to conspicuous hypocrisy.

On July 13, 2009, Judge Sonia Sotomayor, up for the job of Justice of the Supreme Court after her nomination by Democratic President Barack Obama, told the US Senate that "The task of a judge . . . is not to make law, it is to apply the law."[3] The senators, many of them lawyers, received her statement approvingly. Chief Justice John Roberts, a man of the Right, had addressed the senators similarly during his hearing after being nominated by Republican President George W. Bush. Certainly Sotomayor and Roberts know that judges make law all the time.

Common law establishes the foundations for some of the most basic rules of society, such as prohibitions against murder, rape, burglary, and trespassing, as well as important interpretations of those rules. One example is "the eggshell skull rule," which is a common law standard that holds that you are liable for damages to someone, even if your actions cause damages disproportionate to intent; the actual effect of the action, not intent, determines liability.[4] For example, if someone has a skull as thin as an eggshell, and if you cause such a person's skull to break by tapping on it, you are responsible for that damage, even though you didn't know the person's skull was eggshell thin, and even though most people's skulls aren't eggshell thin.

This is probably a pretty good rule. But what's germane for our purposes is that no legislature wrote it. You can't go look it up in a law book, despite its great significance. You can go to "case law," to the records of decisions by judges and juries, which in common law often has as much power as a legal statute. There are similar common law rules for trespassing, burglary, contract interpretation, and other components of social functioning. While legislatures sometimes do modify or change these rules, replacing or overturning them is difficult.

From one perspective, having this huge body of law, worked out over the centuries, is an asset. It stabilizes the law and the society it helps form. On the other hand, it puts the law into the hands of lawyers and judges, and removes it from the legislatures and the voters who are supposed to be responsible for it. It takes part of the social contract out of citizens' hands. To understand it better, we need to look to England.

OUR ENGLISH ROOTS

When my father was a schoolboy around the time of World War I, one of his tasks was to memorize all the English kings and the dates of their reigns. Three-quarters of a century later, he could still do this, and he would occasionally demonstrate this chiseled-in knowledge with amusement. However, there was one quirk to his skill. He had memorized the lists separately—probably for some test—and while he could still recount the names of all the kings, and the dates during which they served, he could not do both at once. That is, he could tell you that King Richard I was followed by King John, who was followed by Henry III; and he could tell you that a king served from 1216 to 1272, and another from 1272 to 1307, but he couldn't tell you whose reign those dates corresponded to, or when a particular king served, without writing the two lists down and matching them up. This amused him.

I mention it here, not only because I like telling stories about my father, but because of how unimaginable it would be requiring schoolchildren to learn the names and tenures of the kings and queens of England now. My dad, John F. Marshall Jr., would have been one hundred years old in 2011 if he were living, and perhaps that explains why a public school in Norfolk, in a genteel neighborhood, was teaching him these things as a schoolboy. He was essentially still living in the Victorian era, when our British roots were still more evident and remembered.

We now are less aware of how our present political institutions evolved from British ones. I theorize that this is because, with the United States now being a world power, it damages our pride to know we are not as exceptional as we tend to think. Our American experiment is really an iteration of the British system the colonists knew so well. Even a cursory examination of history shows that much of what we hold hallowed comes from the British.

America has three branches of government, the legislature (Congress), the executive (the president), and the judiciary (the Supreme Court et al.). This comes from the English. They have the king, who until modern times carried out the law and commanded the armies;

Parliament, which makes (some of) the laws and, like our Congress, controls the purse strings; and the judiciary, which like here is a separate power that can even overrule the king. All of this evolved in Great Britain over the centuries, with numerous key decision points, including the Magna Carta in 1215, through which the nobles managed to get the king, at gunpoint, to guarantee that his power was not unlimited and unchecked; the Petition of Right, passed by Parliament in 1628, which guaranteed English subjects some liberties that the king could not infringe upon; the Glorious Revolution of 1688, which further limited the power of the monarch and began parliamentary democracy, which included the English Bill of Rights; and so on. This stuff is not a secret. But it's been forgotten in popular discourse.

Perhaps the biggest thing we inherited from England was the common law. It comes out of the English tradition of limited government, since even the king could not rewrite common law indiscriminately, or arbitrarily overrule it. It grew out of the unique fragmentation of power in Great Britain, which grew out of the Magna Carta and other events over the centuries. Common law is part of our institutional DNA, arguably even more than our US Constitution. While many lawyers and judges praise common law for its deep institutional permanence and evolutionary character, I am troubled by its antidemocratic attributes.

Most European countries, including Great Britain, trace their law back to the Romans in some form. The series of events that led Great Britain to develop common law were significant, because they would mean that Great Britain and all its colonies—Canada, the United States, Australia, New Zealand, and even India and Singapore—would have a different system of law than the rest of Europe and their colonies.

CHURCH VERSUS STATE: WHO MAKES THE LAW?

With the decline of the Roman empire in the Middle Ages, the Catholic Church moved in to fill the void. The empire ruled from Rome was being replaced, for practical purposes, by Christendom, ruled by the papacy.[5] (I find it fascinating that when we look at the Catholic Church, we are seeing remnants of the Roman empire.) In most places the Catholic Church was the law, more so than the king or the local noble.

That began to change under the Normans in Great Britain, and the struggle between the ascendant Normans and the Church helped plant, almost by happenstance, the seeds that would grow into the common law. Some English words, like "law," have Norse roots. This is because William the Conqueror, who successfully invaded England in 1066, was a Norman, a people originally from in and around Norway and Sweden.[6]

The Normans, says Theodore Plucknett, were great administrators, and many of our contemporary rules have roots in those William and his heirs set up. Just as William had a big hand in shaping private property through the Domesday Book, he and his descendants had a big hand in founding the common law by removing the Catholic Church's dominion over much of the law. This would leave an opening for a more decentralized, lawyer- and judge-based law to emerge.

William put government over what we would now call criminal and civil cases, and relegated the Church to overt religious crimes such as heresy, blasphemy, etc. There was considerable overlap, of course, but a principle had been set and the public side of law would also grow into common law.

The Magna Carta of 1215, which I discussed in Chapter 2, also had a hand in shaping common law by fragmenting power relationships in England—between the king and the Church; the king and his nobles; and the king and other power centers, such as the City of London. Here's a key paragraph from the Magna Carta, translated from Latin:

> First, that we have granted to God, and by this present charter have confirmed for us and our heirs in perpetuity, that the English Church shall be free, and shall have its rights undiminished, and its liberties unimpaired. That we wish this so to be observed, appears from the fact that of our own free will, before the outbreak of the present dispute between us and our barons, we granted and confirmed by charter the freedom of the Church's elections—a right reckoned to be of the greatest necessity and importance to it—and caused this to be confirmed by Pope Innocent III. This freedom we shall observe ourselves, and desire to be observed in good faith by our heirs in perpetuity.[7]

Pope Innocent III of the Catholic Church had excommunicated King John, which made life extremely difficult for him. At that time, royalty was supposed to pledge its fealty to the pope, and to acknowledge and admit that its authority was derived from the Church itself. The pope was a replacement for the Roman emperor and likewise ruled from Rome.

The pope reinstated John in the Church only after King John in 1213 transferred his kingdom to the pope, who then gave title back to him as "feudatory of the Church of Rome," which among other things required a tribute each year of "1,000 marks."[8] This meant that England was just a domain of the Catholic Church, and that the pope was just giving the English king a long-term lease. Things would stay this way until Henry VIII pulled England out of the Catholic Church so he could get a divorce—and not incidentally seize much of the land and wealth of the Catholic Church.

The Magna Carta not only established the Church's authority, something which is difficult for us to remember, given that we think of the Magna Carta's role in protecting individual rights and establishing stronger civil society, but it also protected the rights of corporations, particularly cities.

As we will discuss later in this book, cities at that time had special rights. They were (and usually still are) corporations, the institution that would evolve into the private corporations we know today. The Magna Carta protected the rights of cities. It established that the Crown could not arbitrarily intrude upon or sweep aside the powers and privileges of cities. This is one of the precedents for and foundations of the status of cities as corporations, in effect minigovernments with special powers. In the time of the Magna Carta, this meant principally the City of London, which must have galled Henry III, given that he lived there. Here's some of the pertinent text of the Magna Carta:

> The City of London shall have all her old liberties and customs. And moreover we will and grant that all other cities, boroughs, towns . . . and ports shall have all their liberties and free customs.[9]

This body of what we would now call law grew, but remained an evolving thing, tracing out delineations of power between royalty and competitors such as the Church, the barons, and the City of London. That would grow into our present arrangement of competing power centers, from private corporations to the public Supreme Court. For better and for worse, we don't have a Hobbesian unified state.

Various events influenced the development of common law over the ages, even though overall it should be seen as an outgrowth of fragmentation of power in Great Britain. A section in the Second Statute of Westminster, passed by Parliament in 1285, seemed to create almost offhandedly the right of the courts to look for precedent and then create law when they cannot find a specific law and cannot consult Parliament about it. This section was framed as a way of not leaving people waiting for justice until the next time Parliament met. A few centuries later in the Renaissance, there were attempts in much of Europe to impose old Roman law, "The Digest," over then-contemporary law as a way of rationalizing and ordering the law. This succeeded on some parts of the continent, but not in England.[10]

Kings ruled by divine right. But what about the law, which also came from God? Which had ultimate authority, a king or the law, both deriving their power from God? Plucknett says in early centuries, kings were thought of as subservient to the law, which was divine. The power of kings had limit. But debate about this grew more specific as kings tried to claim the right to rule directly, because they were divine. This in turn prompted the courts and the legislatures to push back.

"The King is subject not to men, but to God and the Law," said Chief Justice Sir Edward Coke, the attorney general under Queen Elizabeth and one of the most significant interpreters of common law and proponents of monarchs having limited, not absolute, authority. With his words, he was looking for a way to limit the power of the king while still allowing the king to save face.[11] Coke was one of the principal authors of the Petition of Right, passed in 1628, which included the writ of habeas corpus, which established that neither the king nor other authorities could hold people without charges.

This debate over whether the law was anything the king said it was, or whether the king was subservient to the law, was a continual one. Thomas Hobbes and John Locke, who bookend each other on state authority and its prerogatives, figure in here.

"Where Hobbes had considered law to be the command of the State, Locke returned to the notion of natural law—a conception which was easily reconciled with the medieval view of law as the will of God," says Plucknett. "Where Hobbes had made law the tool of the State, Locke regarded it as the guardian of liberty."[12] Locke's emphasis on limited monarchical power suited those who wanted the Church to have more power. Locke grounded his philosophical system on God, which is sometimes forgotten.

This back and forth, principally between Parliament and the king, but also between Church and king, between cities and king, continued over the centuries. Meanwhile, the common law continued to evolve and grow.

EVERYWHERE AND NOWHERE: THE HOME OF COMMON LAW

If common law is unwritten, where does it reside?

For some eight hundred years in England, Hamm says, common law lay in a "guild-like" Inns of Court, which was apparently a sort of club of judges, lawyers, and other court officials. (This is strikingly similar to the Stationers Company, the private guild of printers and publishers that was the home and birthplace to what we now call copyrights. We'll learn more about this in the chapter on intellectual property.) This "autonomous institution," the Inns of Court, was a home for the common law, which was sort of an internal record of proceedings and members' thoughts about the law. The Inns of Courts collapsed in the eighteenth century, according to Hamm.[13]

Since then, and even before then to a large degree, common law lives in the casebooks. That common law is officially unwritten law does not mean that there has not been a lot of writing about common law. There has been. And much of this writing gains the force of law because lawyers and judges rely on it.

Blackstone's *Commentaries*, or in its full title, *Commentaries on the Laws of England*, by Sir William Blackstone, is the best-known attempt at summarizing and laying out the body of common law. It was extraordinarily influential for centuries, and still has weight. It is the book that Atticus Finch in *To Kill a Mockingbird* gives to his daughter (and narrator of the novel) "Scout" to learn to read with, to the horror of Atticus's aging mother. Blackstone, who published his book in the 1760s, neatly divided the law into "The Rights of Persons," "The Rights of Things," "Of Private Wrongs," and "Of Public Wrongs." In modern terms, the latter three translate into property law, torts, and criminal law. The first category, the Rights of Persons, is difficult to translate into modern terms and that's telling. It dealt chiefly with relationships among and rights held by the king, Parliament, the military, and citizens, as well as "Master and Servant," "Husband and Wife," and "Parents and Children." Much of it is about divisions of people by status and class. It was considered so elemental that it received an entire book, but much of it now has little relevance because we no longer have classes of people with specific categories of rights. Law governs what is.[14]

To a degree almost impossible for us to imagine today, in the eighteenth and previous centuries in England and in Europe, one was placed in a thick web of relationships that defined one's role in society—

master and servant, husband and wife, freeman or peasant, master and apprentice, king and nobles—and defined one's rights and responsibilities. One had obligations both up and down this chain. Conceiving of society—and a market—as a set of interactions between equal individuals would have been an incongruous assumption, and it took centuries for such a society to emerge. It was part of the design of markets.

The one chapter out of eighteen in Blackstone's first volume, "The Rights of Persons," that is still clearly relevant is telling. It is a chapter on the rights of corporations. The rights of these artificial persons have grown disproportionately since Blackstone's time.

Part of the deemphasis on legally defined social status was an admirable shift that had to do with American democracy viewing people as individuals, and not as mere actors in a social caste system. But some of it had to do with less admirable needs, such as the coming of the big private railroad corporations in the mid-nineteenth century, and their need for easily applicable rules that could be invoked quickly and, not incidentally, with less liability put on their actions. Howard Schweber argues this in his book *The Creation of American Common Law, 1850–1880: Technology, Politics and the Construction of Citizenship*.

Under common law, said Schweber, persons, natural or artificial, had legal responsibility for the consequences of their actions, under rules such as "the eggshell skull" rule. In addition, how much liability individuals had was determined by their role in defined relationships, such as husband and wife, master and servant, and king and commoner. But soon after their advent, corporate-owned trains began killing and maiming, right and left, people who had wandered onto the tracks. Making corporations liable for these deaths and injuries would be a hardship. So, Schweber argues, the interpretation of common law was changed, from focusing on "the status of each person and the precise relationship between the actors"—per Blackstone's detailed commentaries in "The Rights of Persons"—to "a universal set of duties, equally applicable to everyone regardless of his or her social position or role in a transaction, that completely reconfigured the rules for determining legal liability."[15]

In this century of turmoil, when so much of the legal and political landscape was changing, there were various and influential attempts to sum up common law, similar to Blackstone's *Commentaries*.

In the late nineteenth century, a man who would become a US Supreme Court Justice, Oliver Wendell Holmes, produced one of the best summaries of the common law while still a law professor. It is entailed simply: *The Common Law*. Less neatly than Blackstone but more usefully, Holmes divided the common law into eleven different sections, or lectures, and then explained each one.[16] Holmes was a good writer. Here are a few of his bon mots:

> The Substance of the law at any given time pretty nearly corresponds, so far as it goes, with what is then understood to be convenient; but its form and machinery, and the degree to which it is able to work out desired results, depend very much upon its past.

> A very common phenomenon, and one very familiar to the student of history, is this. The custom, beliefs, or needs of a primitive time establish a rule or a formula. In the course of centuries the custom, beliefs, or necessity disappears, but the rule remains.

> Even a dog distinguishes between being stumbled over and being kicked.[17]

CHECKING THE KING, CHECKING THE POPULACE

The common law ended up doing a great job of limiting the power of kings. But as government has evolved from hereditary kings and queens to elected prime ministers and presidents, the common law has also done a good job in limiting the power of citizens and democracy, and putting the power in the hands of usually unelected judges.

In the late nineteenth and early twentieth centuries, a series of judges kept both Congress and state legislatures from enacting reforms that would limit the hours workers worked, give them minimum wages, and restrict corporations from banding together into trusts and then using that market power to extort unfair premiums from shippers and low wages from workers. Courts even made it difficult to pass child labor laws. Many of the decisions were based on interpretations of common law.

In Alabama, the state Supreme Court in 1841 said the state could regulate the size and price of a loaf of bread because "the mode or manner of enjoying property" could be regulated to serve "the public interest." But in 1905, in *Lochner v. New York*, the US Supreme Court invalidated a state law that restricted those working in bakeries to sixty hours a week and ten hours a day. In a 5–4 decision, Justice Rufus W. Peckham said the state should not side with the bakers in their contract dealings with the bakeries.

In 1895, the Supreme Court, in a 5–4 decision, declared illegal the income tax, reversing itself from a previous decision. Said Justice Stephen J. Field, who a few years earlier had played a part in elevating corporations to "persons" and was known as a friend to the railroads: "The present assault upon capital is but the beginning. It will be but the stepping-stone to others, larger and more sweeping, till our political contests will become a war of the poor against the rich."[18]

In the 1920s and 1930s, the US Supreme Court prohibited government from setting minimum wages and establishing other rules to encourage unions and protect labor. While in the nineteenth century the Court had allowed a state to regulate the price of a train ticket or of transporting train cargo, in *Adkins v. Children's Hospital* in 1923, the Court, in a 5–3 decision, refused to allow the District of Columbia to set a minimum wage for women. Only in the late 1930s, with Franklin Roosevelt threatening to expand the Court, would the Supreme Court relent and begin allowing minimum wage laws, mandatory overtime pay, maximum workweeks, and other controls most of us take for granted.

LEGAL REALISM AND THE LAW'S PURPOSE

To watch through the lens of history these judges in the nineteenth and twentieth centuries rule one way, then another way, using only the flimsiest of sustaining logic, leads one to embrace what in academia has been called "legal realism," where the law is viewed as only an instrument of political will. In this school of thought, it is acknowledged that a judge can always find some principle or precedent to support a desired end, so one should just skip the middle step and look at the desired end. If judges (and the elites that appoint them) wanted to squash a minimum wage in the late nineteenth century, well, they could find a precedent somehow and make this legal. If they wanted to abolish child labor, well, they could find a way to do that too, all legally. The most glaring example of legal realism, with barely a fig leaf of law to cover it, was the selection in late 2000 by the US Supreme Court of George W. Bush as president after the disputed national election. Just coincidentally, the five votes handing Bush the presidency corresponded exactly with the political leanings of those five judges.

Legal realism is a useful tool for analysis. I would not use it as a doctrine of prescription. We do want a government of laws, and not of men, even if at key points the desires of those men, and increasingly women, overwhelm what might be called the law.

LAW AND REASON

We habitually think of having clear laws that are applied uniformly as being synonymous with fairness, but of course this is not the case. Laws can be synonymous with unfairness, or simply irrationality. Garbage in, garbage out.

You are guilty if you are bald. You are guilty if you are a Jew. You are guilty if you cross the street three times without looking backwards. These nonsensical statements could all be laws, but not rational or fair laws. The process of the law—the courtroom, the careful weighing of evidence, clear, contemplative discussion—tends to convince us on a subliminal level that we are striving for justice. Not necessarily true, as history shows.

Slavery is one example of how law and justice are not necessarily connected. Until a constitutional amendment outlawed slavery after the Civil War, there was a great body of law dealing with it. When you could beat a slave, handling crimes by slaves, transfers of ownership, all were part of law, much of it common law.

A few years ago I visited Salem, Massachusetts, the locale where the infamous Salem witch trials were held. On display were the actual letters and written proceedings relating to the trials of the "witches," the women and some men who were judged guilty and put to death.

What to me was so chilling about this centuries-old handwriting in cursive script upon faded paper was that the thoughts did not sound old or foreign. These justices were clearly weighing the evidence in a thoughtful, reasoned way. They would note the evidence on both sides. But what they were weighing, from a contemporary perspective, made no sense. Sometimes they would be examining a woman's body for the mark of the devil, which apparently could be a mole in a hidden, intimate place.

Cotton Mather, a learned man, a prolific writer, a Harvard graduate, and a minister, had considerable involvement in the trials. His writing about witchcraft helped set the stage for the events. But if you look at Mather's life as a whole, you'll find that he was a leader in science, having worked on crop hybridization techniques and a predecessor to vaccination called "inoculation."[19] Being "rational" is no defense against being stupid or evil, unless core assumptions are examined.

Most law is rooted in religion, and since religion is a matter of faith, we can say that law has roots in irrationality. This is not just playing with words. As demonstrated in the Salem witch trials, we find at times no particular connection between judging and what is judged.

In the 1200s in England, judging someone guilty or innocent often involved some sort of torture or battle. Actual laws from the time refer to "going to the water," a term encompassing variations on being tied up and thrown into the water to see if you floated, which proved one's guilt or innocence. Another common method was "The Ordeal." You had to grasp a red-hot iron or stone, carry it for a set distance, and then have your hand bandaged up. In a few days, typically three, the bandage was opened up. If your hand was infected, you were guilty. If it was "clean," that is, not infected, then you were innocent.

Ordeals gave way to trials by jury, but the accused did not have a lot of rights here. The Crown insisted that the accused consent to trial by jury. Among the remedies for refusing were being placed between two boards upon which stones were piled until either the accused died or gave consent. Some let themselves be killed this way, because if they didn't consent they technically did not lose the trial, and their heirs got to keep their property. This barbaric practice was only abolished in 1772.[20]

Still another common method was the battle, where you had "champions" fight it out for you. If I disputed something, say that I owned such and such piece of property, or if I accused you of stealing, then our "champions" would fight. The guy who won, as proxy, won the case for his employer. These fights were sometimes to the death. Big landowners had professional champions, and there were roving champions who made a living by fighting.[21]

This foundation of law on superstition was more obvious to those of the Enlightenment in the eighteenth century, because they were closer to it. In his *Notes on the State of Virginia*, Thomas Jefferson points out that heresy had been a crime punishable by burning under common law. He then noted that while the Virginia legislature had circumscribed this, there still was on the books the possibility of being prosecuted for heresy.

I doubt whether the people of this country would suffer an execution for heresy, or a three years imprisonment for not comprehending the mysteries of the Trinity. But is the spirit of the people an infallible, a permanent reliance?

Jefferson complains about this, and the section contains this famous declaration: "The legitimate powers of government extend to such acts only as are injurious to others. But it does me no injury for my neighbor to say there are twenty gods, or no god. It neither picks my pocket nor breaks my leg."[22]

CONCLUSION

I don't want to throw out common law, despite my dislike of its undemocratic nature. But we should hold it up to light and air. In so doing, we give a better chance for "We the People" to overwrite the common law through our elected legislators, as we learned in civics.

CHAPTER 4

I AM MY BROTHER'S KEEPER: COOPERATIVES

Experiment. Make it your motto day and night.
Experiment. And it will lead you to the light.
The apple from the top of the tree is never too high to achieve.
So take an example from me.
Experiment. Be curious, though interfering friends may frown.
Get furious, at each attempt to hold you down.
If this advice you'll only employ, the future can offer you infinite joy
and merriment.
Experiment, and you'll see.
COLE PORTER, "EXPERIMENT," 1933

IF THIS CONVENTION outside Minneapolis had a color, it would be brown. The men wear brown jackets and brown pants. Their hair is brown. The women are restrained sartorially. I, in my pinstriped flannel suit, with rectangular two-color framed glasses on my face, and sporting a jaunty cane due to a recent injury, must look like I have a sign on me saying "Visitor, Visitor, probably from New York!" The setting for this convention is equally staid, the Sheraton Bloomington Hotel, a set of large white boxes on a parking lot off a freeway exit ramp near some strip shopping centers. Just a few miles down the road is the Mall of America, the mammoth 4-million-square-foot shopping center with an amusement park in the middle.

Which makes the activities of this bunch all the more ironic. This group of middle-aged men and women, who in their dress and Scandinavian-tinged accents and names look and sound like they walked out of Garrison Keillor's Lake Wobegon from *A Prairie Home Companion*, are a revolutionary bunch, engaged in an alternative form of capitalism with an alternative arrangement of markets, one that works better than the conventional kind. They show how the kind of market economies we inhabit is a matter of choice. The name of this alternative form of capitalism and markets is—get ready—cooperatives. This is a convention of the Cooperative Network, a trade association for more than six hundred cooperatives in Wisconsin and Minnesota. For various reasons, cooperatives are particularly strong in these Scandinavian-rooted states.

At this convention, and in my wanderings around the region, I could see the beginnings of a solution to many chronic problems bedeviling the United States right now, including inequity of income and wealth, loss of community and related social and family ties, the decline of manufacturing, and the rising price and dearth of necessary services such as health care. Cooperatives offer ways forward on all these problems. But leaving aside their merits, cooperatives also show that there is not just one way to organize a market economy, but many. Markets and capitalism could be more democratic and more experimental, if we chose to make them so, and cooperatives are a good example of how. It's telling that I found cooperatives maddeningly difficult to understand—not because they are complicated, but because I had to move around various pieces of mental furniture to make space for them.

WHAT IS A COOPERATIVE?

If you are like me, you have vaguely heard about cooperatives without really understanding what they are. Although they are particularly big in Minnesota and Wisconsin, cooperatives can be found all around us. In the grocery store we see their products, including Land O'Lakes, Ocean Spray juices, Sun-Maid raisins, Minute Maid orange juice, Sunkist oranges, Cabot cheese, Organic Valley milk, and Blue Diamond almonds. On the highway we pass by True Value hardware stores and Best Western hotels. We may get a catalog in the mail from REI outdoor equipment purveyors. Your town might feature a food cooperative, such as the Park Slope Food Co-op down the street from me here in Brooklyn. You might know someone who belongs to a credit union, which is a cooperative. In the daily newspaper you see stories from the Associated Press, a cooperative of newspapers that runs this prestigious wire service. And these are just the familiar ones. There are cooperatives such as Agribank, which supplies credit to farmers but is little known outside agricultural industries. There are tiny cooperatives and enormous ones. The cooperative sector in Western Europe is stronger and more diverse than here. As I studied co-ops, I realized that the basic model allowed for an almost infinite variety of aims, structures, and priorities.

And just what is the common denominator or principles for these diverse businesses? There are officially seven co-op principles, but two are crucial rules that make a cooperative business distinct from conventional ones.

First of all, a cooperative is a business where its users or members are the owners and managers. A co-op is "member-controlled." So with Land O'Lakes, for example, the farmers own the company that sells the butter made from their milk in the supermarket. This is what is called a "producer" co-op. But users or members can be also be consumers in a "buyer's co-op," as in a grocery store co-op, or employees in a worker-owned co-op. Many co-ops are hybrids, where members can occupy one or more of these roles—producers, buyers, sellers, or employees. Because of this, co-op member/owners often cooperate with one another, where they typically might compete with each other in conventional businesses.

The second crucial principle, or rule, of cooperatives is the relationship they have with money itself, which is capital. In co-ops people vote, not their money. Cooperatives are "democratically controlled." Management is based on votes by individuals, regardless of how many shares they have or how much they use a co-op. A farmer who sells Land O'Lakes or his local cooperative a million gallons of milk a month has the same vote as one who sells it a thousand. Control of cooperative businesses is based on a one-person, one-vote principle, instead of the one-dollar (or one-share), one-vote principle of conventional corporations.

Under conventional capitalism, markets and economic institutions are organized to make the most money for capitalists who have the spare cash. That's why it's called capitalism. In cooperatives, capital and capitalists are still employed, but they are the servants of the owners, or "members," of the cooperative. Yet like traditional businesses and markets, cooperatives still rely on pricing and supply and demand to distribute goods. There is still profit. But the different structure changes the relationship of buyer and seller, and of owner to owner.

THE LAND OF COOPERATIVES

Minnesota and Wisconsin have been called the land of co-ops. In these two states, a cooperative might provide a family their electricity, telephone, and cable television service. Another cooperative might provide them health care, including employing the doctor that prods and pokes them and building the hospital where they are treated. An insurance cooperative might provide life insurance, as well as other types of insurance. A credit union might provide the family banking. Another cooperative might help the public schools the family's children attend buy textbooks and supplies in bulk. If the family owned a farm, then cooperatives would buy their grain and milk, while another sold them seed and supplies and advanced them credit for next year's crop. When a family member died, a member-owned cooperative would put him or her in a coffin and handle the services. About 3.4 million of 5 million people in Minnesota are members of at least one co-op.[1]

So to many people here, cooperatives are as natural as butter on bread, even though their growth here has hardly been placid. Cooperatives in these states have battled it out with big banks, agricultural companies, and private utilities, which feared cooperatives and the independence they gave their customers/members. It's clearly no accident that co-ops are popular in a region dominated by Scandinavians, who have a community-oriented culture that puts a premium on working together to solve common problems.

"Cooperatives were very often started by and for German and Scandinavian farmers who wanted to share their risks," said Jan Eliassen, a consultant based in Maryland who works with agricultural cooperatives. "They have an ethos that says, 'I am my brother's keeper.' Anglo Saxons have a look-out-for-yourself and 'I am not my brother's keeper' ethos."[2]

MINNESOTA GOTHIC: CO-OPS IN ACTION

To get a better feel for co-ops in action, I visited Cheryl and Bruce Mohn, who own a small dairy farm in Lakeville, south of Minneapolis off I-35. I was introduced to them by Lee Egerstrom, a former reporter for the *St. Paul Pioneer Press* who has written several books about cooperatives. Now in his late sixties, Egerstrom is a fellow for a regional planning group called Minnesota 2020.

Farms are just one arena for co-ops, but they are a large one. The Mohns' dairy farm consists of about 300 acres (they own about 120 acres and lease the rest) in a rural area that is beginning to experience a suburban creep of houses and subdivisions. This is a small farm by Midwestern standards. It consists of two older farmhouses, a shed for the family's fifty cows, a barn for milking, storage houses for corn and hay, an office/warehouse for Cheryl's entrepreneurial mail order business, Uddertech, for cow milking equipment, and a few other buildings I couldn't identify. Beyond that were fields, many of them planted with corn, much of which would be ground up to feed the cows that produce the farm's milk.

The farm has been in the Mohns' family since his great-grandfather came from Norway in the 1850s, says Bruce Mohn, a man with a weathered farmer's face. Continuing his family's tradition is one of the prime satisfactions he gets from farming, he said, and one of the prime reasons he keeps the farm small and doesn't take on too much debt for more rented land or more cows and equipment.

"I don't want to be the one that loses it," he said, as we walked between buildings in the brisk late November afternoon.

The farm and its operations are embedded in the co-op system, and most likely that's the reason the farm is still operating independently. The Mohns sell the roughly 475 gallons of milk their fifty cows produce every day to Hastings Co-op Creamery, which sells its milk, cream, butter, and cheese in supermarkets and convenience stores, as well as to schools and commercial users. Under the co-op structure, the Mohns are among the owners of the Hastings creamery, and help manage it. Neither has ever served on the board, but they could, if they chose to run and got elected. As with most people I spoke with on the subject, for them, serving on a co-op board seemed to combine a curious mix of business, social, and community purposes. As board members, they would be looking after their own business interests, but in conventional market terms they wouldn't be compensated enough. But people did it anyway. These board members tended to be the ones who serve also on the school board, the church board, and so on.

"Some people do it and enjoy it," said Cheryl Mohn. "Of course, you get paid, but it's not much, considering how much work it is."

The Mohns are users—and thus owners—of a half dozen or so other cooperatives besides the creamery in their lives and business. They get financing for their farm operations through Agribank, the major co-op bank that is part of the co-op–based Farm Credit System. They buy semen to impregnate their cows through Genex, a cooperative that sells, yes, semen. The Mohns have insurance on their farm through a cooperative insurance company. In their personal lives, they get their health care through a co-op. They used to get their electricity and telephone service through co-ops. Until recently, the Mohns used the grain elevator that bought members' grain through a co-op structure, although now they usually drive farther to sell their grain directly to Cargill, which is not a cooperative, at a nearby Mississippi River barge terminal port. Because this Cargill port is a step up the food chain in the farm-to-market staircase, they get a better price.

The Mohns are strong supporters of co-ops. When they do criticize co-ops—which they do—it's because they believe co-ops sometimes diverge from the priority of protecting the interests of the small farmers like themselves. Land O'Lakes, for example, has a program that helps small farmers get bigger, they said. While this may be well and good for those farmers, it can hurt the interests of small farmers like the Mohns who depend on small-scale distribution systems being there for them. I didn't know enough to judge whose side to take in this, but the debate certainly showed that co-ops were not static creatures.

The Mohns' perspectives were probably colored by the fact that the price for milk was brutally low nationally when I interviewed them in late 2009, about $14 per "hundredweight" (meaning one hundred pounds of milk), down from close to $20 per hundredweight in 2007. It had been a hard few years.

CO-OPS: THEIR HUMBLE ROOTS

Although people have long banded together to solve common problems—guilds, unions, associations, and even the corporation itself are examples—the unique structure of co-ops that balances power and fairness is generally said to date back to the mid-nineteenth century in England.

In 1844, a group of weavers in a cotton mill in England, struggling to make ends meet, got together to buy butter, milk, and other staples. This was the start of the Rochdale Society of Equitable Pioneers, one of the first cooperatives and one on which the organizational form of others has been modeled. Want to change the world? This humble group provides an example. Without guns, without force, you start something that can improve people's lives and that can grow organically over the decades and centuries. The Rochdale Pioneers wrote the seven principles of cooperatives, which are, amazingly, with just some slight modifications, still the seven principles of cooperatives around the world today. Many of these principles, such as one member, one vote, were directly reacting to what the cooperative founders saw as oppression by a status quo in which only property owners could vote, and they exercised influence according to the size of their estates.

The original Rochdale principles were:

1. Open membership.
2. Democratic control (one person, one vote).
3. Distribution of surplus in proportion to trade.
4. Payment of limited interest on capital.
5. Political and religious neutrality.
6. Cash trading (no credit extended).
7. Promotion of education.

The principles of the International Co-operative Alliance, a global coalition of co-ops that credits the Rochdale Pioneers for beginning the movement, are:

1. Voluntary and open membership.
2. Democratic member control.
3. Members' economic participation.
4. Autonomy and independence.
5. Education, training, and information.
6. Cooperation among cooperatives.
7. Concern for community.

As you can see, the two sets are pretty similar, despite the passing of more than 160 years. The International Co-operative Alliance, founded in 1895, says it represents more than 800 million people in co-ops around the world. It has updated the principles three times, in 1937, 1966, and 1995, and the changes were each time pretty minimal from a historical perspective. Its principles are seen everywhere in co-op land. The National Rural Electric Cooperative Association, which according to its website represents 864 power distribution systems that serve 42 million people in forty-seven states, lists the seven principles on its website. At the co-op convention in Minnesota, members of co-ops often mention "the seven principles." There was something magical about these conventioneers, typical businessmen and -women in appearance, referring to principles that trace back to a bunch of struggling self-helpers in 1844.

And how has the co-op of the Rochdale Pioneers fared? Very well. It still exists as part of the Co-operative Group, based in Manchester, England, a huge cooperative that sells everything from potatoes to banking services to electrical services to funeral services. It is "one of the world's largest consumer-owned businesses, with over three million members and 85,000 employees across all its businesses," says the group's website.[3]

IN EUROPE

Cooperatives are more common in Europe than the United States. Cooperative owners in France grow and sell wine. In Holland, which has a surprisingly large and vital agricultural sector for such a small country, cooperatives make a variety of specialized products out of milk, grains, and other agricultural commodities.[4]

"Denmark is full of them. Finland is full of them," said Lee Uldbjerg, sixty-one, a Land O'Lakes executive wearing a tweed jacket. "It's an old, old model. The Danes figured out a couple of hundred years ago that it paid to work together."

Mondragon, a network of cooperatives started in the Basque country of Spain in 1956 in the town of that name, is particularly noteworthy because it's an employee-owned cooperative that has steadily grown in size since its founding a half-century ago.[5] With 85,000 employees, it generates €15 billion in sales, from over two hundred worker cooperatives. These co-ops are in five major groups: consumer goods, financial services, construction, industrial components, and management consulting. Among their many activities, Mondragon co-ops sell high-end machine tools to Germany, helped build the Frank Gehry–designed Guggenheim Museum Bilbao, and run the largest grocery store chain in Spain. They do so with wages set on a scale of highest to lowest of 6:1, with occasional exceptions up to 8:1.[6] In contrast, the average CEO of a company within the S&P 500 in recent years has made anywhere from three hundred to five hundred times more than the average American worker, up from twenty-four times more in 1965.[7]

FORMED IN BATTLE: COOPERATIVES IN THE UNITED STATES

Just as the Rochdale Pioneers in England formed in an alliance against poverty, co-ops in the United States often have their roots in defensive actions against common adversity. That adversity can come from banks that overcharge or don't lend, low-ball wholesalers, low-quality, low-price competitors, grain storage companies, and unresponsive power and telephone companies that don't serve rural areas or only do so at exorbitant prices. From these defensive beginnings, take-charge profit-making companies were born.

In the early twentieth century, farmers began many cooperatives to gain a greater share of the money spent on their products. The Capper-Volstead Act in 1922 was a key piece of legislation, still relevant today. It exempted cooperatives from antitrust legislation that would have prohibited voluntary association among producers. Federal agencies were given power to intervene against a cooperative if it actually gained monopoly power in a market.

Co-ops took a leap in number in the Great Depression in the 1930s. Rural electrical co-ops were given a big boost by President Franklin Roosevelt in 1935 when he created the Rural Electrification Administration to expressly encourage the formation of cooperatives to spread electrical service to rural areas. These power cooperatives were given loans to start businesses, which were paid back. These electrical cooperatives, many of which still exist, proved that service could be provided to rural residents not only at a profit, but also at a reasonable cost.

But all this did not come easy. Banks, big grain companies, and power companies did not like co-ops and sought to prevent their formation. A big conventional grain company would rather buy wheat from a small farmer to whom it can dictate price than compete with a co-op of which the farmer is an owner. A local bank doesn't like being undercut on interest rates by a credit union.

Although formed in adversity, co-ops have a history of slowly turning the tables and becoming powerful commercially, while still keeping their values of fairness and equity. One example in Canada is the co-op Credit Desjardins in Quebec, perhaps the leading banking institution in the province. It was started by the journalist Alphonse Desjardins in 1900 as an effort to spread credit to the poorer French-speaking majority that had historically been denied it.[8] It is now a powerhouse, with its branches and ATMs seen in seemingly every small town and on many big city streets.

In 1921 one of the best-known cooperatives in the United States, Land O'Lakes, was formed, as an effort to keep the incomes of farmers up while also keeping quality up. Land O'Lakes, whose butter is familiar for the pretty Indian maiden on its yellow box, had $12 billion in sales in 2008 and is headquartered outside Minneapolis. Formed by some already existing dairy cooperatives in Minnesota as the Minnesota Cooperative Creameries Association, it is actually a cooperative of cooperatives, being owned by more than one thousand local cooperatives as well as individual farmers.[9]

Here's how it works. The Pulaski Chase dairy co-op in Wisconsin buys its members' milk, and then turns around and sells it to Land O'Lakes, of which the Pulaski Chase Cooperative is an owner. The local farmers who comprise the owner membership of Pulaski Chase, in turn, elect its board of directors. These directors, and thousands like them around the country, elect the board of Land O'Lakes.[10]

Land O'Lakes not only buys milk and sells butter, but sells farmers animal feed through its Purina arm, and fertilizer, insecticide, and technical services. It is an example of a common practice with cooperatives, in that a co-op can both buy from and sell to its owner/members. Land O'Lakes buys its members' milk, while also selling them feed for their cows. There's no contradiction here, because since its customers are also its member/owners, it does both at the best price it can.

If Land O'Lakes were a conventional corporation, it would be pricing what it buys and sells to maximize the profits of its investor/owners, who would probably not be the farmers who sell it milk to make the butter. In this sense, its owners and its producers would be in a competitive, antagonistic relationship, where each tried to maximize its advantage at the other's expense. At Land O'Lakes, they are in a cooperative relationship, because the producers are the owners.

Farming and farm-related services have been the special province of cooperatives for a century or more. Making milk or butter and then selling it are uniquely suited for cooperatives, because conventional market structures push both profits and quality down. A farmer selling corn or soybeans can see all his profit go to the man who operates the sole grain elevator in the region, or the local bank. He can see his product sell for at or below cost, because his product is a commodity and lacks "market power," which means the ability to set the price of one's product.[11] He can end up at the mercy of large food companies like Perdue Foods or Smithfield Foods. He can see low-quality, low-price butter or milk undercut his goods. Land O'Lakes is a huge company, but the farmers who sell it milk are empowered by its size, not diminished.

TOWARD EQUITY, COMMUNITY, AND PRODUCTIVITY

Because cooperatives are a type of business set up to be both productive and fair, they offer a way forward for a lot of the problems bedeviling the United States, and indeed, much of the industrialized world.

Take equity. As has been noted many times, in the United States income inequality and inequalities of wealth have been steadily rising for a generation. According to some analyses, the wealthiest 1 percent of the country are worth more than the bottom 90 percent. As of this writing, many CEOs have compensation packages of $10 or even $100 million a year. This means the pay of top executives is now not just dozens, but hundreds, of times more, even a thousand times more, than the pay of the lowest-paid employee in a company.[12] There are those who fear, accurately I think, that our democracy is threatened when so few have so much wealth, and thus so much power. Co-ops can counter this, because the rewards of a cooperative company are distributed more equitably. Why this is so relates to how co-ops operate.

Cooperatives apply democracy to the market, as I have said. With cooperatives, all owners get the same vote, regardless of their size and rate of participation in the co-ops. Every co-op, whether it be a small local dairy cooperative or one of the giants like Land O'Lakes or CHS that are in the Fortune 500, adheres to this principle. This arrangement helps block one of the common trends of conventional capitalism, which is that capital concentrates and the big owners, producers, buyers, or sellers gradually take over the little ones and subordinate their interests.

"It's the way we run our church, the way we run our government," said Gary Tomter, an executive at energy, grain, and food giant CHS who oversees its northern territories, in yet another of my many hallway conversations at the convention. "It's a democracy."

CHS had $17 billion in revenue in 2008 and was situated in size between US Steel and Xerox on the Fortune 500 list. It was established in 1998 with the merger of two already large cooperatives, Cenex and Harvest States Cooperatives. It refines and sells gasoline. It sells fertilizers and grain, manages oil pipelines, and even operates a chain of convenience stores. It is a very, very large company. Yet here was this top executive saying his company operated like a church.

Because co-ops are oriented toward the middle and smaller members, the profits or payments of the co-op go to them in larger proportions. Cranberry growers with Ocean Spray get a bigger portion of the $3 spent on cranberry juice than, say, what corn producers receive for their contribution to a box of Kellogg's Corn Flakes.

This market democracy is also reflected in the absence of the mega pay packages for top corporate executives that have earned the ire of so many commentators, but continued regardless.

"Co-ops are conservative." Bill Oemichen, the president of the Cooperative Network, was a hearty man who, as he dealt with convention duties, answered my many questions about how co-ops work. "They are not going to pay those salaries you hear about. You would never get that kind of salaries in a co-op."

Oemichen said co-ops avoid much of the rancor and corruption that plague conventional businesses. "When I was head of the consumer protection agency [in Wisconsin], I would get two hundred thousand complaints a year. Fewer than ten of them were from co-op members or about co-ops."

When you compare Wisconsin dairy farmers to, say, North Carolina hog farmers, or Massachusetts cranberry growers to Arkansas chicken growers, you see that control by a few in the interest of the few is indeed what has happened in other areas of agricultural production. Giant companies like Perdue and Smithfield Foods have converted once proud independent farmers into little better than employees. The nominally independent chicken farmer resembles a sharecropper or peasant, toiling for his master in a faraway mansion. This is not to single out Smithfield or Perdue for special criticism. It is to say that their business model puts them in an adversarial relationship with their suppliers. All this would be different if hog or chicken farmers were members of a cooperative. Cooperatives are designed to steer profits and benefits to the producers, including the smallest ones. "Control goes from the bottom up, profit goes from the top down," says Tomter.

The opposite is true of conventional capitalism. Smithfield Foods, for example, extracts the maximum profit from its hog farmers while giving them minimal control. In a cooperative, ideally at least, the members at the lowest level control the direction and priorities of the company they belong to. The profits it earns are in turn passed down back to those members, including to the smallest of them.

Because of this structure, and for cultural reasons as well, there is an emphasis within cooperatives on consensus, not blunt majority rule. Most cooperatives in fact have rules that require a supermajority to actually change the core architecture.

CAPITAL AS SERVANT

Typically co-ops do not allow outside investors. Or if they are allowed, they are given no say in management. Combined with the one member, one vote rule, the member-owner rule means a cooperative practices a kind of capitalism that works for the interest of the people who make or buy stuff, rather than those who simply invest.

"It's the ownership that makes a co-op different," Uldbjerg says. "With co-ops, the profits go to the people who make the stuff the company sells."

This "member-owned" rule keeps a health-care cooperative like Health Partners, the billion-dollar company that is a big player in health care in Minnesota, working in the interest of the patients, not the doctors or hospital administrators. It keeps cooperative utility corporations working in the interest of their customers. It is, like the rules that create all kinds of markets, just a rule, but one that can be learned from, and copied.

One contemporary challenge for cooperatives is how to raise enough money for today's capital-intensive endeavors. Even farming today can involve tractors that cost half a million dollars, while production and distribution systems can run into millions if not billions. Historically, cooperatives raised their capital from within their membership. Many still do this. This dates back to the Rochdale Pioneers in 1844 struggling and succeeding in raising a pound each to fund the start-up costs of their cooperative.

In recent years, some co-ops have begun allowing outside investors, as long as no essential voting rights are given to them. These are being called "hybrid co-ops," or in Minnesota, "308B co-ops," after the section of Minnesota law allowing them. This is the frontier of co-ops, I was told at the convention. Letting in more outside money, while not ceding control. It's clearly a dangerous game, because co-op values depend on not allowing independent capital to gain control of a co-op. So far, though, co-ops are keeping capital in its place. Here's how the website of CHS, a huge cooperative company listed on the New York Stock Exchange, addresses the issue:

Since 2003, the list of stakeholders at CHS has included non-voting preferred stockholders. This provides CHS with additional capitalization to maintain a strong balance sheet, position our businesses for the future and provide timely investment returns for *stockholders. CHS preferred stock represents an equity interest in the company, but does not carry voting rights.*[13] [emphasis mine]

In other words, we'll take your money. We won't give you control.

REVIVING COMMUNITY

There has been much lamenting that community as a whole has declined in this country in the last half-century, resulting in a loss of what Robert Putnam calls social capital. Although it's easy to lapse into nostalgia, research by Putnam and others, as well as my personal experience, shows community really has declined. People know their neighbors less. There are fewer bowling leagues, and more "bowling alone." Co-ops could help counter this.

Co-op members tend to be engaged citizens, to care more about the quality of schools and the stability of a town or city in which their business is located. They are "community-focused," in accordance with one of the seven co-op principles. There are a lot of reasons for this. One is because the one member, one vote rule, allowing no control to outside investors, creates a community-based model of capitalism that is tied to the land, to a particular place on the map.

"It's a lot like the Green Bay Packers, even though the team is not a cooperative," says Oemichen, naming the famous National Football League team that is owned by a city of a mere 100,000 people, and is now tied to that city, probably forever. "The town owns the team. That keeps the team in the town. I'm a Packer shareholder. And the team does very well, despite being in a city of only 100,000 people."[14]

At the convention, I lost count of the number of people who mentioned "community" as one of the core values of cooperative members in a matter-of-fact way.

"Co-ops are committed to the communities they serve. It's one of the seven principles of co-ops," said Ron Schmidt, a director of Clark Electric Cooperative in Wisconsin, which dates back to 1937 and President Franklin Roosevelt's efforts. "They give back to the community, they are part of the community."

Terry Ebeling, age fifty-three, a tall, thin man in a red shirt, talked of why he had been for seventeen years on the board of AgStar, the large cooperative bank that supplied farmers with credit. Ebeling said he was a farmer in southern Minnesota, and he had the worn and slightly fleshy face typical of the tribe.

"AgStar has been there for me," said Ebeling. "I want it to be there for other people. I want to leave it better than how I found it. I want our co-op values to stand. We want loans available to anyone who has a plan, be they a big, medium, or small farmer. They just need a plan."

I found this blending of service and profit motives worth noting. Many years ago, one of my role models, Stewart Brand, said that businesses work best if run like services, and (nonprofit) services work best if run like businesses. A cooperative blends the best of both of those functions. Cooperative businesses generate both actual capital and civic capital.

Money, or capital, we are told, is rootless, amoral. It goes anywhere, seeking out the highest return, whether it be bread baking in Timbuktu, silicon chips in California, or coffee beans in Colombia. This very neutrality of capital is said to be its greatest strength. Capital does not play favorites. It abandons old friends like Bell Atlantic or IBM or General Motors after a few bad quarters. This footlooseness of capital leaves towns, cities, and countries vulnerable to its fickle ways. I envision a dollar bill behind the wheel of a car or airplane, relentlessly searching for greater return and touching down wherever it is found, be it in Oklahoma or India, be it producing nails or nitrogen fertilizer. Capital has no allegiances, its proponents and critics say. Co-ops do.

A BIAS TOWARD MAKING STUFF

Along with a loss of community, there has been a long-term decline in manufacturing in this country. Co-ops can help counter this as well because co-ops excel at making stuff of high quality and maintaining market share over time. Indeed, co-ops often create markets.

A cooperative like Ocean Spray starts with its members, the cranberry bog growers in Massachusetts, who want to keep growing cranberries. In an effort to make more money at it, they then invent new products like Ocean Spray Cranberry Drink, one of the most successful product inventions of all time. The bog owners do not seek to invest their money in Argentina. They are seeking to be profitable cranberry growers. Toward that end, they invent. Ocean Spray, which dates back to the 1930s, has converted cranberries from something eaten once or twice a year with turkey to something "drunk" continually, from the bottle of cranberry "juice" (actually cranberry juice mixed with a considerable quantity of sugar to offset the intense sourness of cranberries) in the refrigerator to the well-stocked bar that would never fail to stock cranberry juice for the de rigueur Cosmopolitan and other cranberry-flavored and -colored drinks. Ocean Spray has about $2 billion in sales annually and is still owned by six hundred cranberry growers sprinkled around North America. And growing cranberries, unlike many agricultural products, is in no danger of moving to Brazil, because the company is tied to the land of its cranberry-growing families in Massachusetts, Oregon, Wisconsin, and British Columbia.

You see this dynamic in Europe as well, where cooperatives have managed to keep agriculture profitable in many high-wage, high-cost-of-living nations. The saga of potato starch is illustrative. A cooperative named Avebe operates in multiple countries and manufactures more than a thousand pharmaceutical and industrial products from potato starch and other potato products.[15] It all dates back to a bunch of potato farmers in Germany in 1919 seeking some new use for all those damn potatoes, which could only be mashed and eaten in so many ways.

One factor in co-ops that helps keep them creative and prevents ossification is that membership is open. Anyone can join a co-op as long as he or she meets the membership requirements. A co-op is not a union, a guild, or the American Medical Association. The wages of co-op members are not enhanced by keeping people out. If anything, co-ops gain market power as they gain members. Open membership is one of the seven co-op principles. This aspect of co-ops can turn potential competitors into neighbors, which in turn enhances the community orientation of co-ops. In a conventional business environment, if you are the seller of maps, marigolds, or marijuana, then your neighbor selling a similar product is your competitor.

Another factor that keeps co-ops healthy long-term is their low emphasis on profits. Co-ops often don't talk about profits, only "surpluses." Maximizing "service" is also a common priority. This is not just semantics. An electrical co-op is not trying to make a profit, but to deliver the best service at the lowest price to its members. A credit union is attempting to lend money to its members at the lowest possible interest rates. A traditional bank operates in opposite fashion. It is attempting to lend money at the highest possible interest rates.

Finally, co-ops often have high-quality products because the interests of producers are more aligned with retailers. In conventional markets, competition pushes sellers to cut quality to reduce costs. This is particularly true for wholesalers, whose name is not attached to the end product. Just the opposite dynamic is at work in a cooperative, both actually and psychologically. A farmer in a cooperative is selling milk to a business he owns; it is his business that is selling that product in the supermarket. The farmer wants to keep quality high so that his products can be the best.

In 1995, Florence Fabricant and Ruth Reichl, the well-known food writers for the *New York Times*, conducted a taste test of butters, with most of the focus being on expensive, boutique butters. You could almost see the reviewers' raised eyebrows when Land O'Lakes sweet butter, then at $2.49 a pound, proved to be at the top in taste and feel, the equal of a boutique butter nearly three times the price.[16]

Robin Partch, the winemaker at Northern Vineyards cooperative winery at Stillwater outside St. Paul, whom I visited there, explained how the cooperative organization helps compensate for a traditional vineyard-winery dynamic that tends to undermine quality.

"The dynamics in most of the industry is that the wine grower wants to maximize production, and wants to pick [grapes] early to minimize losses from weather," said Partch from his storefront, which was on the main street of Stillwater, a pretty, historic river town. "But the winemaker wants the grower to pick as late as possible [so the fruit is riper] to maximize quality." A cooperative, he said, aligns the interest of the two.

THE FUTURE OF COOPERATIVES

During the great health-care-reform debate of 2009–2010, cooperatives emerged for a while as an option, and Cooperative Network president Bill Oemichen briefly made the rounds of the political talk shows explaining how cooperatives, and health-care cooperatives in particular, work. But the debate moved on, and I suspect one reason was so many players did not really understand how cooperatives worked. This is a shame, because encouraging more cooperatives nationally might have really helped put some of the pieces together in the health-care puzzle of reducing costs and improving service.

At the convention in November of 2009, former Republican Senator David Durenberger from Minnesota spoke about the hot issue of health care to a crowded room. The US Senate would eventually approve a health-care bill in 2010 without a single Republican vote. So it was striking to see this former Republican senator speak of the necessity for national health care, and the possibilities for co-ops to be part of the solution. To me, it was an example of how co-ops can be bridges or paths out of some sticky societal problems, something Durenberger himself noted.

"They balance the 'mutuality of interests' of doctors, patients," administrators, drug suppliers, and so on, Durenberger said in his speech about co-ops and health care. The former Republican senator also said, in response to a question, that he would "certainly" have voted for universal health insurance, in whatever form it took, if he had still been in the Senate. He called universal health care a moral and economic imperative.

Cooperatives have enormous potential to be used further in various sectors of the economy. They are a fairer, more stable form of capitalism. In health care, they would put doctors and patients on the same side, for example. Being treated by a doctor who is employed by the health-care co-op you own is a different experience than being treated by a doctor who owns his own business, with you merely the customer. The doctors make different choices when their patients are their employers.

But one difficulty with co-ops is simply understanding how they work.

"You need enough farmers to teach the city folk how to do it," said Egerstrom, the former reporter for the *St. Paul Pioneer Press*.

Hearing similar stories from others, I become more and more convinced that capitalism and markets depend on the structures in people's heads, as well as those in the law books. Our standard model of capitalism is so well ensconced in our heads that it's difficult to make room for another model.

Should there be the desire, cooperatives could spread to other sectors of the economy.

"A co-op is a business," said David Holm, executive director of the Iowa Institute for Cooperatives. "The only thing that makes it different from a regular business is who controls it, and who gets the profits. In a co-op, the users control it, and get the profit. In a regular company, it's the investors who get the control and the profit. The users, be they suppliers or buyers, may get none at all or very little."

Employee-owned co-ops, like REI, are a fertile sector, said Holm. He could see opportunity in, say, a hardware store or other small local businesses that are in danger of going under. "The employees need a job, the town needs a hardware store," Holm said. When an owner puts it up for sale on retirement, Holm said, often it can't fetch much.

Towns could facilitate the cooperatization of the hardware store, with employees owning it.

I can see cooperatives operating in high-technology sectors like software writing. A team of writers could pool their resources, and share the profits among them equally.

Politically and culturally, co-ops are all over the map. Land O'Lakes, Ocean Spray, Borden, and energy and communication co-ops have traditionally been rural, conservative, and to some degree Republican. Newer co-ops like Organic Valley milk, a cooperative of more than a thousand organic farmers, are culturally, at least, more liberal and Democratic. Historically, co-ops have had a foot in both political parties. Oemichen, the Cooperative Network president, previously served as consumer affairs representative under Republican governor Tommy Thompson of Wisconsin. Many at the convention undoubtedly had ties to Democratic and liberal administrations. But to a remarkable degree, these two worlds of cooperatives have functioned harmoniously together without visible differences.

Egerstrom, in *Make No Small Plans: A Cooperative Revival for Rural America*, alludes to this generally peaceful mix of liberal and conservative philosophies as reflected in the way co-ops regard government:

> They turn to government, at one level, when they need help to develop resources and infrastructure they can't develop themselves. They pool resources at the community level to do things when cooperative, collective action and capital are needed and possible. They share a culture that allows them to be both liberal and conservative, usually at the same time.[17]

The cooperative model, which puts capital in the service of people, which runs commercial enterprises in a democratic fashion, is an optimistic model for markets and capitalism. It deserves to be copied and encouraged, not just in its particulars, but in the willingness of its founders from long ago, the Rochdale Pioneers, to try something different as a way to make life better for themselves and their neighbors.

CHAPTER 5

TRUST: HOW WE COOPERATE TO COMPETE

I am affected, not because you have deceived me, but because I can no longer believe in you.
FRIEDRICH NIETZSCHE, *BEYOND GOOD AND EVIL*, 1886

PARK CITY, UTAH, is a surprisingly unappealing little city, given its status as home to the sexy Sundance Film Festival. I was expecting a historic town with an overly cutesy main street lined with expensive shops. Instead, what I find are strip shopping centers with parking lots, groups of pointy-topped mountain-style condos on parking lots, high schools and other civic buildings on parking lots, and wide suburban-style boulevards connecting them. There may be a historic town some-where here—I was later told it was an old mining town—but I never found it.

As I drive around on a snowy day in January during the Sundance Film Festival, I watch festivalgoers in baggy coats trudging through the snow or waiting for shuttle buses. All quite ungainly.[1] But it works well enough, which is all that is necessary. Most people are not here for fun, but as part of their careers, to make, buy, distribute, review, or appear in independent films.

The Sundance Film Festival showcases "independent" films, a term that means films produced not by major studios, but by "independent" producers. The term has blurred some now, as big companies have cre-ated or sponsored independent film companies, such as New Line or Miramax. The festival was created by the famous actor Robert Red-ford in the 1970s, and was his way of giving momentum and attention to efforts worthy of more support, while taking attention away from something he was less enchanted with, the big Hollywood studios and the industry there. The festival is now critical to the fortunes of large companies that come here every year and pick a few "independent" movies to showcase and promote in mainstream theaters.

I talk about the Sundance Film Festival here because it is an example of how many profitable industries and markets have nonmarket foundations. Some of these foundations include literal nonprofits; others are arrangements where profits assume secondary importance, or are the government itself. In essence, in many areas, we cooperate first to compete later. In this chapter, I lay out this premise and give some examples of it, including not only the Sundance Film Festival and the independent film market, but public radio, newspapers, and the Internet. Chapter 4 in this book is about cooperatives, but it's also significant to see how cooperation underlies many industries in ways that are not overtly termed "cooperative."

In a larger sense, we all agree to cooperate first, and then compete later. We agree not to bash our neighbor on the head, and to live our lives in civilized ways. Although there are laws to prescribe and proscribe activities, the reasons we behave aren't primarily legal. It's a social contract that we are following. Respecting this social contract and understanding it as a necessary precondition for markets is, or should be, part of learning about and understanding capitalism.

JOY AND MONEY: WHICH COMES FIRST?

Robert Redford helped start the Sundance Film Festival because he was trying to create a better "market" for independent films. But he was not trying to make himself any richer when he started the Sundance Institute. Quite the contrary, his festival work probably consumed large chunks of his revenue-producing time. Yet another example of how real people do not conform to the behavior of *Homo economicus* that conventional economists use as a model.

The festival emerged in the 1980s as the premier showcase for independent films. As with a medieval trade fair, industry leaders flock to this market town every year, and review and eventually buy millions or even billions of dollars' worth of films. So important is the festival that just getting into the Sundance Film Festival is a big deal for a filmmaker.

Although the festival generates hundreds of millions of dollars' worth of films each year, judged by what is paid for them or by future ticket and popcorn sales, the sponsoring Institute is legally a nonprofit.

Typically people say that Robert Redford started the festival, but the story is more complicated than that. Basically it was started by a few people getting together, including Sterling Van Wagenen and John Earle, a Utah state film commissioner, and getting a little state and foundation money plus a famous actor's backing (Redford). The festival in its first few years went ever deeper into debt, even as it attracted attention from film executives and the public. It went by several different names in its first years, including the United States Film and Video Festival. It started out in Salt Lake City before moving to Park City in 1981. It might have ceased, had the Utah Film Commission not first given it financial support later in 1981, and then perhaps more importantly, had it not come under the stewardship of the Sundance Institute in 1985. It was then that the festival gained the moniker of the Sundance Film Festival, although it would take a few years for the name to evolve to being simply that. On a parallel track, the Sundance Institute was set up as a nonprofit in 1981 by Redford to encourage the development of independent films. The association of the Sundance Institute with the film festival would seem to be a natural, but it actually took a bit of doing to combine the two.[2] To sum up, a slew of nonprofit entities helped get this little film festival off the ground, which in turn helped build a more robust market for independent films.

MARKETS ON NONMARKETS

Many industries and institutions are built on cooperative or nonmarket foundations.

Public radio is one, including National Public Radio, its most famous member. Here we have an industry, long-form radio, that has significant impact on policymakers and the public. National Public Radio's primary shows, *Morning Edition* and *All Things Considered*, are major journalistic undertakings. They get millions of listeners every day, higher in number than most for-profit network news shows, from what I can tell. Exact numbers are actually difficult to get because the commercial radio stations put pressure on the primary rating service, Arbitron, not to include public radio in its figures. NPR, Public Radio International, and other members of the public radio family rest on a thoroughly nonprofit entity—the Corporation for Public Broadcasting—and Congress's decision in 1967 to establish it and devote some of the radio spectrum to nonprofit radio.

If you poke into public radio more deeply, you actually find a market economy. Although virtually every aspect of public radio is nonprofit, from the stations themselves to the production of shows, there is a vigorous market mechanism exercised to decide distribution and exposure. Essentially, shows compete to get picked up by individual stations, which in turn compete to get their shows picked up by aggregators, like National Public Radio or the lesser-known American Public Radio or Public Radio International. The individual stations then select, from the available offerings, shows for themselves, picking up shows of other stations through National Public Radio or another service. They pay NPR for the rights, and a portion of the payment goes back to the producer station. So a show like *Car Talk*, an oddity where Tom and Ray Magliozzi, otherwise known as Click and Clack, the Tappet Brothers, talk in thick Boston accents about vehicular matters, will emerge from a local station (in this case, the prominent WBUR in Boston in 1977), get picked up by NPR (in 1987), and then eventually be listened to nationwide, depending on whether it is selected by the program managers at more than 350 individual stations.[3]

The industry where I got my start in journalism, newspapers, is suffering right now, and by the time this book comes out, who knows what form newspapers will take or how many will be left? But if you view the history of newspapers from World War II to 2000, what you find behind the prestigious newspapers is a large institution with monopoly-level profits that in effect subsidized long-form and civic-minded journalism, of the kind I used to produce on occasion for *The Virginian-Pilot* in Norfolk. These exercises in public service and professional pride were only vaguely related to profitability or even readership, if truth be told. It's debatable how many readers actually wanted to read the prizewinning series on migrant worker safety or city hall finances. An elite did, surely, and such series helped government and society function better. But they probably didn't make that many more people buy the newspaper, not compared with the high cost of such projects.

Few people realize how resource-intensive serious journalism is. Though rarer now, it was not atypical for a newspaper to allow a reporter or two to spend three, six, or even twelve months on a project, supported by the associated time of editors, photographers, and other staff. This was a hefty investment, which in the heyday of newspapers sometimes reached absurd amounts. *Newsday*, which formerly was one of the best newspapers in the country but not widely known outside Long Island and the industry, in 1972 sent a team of reporters, led by

Bob Greene and rounded out by Les Payne and Knut Royce, to Turkey, France, and other parts of Europe to investigate the heroin trade. Any connection to its readership of affluent suburbanites on Long Island was tenuous at best. Even the reporters doubted that anyone read the entire thirty-two-part series "The Heroin Trail" that was published in 1973. The expense, which included a thirteen-year libel lawsuit that the newspaper ultimately won, was enormous.[4] Why did *Newsday* do such a thing?

As with most great and good newspapers, it seemed to be a combination of pride and pressure. Writers wanted to work for the "good" newspapers, papers like the *San Jose Mercury News*, the *Charlotte Observer*, or the *Hartford Courant*. *Newsday* picked up a Pulitzer Prize for Public Service in 1973 for the story, which won it esteem, thereby attracting better reporters and editors. There was a pride these owners and editors had in working at a "good" newspaper.

While these top-quality newspapers had a passion for journalism (and some still do), it's not immaterial that they were still able to make profits of 25 percent or more on revenues, even while incurring these big expenses. Unglamorous departments, particularly the classified ads, would generate millions of dollars in easy profits. As these profits have declined, so has long-form and civic journalism. It still survives, though. The *Washington Post*, an economically strapped newspaper now, in 2010 published "Top Secret America," a report on the explosion of secret government after the attacks of September 11, 2001. The Introduction to the series states that more than a dozen journalists worked two years on it.[5] Thank you, Donald Graham.

Perhaps the most significant example of a market mechanism with nonmarket foundations is the Internet itself, which is now the basis of global commerce. DARPA, which stands for Defense Advanced Research Projects Agency (in the US Defense Department), invented and set up the Internet's principal predecessor, ARPANET, beginning in the 1960s.[6] Today a nonprofit company set up in the late 1990s by the US government, ICANN, the Internet Corporation for Assigned Names and Numbers, manages large areas of the Internet's governance. Although the specifics of the Internet are too extensive to go into, it's significant that this revolution in commerce and lifestyle was not started for any reason having to do with profit. This, too, is typical. The silicon chip was invented because of defense dollars, and throughout history other significant commercial revolutions have had their roots in military and other types of government work.

ALL TOGETHER NOW: HOW WE COOPERATE TO COMPETE

If we move beyond specific endeavors like film festivals, newspapers, and the Internet, we come to the larger point, which is that in reality, all of us cooperate in dozens of ways every day to make a competitive capitalistic, market-oriented system possible.

"We acquire legal rights in a market economy by statute (a relationship between the individual and the state) or by contract (a relationship between two individuals)," said John Kay in *The Truth about Markets: Their Genius, Their Limits, Their Follies.* "But most transactions in a market are governed by expectations and conventions, not the law. We are rarely conscious of making contracts. When Bill bought the Mars bar from the shopkeeper, the law inferred a contract."[7]

Healthy markets rely on trust and deteriorate if that trust erodes. Bruce Scott of the Harvard Business School, in his 2009 book *The Concept of Capitalism,* compares economic markets, where people meet either physically or virtually to buy and sell, to "the common," the piece of pasture or grazing land used collectively by a village. Scott argues that just as the classic "common" depended on villagers not abusing it by overgrazing, so the commercial commons depends on some sense of restraint and fair play by individual buyers and sellers.[8]

Says Scott:

> Prior to the advent of long distance trade, circa 1500, people all over the world were able to manage their various local physical commons because those commons were small enough for the actors to see the damage that resulted from over-hunting or over-grazing. These actors would then govern themselves accordingly and maintain a stable system whose output was limited. . . .
>
> Successful globalization depends upon successful regulation of a global common, including successful regulation of atmospheric pollutants and of the harvesting of marine life. While excessive regulation has stifled many economies for long periods, inadequate regulation is also a threat to effective decentralized decision-making throughout the global common. Abuse of the common is an ever-present temptation that comes with economic freedom. Effective use of a commercial common, as well as its effective protection from abuse, depends upon the maintenance of an effective system of economic governance, and, for all practical purposes, today that means governance through a capitalist system headed by a legitimate political authority.[9]

CONCLUSION

What is needed in our nation is a renewed respect for the noncompetitive, more cooperative parts of our society that the competitive, for-profit parts rely upon. Rather than trying to "marketize" everything, we should realize and teach that for-profit markets and capitalism itself rest on our willingness to do certain things without immediate individual benefit.

CHAPTER 6

STAKING CLAIMS ON THE MIND: INTELLECTUAL PROPERTY

Americans have been selling this view around the world: that progress comes from perfect protection of intellectual property.
LAWRENCE LESSIG, STANFORD LAW PROFESSOR AND AUTHOR OF *THE FUTURE OF IDEAS*[1]

IN THE EARLY 1600s, the English Parliament was growing increasingly aggravated with the king, because he and his predecessors had been handing out favors in the form of monopoly rights to sell or produce things. One historian described life in the 1600s in London this way:

It is difficult for us to picture for ourselves the life of a man living in a house built with monopoly bricks, with windows (if any) of monopoly glass; heated with monopoly coal (in Ireland monopoly timber), burning in a grate made of monopoly iron. His walls were lined with monopoly tapestries. He slept on monopoly feathers, did his hair with monopoly brushes. He washed himself with monopoly soap, his clothes in monopoly starch. He dressed in monopoly lace, monopoly linen, monopoly belts, monopoly gold thread. His hat was monopoly beaver, with a monopoly band. His clothes were held up with monopoly belts, monopoly buttons, and monopoly pins. They were dyed with monopoly dyes. He ate monopoly butter, monopoly currants, monopoly red herrings, monopoly salmon, and monopoly lobsters. His food was seasoned with monopoly salt, monopoly pepper, monopoly vinegar. Out of monopoly glasses he drank monopoly wine and monopoly spirits; out of pewter mugs made from monopoly tin he drank monopoly beer made from monopoly hops, kept in monopoly barrels or monopoly bottles, sold in monopoly-licensed ale-houses. He smoked monopoly tobacco in monopoly pipes, played with monopoly dice or monopoly cards, or on monopoly lute strings. He wrote with monopoly pens, on monopoly writing-paper; read (through monopoly spectacles, by the light of monopoly candles) monopoly printed books, including monopoly Bibles and monopoly Latin grammars, printed on paper made from monopoly collected rags, bound in sheepskin dressed with monopoly alum. He exercised himself with monopoly golf balls and in monopoly licensed bowling alleys. A monopolist collected the fines which he paid for swearing. He travelled in monopoly sedan chairs or monopoly hackney coaches, drawn by horses fed on monopoly hay. He tipped with monopoly farthings. At sea he was lighted by monopoly lighthouses. When he made his will, he went to a monopolist. (In Ireland one could not be born, married, or die without 6d. to a monopolist.) Pedlars were licensed by a monopolist. Mice were caught in monopoly mousetraps.[2]

And the name of the means by which the king handed out these monopolies? Patents. "In 1621 there were alleged to be 700 of them," said historian Christopher Hill.[3] And the interesting thing is that when you consider our present era, we live lives not that dissimilar from the man in the 1600s in literally being surrounded by a cloud of monopolies in the form of patents and their cousin, copyrights, and to a lesser extent, trademarks. Except they surround us now not by the hundreds, but by the thousands.

As I write this chapter at my desk, I write on a monopoly computer that runs on monopoly software; I use a monopoly pen and I answer the telephone with a monopoly cell phone. I snack on monopoly chips made from monopoly soybeans, and I read monopoly books and watch monopoly movies that are filled with monopoly images and monopoly songs.

The thou shalts and thou shalt nots of intellectual property are all around us, yet mostly unnoticed. They are a kind of white noise, cluttering our toasters, phones, computer screens, and books with little symbols and numbers representing rules and regulations that people are able to ignore most of the time. Virtually all of us have clicked on an "I agree" icon on their computer saying they have read and understood pages upon pages of prose about software they were using, prose usually meant to help secure a company's intellectual property.

Intellectual property rights are, like a city's water system or the public schools, key parts of a society's infrastructure system and are designed by the state. They are a market and a cornerstone of how our market economies are constituted now. In this chapter I look at their origins and future.

Speaking very generally, the history of intellectual property is similar to the history of corporations and of property itself, in that what for centuries was a privilege granted by the state eventually became a right, and then finally property itself, to be protected by the state. As has so often happened, eventually the origins of this "property" as a creation of the state were forgotten. What was perhaps more clearly recognized in the past is that creating these little state-protected monopolies, whether they're called property, a patent, a copyright, a trademark, or a privilege, has ill effects as well as beneficial ones, and what the balance is, is always a matter of debate. Too much protection, which we probably have now, can actually stifle innovation and inhibit creativity, the very social goods that intellectual property was meant to stimulate. What's telling is that historically the great promoters of the "free market," from Adam Smith to Friedrich Hayek, have regarded intellectual property as an intrusion on the free market, not part of it.

"If we did not have a patent system, it would be irresponsible on the basis of our present knowledge of its economic consequences, to recommend instituting one," said Fritz Machlup, an economist, in overview remarks in a history of the patent system he wrote for Congress, as it prepared in the 1950s to do one of its periodic overhauls of the system.

> But since we have had a patent system for a long time, it would be irresponsible, on the basis of our present knowledge, to recommend abolishing it. This last statement refers to a country such as the United States of America—not to a small country and not to a predominantly non-industrial country, where a different weight of argument might well suggest another conclusion.[4]

One promising development in recent years is that public debate has begun over to what extent books, images, and inventions should be regarded as private inventions, and when they should enter the public domain for all to use freely. It is becoming apparent that we are at a place similar to that occupied by that man in the 1600s, hemmed in on all sides by monopoly goods that enable but also curtail our movements. We need to remember that intellectual property, more than others, is clearly a social good invented and protected for the benefit of the public. God did not come down from heaven and institute copyrights and patents; humans did. That being the case, we should be open to changing these systems to suit changing times, changing technologies, and the changing needs of the public, whose welfare is why we have intellectual property in the first place.

GLORIOUS BEGINNINGS

All important things began in Venice, say some fans of that antiquarian city, and it's arguable that the patent system did. Although now a glittering antique, this improbable collection of mansions and churches perching on canals interlacing some marshy islands in a lagoon on the eastern coast of Italy existed for 1,100 years as an empire and a republic—until 1797, when Napoleon ended what still stands as almost certainly the longest-running self-governing nation in history. With its thousands of state-built ships, Venice once ruled the Adriatic Sea and much of the trade between East and West. At one time, the Venetian shipbuilding factory, the Arsenal, employed sixteen thousand workers, who could churn out a fully equipped galleon every few hours.[5] (A galleon was no rowboat, but a merchant or war vessel, equipped with scores of oarsmen, that could travel across the sea.) Venetian wealth was built on trade, and so it is no surprise that the city was a center for innovation in trade-enhancing mechanical devices. Venetians, for example, invented the rudder, unknown until the 1400s, which made their ships more maneuverable and steadier.[6] Because it was a republic with a stable government, Venice also had the time to develop a full body of commercial law, including a patent system, which in turn helped it dominate trade even more.

A patent was originally synonymous with state authority, and patents existed for many centuries before Venice created a patent system. The word "patent" comes from the Latin phrase "Litterae patentes." "Litterae" means "a letter," and "patentes" comes from the Latin word "pateo," meaning "open." A patent was an "open letter" from the king or emperor, a kind of free pass granting entry and special powers, and it dates back to Roman times. A "letter patent" could grant safe passage through hostile territory, the right to conquer another city, or freedom from prosecution for certain acts. There were "patents of nobility," meaning the king had granted you a title. Eventually, they came to be used for special rights or privileges of trade. A man with a "letter patent" might be given exclusive rights to own land, sell tea, or trade with a neighboring city. In medieval times, various kings and princes had begun using patents to reward an ally or lure away a competitor nation's top talent. In 1331, for example, the English king Edward II gave "letters patent" to John Kempe, a Flemish weaver who had brought to England improvements in weaving technique.[7] In the development of the New World, nations gave "land patents," which were big grants of territory as private property in North America, South America, and the sugar islands like Barbados, Montserrat, and Jamaica. Originally a patent was just any exclusive grant of privilege given by a king or other government authority.[8] A "patent of invention," which today is pretty much the only type of patent people mean when they use the term, was originally just one of many ways an executive or legislative branch could use the power of a "letter patent."

Venice's big conceptual leap was to conceive of using patents not just as special favors to be granted on a case-by-case basis, but to compose a system under law that would encourage future innovation in a predictable way. If you did this, you would get that.

Meeting in its regal chambers inside the ducal palace that still sits on St. Mark's Square in Venice, the Venetian Senate passed the world's first patent act in 1474, at the zenith of the city's power and wealth. As the economic historian Luca Mola explains in *The Silk Industry of Renaissance Venice*, this move to establish a patent system emerged in the wake of costly wars during that century, and from the need for the state to raise more revenue by making the Venetian economy more dynamic and competitive. The Venetian Senate had been awarding patents regularly to innovators, including those who could be lured from other city-states and nations, and it occurred to someone to create a more predictable system.[9] The Venetian Patent Law, passed on March 19, 1474, states, according to this translation of text written in Latin and old Venetian:

> We have among us men of great genius, apt to invent and discover ingenious devices. . . . Now, if provisions were made for the works and devices discovered by such persons, so that others who may see them could not build them and take the inventor's honor away, more men would then apply their genius, would discover, and would build devices of great utility for our common wealth.[10]

The law goes on to establish penalties for patent infringement, and to say that the state itself could use a patented invention as it liked, as long as the inventor himself were employed to operate it. You could get a patent of ten years simply by applying to the Provveditori di Comun, a municipal administrative office that was given the power to decide, like our patent office today, whether or not an invention was truly novel. But lengthier terms could be gained by applying to the Senate itself.[11] The Venetian Senate would award close to 100 patents over the next three-quarters of a century.[12] From 1474 to 1788, or three centuries, the Venetian Senate would award 1,904 patents—fewer than 2,000.[13] This compares to the more than 185,224 granted by the US Patent and Trademark Office in one year—2008—a figure that includes 1,240 patents granted just for new plants.[14]

Venice at this time was one of the few republics in the world. The Doge, the Senate, and hundreds of other, lesser officers were elected by those who held the right to vote, which was limited to members of about a thousand families (the number varied over the centuries), written up in the Libra D'Oro, or Book of Gold. The right to be in this Book of Gold was passed down by hereditary right. These men (for they were certainly all men at this time), who gathered in the enormous room of the Great Council and in the Senate chambers, came up with the world's first patent law in the spirit of enhancing the general health and prosperity of their society. As we will see in the following centuries, the use of patents has vacillated between attempts to help enrich society and attempts simply to make a few well-placed individuals rich. It's significant that the wording of the Venetian Patent Law indicates that the rationale for the act was to benefit the commonwealth.

People build on what they know, and the patent system was modeled, perhaps unconsciously, on the guild system, which then structured many aspects of working life in Venice. The Senate, after initially setting the term of a patent at ten years, soon changed it to fourteen years. Not coincidentally, this was the same length of time as the standard two terms of seven years each that an apprentice served under his master in the guild system. The Venetian Senate was awarding an inventor a kind of commercial bondage over his invention for a set period of time, the same way a master had dominion over his apprentice.[15] England would later copy the Venetian law, and then the newly formed United States would copy the English law. This term of fourteen years would be the standard for patent and other forms of intellectual property rights into modern times. The United States initially awarded patent rights for fourteen years. In 1836, Congress would change this to twenty-one years—another multiple of seven—and today patents are awarded for terms of twenty years. The fact that into the twentieth century the United States had patents awarded for multiples of seven years, because that's how the guild system operated in Venice in the 1400s, is an example of path dependence, a subject we'll talk about in Chapter 14.

While the Venetians awarded patents, an invention had not yet become property.

"An inventor had no right to a patent, moreover," said Adrian Johns, writing in *Piracy: The Intellectual Property Wars from Gutenberg to Gates*. "It was a gift, arising from the voluntary beneficence of the ruler, and its recipient was a beneficiary of state prerogative."[16]

THE GLORIOUS REVOLUTION AND ITS CHILDREN

The honor of inventing intellectual property, if it is that, goes to Great Britain a few centuries later. Intellectual property as such grew out of the battles between the Crown and Parliament, and to some degree between the Crown and what we would now call the private sector, over who would control trade and commerce, and profit from it. This series of events built to a crescendo that culminated in the Glorious Revolution of 1688, when William of Orange sailed over from Holland with his troops and deposed King James II. But this had been preceded by a century of turmoil, including the English Civil War and the beheading of Charles I. What would come to be called intellectual property was part of this war.

In 1623–1624, a half-century before the Glorious Revolution and a generation before the English Civil War, Parliament fired an opening salvo when it passed a law saying the Crown could only grant patents to the "first and true inventor" of a product or process, as opposed to the king handing out or selling a patent monopoly to friends and supporters to sell salt. The act that Parliament passed was called the Statute of Monopolies. This landmark law still figures into present British patent law.[17] Limiting the authority of the king to dispense patents was part of a whole range of attempts to check royal power, including establishment of habeas corpus, trial by jury, and the right to counsel.

According to Johns, intellectual property as such grew out of a particular battle involving the Stationers Company, a guild, or union, of printers and publishers, and the holders of patents from the Crown. Today we give authors and publishers copyrights on books, and inventors patents. But back then the distinction was not so bright. The copyright had not yet been invented, and patents were used to designate any dispensation of royal privilege.

One of the patents the Crown had given out was the exclusive right to print law books, a valuable right when such books were needed in every town and circuit court. But during the turmoil of the English Civil War, the rights of the patentee and his privilege from the Crown had been ignored. For much of this period, after all, there was no king—Charles I had lost his head—only Oliver Cromwell. In the vacuum, someone from the Stationers Company had begun publishing the law books, and had written down his right to do so in the Stationers official registration book. It was these registrations, Johns says, that grew into what we now called copyrights. But in the late 1600s this book was simply a set of internal records kept by the Stationers Company, used by guild officials to keep track of who had the right to print what, and to discipline members who printed works that other printers had a contract on first. It's worth mentioning that authors didn't figure into this debate yet. Only printers and publishers.

After the restoration of the monarch Charles II in 1661, a certain Richard Atkyns, whose patrician family had held the patent to publish law books for several generations, sued to have his patents restored and to stop the Stationers Company from publishing them at all. The case soon became not just about law books, but about who had the right to publish something and who profited from it. The Crown envisioned a system, quite imaginable for the times, of the Crown getting a cut from every book published through a system of licensees, its patent holders. It was to be part of a system of expanded monarchical power, where the Crown would profit even more than it had already through patent holders in the slave trade, the explorations of new land, and so forth.

To counter this argument, and in a bid to hold on to their livelihood, the Stationers came up with a novel and desperate idea: that authors "owned" rights to their books and that the printers and publishers of the Stationers Company were mere facilitators of those rights. According to Johns, such an argument had never been made before. The rationale was that this would be more politically palatable to the Crown, which viewed the printers and publishers as mere tradesmen opposing the king, while the authors tended to be of more gentlemanly rank. This was the start of an author having "rights" to his (or her) book.

But King Charles II did not buy it. In 1680 Charles II found for Atkyns and set about reorganizing the Stationers Company to be less of a threat to kingly ways. And if history had proceeded more linearly, we might be now living with state-authorized publishing with royalties going to the state. But then something unexpected happened eight years later in 1688: the Glorious Revolution, which threw out Charles II's young brother, James II, who by that time had become king. A faction of the English nobility encouraged William of Orange of Holland, accompanied by his wife Mary, the sister of James II, to invade England and make himself king and his wife queen of England—which William did. After his military victory, William restored the Stationers Company in its old form. And with the restoration, the idea that the Stationers had come up with returned, that authors "owned" their works. Thus intellectual property was born. The idea soon spread to other forms of intellectual creativity, such as inventions. This would eventually result in the Statute of Anne in 1709, which gave publishers and authors fourteen years of exclusive printing rights, renewable for another fourteen years (echoes of the guild system again). The full title of the law was "An Act for the Encouragement of Learning, by vesting the Copies of Printed Books in the Authors or purchasers of such Copies, during the Times therein mentioned."

The twin rallying cries of the Glorious Revolution were Liberty and Property. But even supporters of the revolution, Johns says, knew these two principles were in conflict with each other much of the time. When it came to books, to give an author his text as "property" also impinged on the liberty of someone else to print it or read it without paying what many would view as a monopoly tax. We wrestle with this balance today when a filmmaker is ordered to pay to use a piece of art or a brand name in a film, or when a musician is prohibited from using bits of other songs to craft a new one. In 1774, the House of Lords rebalanced this relationship, in the case of *Donaldson v. Becket*, by allowing Scotsman Alexander Donaldson to reprint books without royalties. Essentially, the House of Lords found that these copyrights were not official property, but mere privileges, to be controlled and limited by the state. It is in recent decades that the term of this "limited" period has grown so long as to raise the question of whether the word "limited" is still appropriate.

1776–1900: THE EMERGENCE OF THE MODERN PATENT SYSTEM

While the rights and privileges of booksellers, printers, and authors were being defined in England and its colonies, the dispensing of patents, in the older sense of the word, continued, as a royal favor. This aroused the ire of the people, who saw the costs of their daily goods and services raised by all these monopolies handed out by the king, and sometimes the Parliament. The Stamp Act that American colonists protested, which required an official stamp on a newspaper or other printed good, was similar to a patent in its effects, because it raised the cost of a basic good, newspapers, for the benefit of the Crown. You can sense some of this hostility to state monopolies in the constraining language of the US Constitution, Article I, Section 8, Clause 8. It says that Congress has the power "To promote the Progress of Science and useful Arts, by securing for limited Times to Authors and Inventors the exclusive Right to their respective Writings and Discoveries."

Notice how similar the phrasing of the section of the US Constitution is to the phrasing of the patent law passed by the Venetian Senate in 1474. The emphasis for patents is on the common good—not individual wealth or property.

"I think the clause is correctly read as outlawing all general patents (no patents on salt, tea, pepper, paper were to be allowed)," said Lawrence Krubner, a writer and blogger on economic policy.

> The colonists had suffered too much from those kinds of patents. They were afraid of patents. They were so afraid of patents that they were only willing to allow them for one very specific purpose: That is, you could only have the exclusive use of an idea if you were an inventor or writer, and then only for a brief time.[18]

Thomas Jefferson, himself a prolific inventor, was not a fan of what would be called intellectual property and never took out a patent on any of his many inventions. (His later money troubles would have been fewer if he had.) Ironically, Jefferson would go on to lead the country's first patent office, because it fell under his duties as secretary of state under President George Washington. Jefferson would set up many of the initial procedures and policies for patents. He reportedly examined personally all of the 114 applications that came in from 1790 to 1793. (At Jefferson's request, Congress in 1793 established, although not in the form he wanted, a more formal patent office with its own head, so as to relieve the secretary of state of this workload.) As head of the patent office, Jefferson usually tried out the inventions himself to see whether they worked as advertised, and granted only about half of the applications.[19]

His unease with patents stemmed from his belief that they were contrary to "natural rights."

Said Jefferson in 1813:

Inventions cannot, in nature, be a subject of property. Society may give an exclusive right to men to pursue ideas which may produce utility, but this may or may not be done according to the will and convenience of society, without claim or complaint from anybody.[20]

It was in this spirit that a few years earlier a writer on what would come to be called economics, Adam Smith, released his *The Wealth of Nations* in 1776, two years after the *Donaldson v. Becket* court case, in which Donaldson, a "reprinter," won the right to publish books that had been copyrighted. It's germane to point out that Donaldson was, like Smith, a Scotsman. Like Donaldson, Smith was skeptical of any system of state privilege, even of patents for inventions or copyrights for books, and viewed them as impositions on what would come to be called the free market. Although Smith was certainly a brilliant theorist, he also seemed to be reflecting the tenor of the times, which was alive with the notion of freedom, including in economic life. Peculiarly, to a modern eye, this meant a bias against patents and copyrights.

This tension about what would be called intellectual property, in particular patents, continued throughout not only the eighteenth century, but the nineteenth century as well. It was not until 1852 that Great Britain organized something akin to a system of intellectual property, and other nations struggled to work out their positions on this. As with emerging nations in the developing world today, it was somewhat clear in the nineteenth century that it didn't necessarily help a developing country to send royalty checks to Great Britain for books or inventions.

This set up a practical and ideological battle that was waged throughout the nineteenth century as Europe and the Americas industrialized. Many of these arguments came to a head during the debates surrounding the Patent Law Amendment Act of 1852. The *Economist* magazine in 1851, around the time it was also arguing against a new device called the limited liability corporation, opposed a stronger patent system as being a tax on the public and a violation of free trade.[21]

Said Johns, summarizing such arguments:

Patents were therefore charged with several offenses at once. They projected an artificial idol of the single inventor, radically denigrated the role of the intellectual commons, and blocked a path to this commons for other citizens—citizens who were all, on this account, potential inventors too. . . . Patentees were the equivalent of squatters on public land—or, better, of uncouth market traders who planted their barrows in the middle of the highway and barred the way of the people.[22]

Despite the arguments, a revised Patent Act passed in 1852, but the debate continued in the rest of Europe. Some of the arguments and events are worth recounting, because they show how people grappled with this most nebulous form of property.

The French Constitutional Assembly, as the smoke was still clearing from violent revolution, declared in 1791, in a preamble to a patent law, that patents were part of the natural rights of man (like those described by Englishman John Locke), and the legislature was only helping ensure them. "Every novel idea whose realization or development can become useful to society belongs primarily to him who conceived it, and that it would be a violation of the rights of man and their very essence if an industrial invention were not regarded as the property of its creator."[23]

In 1820 Austria argued, to the contrary, that there existed a natural right to copy other people's ideas, or "a natural right to imitate." This was Thomas Jefferson's view as well. Patent lovers might consider this akin to there being a natural right to steal.

Another idea was that patents were not a right, but a just reward, which government was helping ensure by the granting of a monopoly. A similar but distinct argument was that patents were purely a practical measure by a society to spark invention of socially useful devices by the creation of an incentive to do so. Finally, there was the concept that society is simply paying for secrets, giving an inventor an incentive to release his invention into the public sphere. "The patent constitutes a contract between society and inventor; if society grants him a temporary guaranty, he discloses the secret which he could have guarded; quid pro quo, this is the very principle of equity," said French economist Louis Woolskin in 1869.[24]

The nineteenth century was marked by a hodgepodge of nations for and against patent laws.

Russia enacted patent laws in 1812; Prussia in 1815; Belgium and the Netherlands in 1817; Spain in 1820; Sweden in 1834; and Portugal in 1837. But toward midcentury the pendulum seemed to swing the other way, against patents and intellectual property. In 1868 Chancellor Bismarck of the emerging nation of Germany declared he was against a patent system "on principle." The legislature of Switzerland rejected proposals for a national patent system in 1849 and twice in 1863. The last time, the legislature said that "'economists of greatest competence' had declared the principle of patent protection to be 'pernicious and indefensible.'" The Netherlands repealed its patent laws in 1869, saying "a good law of patents is an impossibility."[25]

Said Machlup in summarizing this era:

> In the attacks on patent protectionism, free-trade arguments were used more than they were in England, and economists were almost unanimous in the condemnation of the system. Trade associations and chambers of commerce submitted reports recommending reform or abolition of the patent laws. The debate was carried on in books, pamphlets, journals, and in the daily press; in various societies of lawyers, engineers, and economists; and in the legislatures. Engineers, inventors, and would-be inventors, industrialists with a vested interest in patents, patent lawyers, and others who felt they stood to profit from the patent laws were wholehearted advocates of the system. They were opposed by commercial interests, by industrialists and inventors who felt their activities directly restricted, and by economists.[26]

But gradually the advocates of patents won out. A German bill in 1871 said that it was fortunate that an economic crisis had caused backers of "the pernicious theory of free competition and free trade" to turn away from such foolishness and embrace patents. Many regarded the strengthening of patents as a triumph of special interests, which perhaps it was. But the International Patent Congress was held in Vienna in 1873, and follow-up sessions in Paris in 1878 and 1880. The work of these assemblies was the basis for the Paris Convention for the Protection of Industrial Property, which was established March 20, 1883. The United States formally signed on in 1887. But some nations would remain outside this club for decades. The Netherlands, after repealing its patent law in 1869, did not pass another until 1912. Swiss voters in a national referendum rejected a national patent system in 1882, but then passed a revised law in 1887.[27]

INTELLECTUAL PROPERTY IN THE
TWENTIETH CENTURY: NOT SO SACROSANCT

By the first decades of the twentieth century, as the Wright brothers flew the world's first plane and the terrible carnage of the First World War began, most countries had their own patent systems and had signed on to international treaties establishing standards respecting some form of patent internationally. But many economists continued to frown on patents and their brethren.

Friedrich A. Hayek, a classic free market economist with continuing influence, criticized both the patent system and the corporation system as infringements on competition in his 1944 classic, *The Road to Serfdom*: "Serious shortcomings here, particularly with regard to the law of corporations and of patents, not only have made competition work much more badly than it might have done, but have even led to the destruction of competition in many spheres."[28]

This critique persisted when Congress overhauled and updated the patent system in 1952. "The patent system has, from its inception, involved a basic economic inconsistency. In a free-enterprise economy dedicated to competition, we have chosen, not only to tolerate but to encourage, individual limited islands of monopoly in the form of patents," said Sen. Joseph C. O'Mahoney, who led the committee revising the US patent system.[29]

Congress revised the patent system in 1956, and in so doing it kept multiple objectives in mind. As the leading industrial power on earth, the United States had an interest in having as much trade as possible, and it was thought that enforcing the patent system too vigorously impeded that goal. In the 1970s, the Justice Department largely ignored the fact that Taiwanese firms regularly ripped off the design of American television and hi-fi sets. Up until 1980, the Justice Department regarded enforcement of the patent system as less important than antitrust laws, with which it often conflicted.

In the last two decades of the twentieth century, though, the stock of patents as an institution rose. The causes were many. One was the 1980 election to the US presidency of Ronald Reagan, an ardent free marketer whose team thought antitrust law unnecessary. The old belief by Hayek and others that patents and other forms of intellectual property violated economic freedom was not in their gaze. Another reason was that the nation's economic interests were less and less tied to producing cars and trucks, and more and more tied to producing software, films, and other "soft" goods that relied on patents and copyrights to reap greater monetary value across a large world.

Ralph Oman, writing in 1994, summed up the changes in attitude toward intellectual property that had taken place during his professional career.

"In my twenty years in the intellectual property field," Oman said in the foreword to a book on intellectual property law,

I have lived through a dramatic transformation. Back in the 1970s, patents, copyrights and trademarks cowered in the shadow of the anti-trust laws. They were disfavored monopolies, and the courts, the Ford and Carter Administrations, and Congress took every opportunity to limit their scope and expand the ambit of unbridled competition.

Then it slowly dawned on Congress and other U.S. policymakers that the world was changing.[30]

INVENTING WHEELS AND PENALIZING CAMPFIRE SONGS

In contemporary times, we have a strange paradox. The rules of intel-lectual property are ignored more flagrantly than at any time since Harper's and other publishers in the eighteenth and nineteenth cen-turies sold best-selling English novels without compensation to their authors. Music listeners download individual songs by the billions without payment; software and movies are copied and sold on pirated DVDs on the streets of Beijing and New York City routinely. Yet at the same time, some forms of intellectual property have been liberally cre-ated, and then more rigidly protected than ever before—too much so.

The current patent system is clearly a mess. In mid-2011, Google, Apple Computers, and Microsoft paid tens of billions of dollars for thousands of patents, not to improve the technology of their devices or services, but simply as a defensive or offensive weapon in court. The US Patent Office is so liberal in awarding patents that on any piece of technology, it can be argued that dozens or even hundreds of patents are relevant. This has given rise to "patent trolls," companies with no or few employees that exist only to sue actual manufacturing com-panies, often successfully, for millions of dollars. The rationale that patents exist to spur creativity and foster social good is seldom men-tioned. James E. Bessen and Michael J. Meurer of Boston University's law school and authors of the book *Patent Failure* estimated in a re-search paper in 2011 that such patent trolls had cost technology com-panies a half a trillion dollars, with most of the money not going to inventors, but to the suing companies.[31] Congress, caught between the pharmaceutical companies, which at present want liberal patent granting and tight enforcement, and software companies, which want the opposite, has shown itself unable to sort things out for the public good. In September of 2011 President Barack Obama signed into law a patent reform act, but most of the larger issues were left untouched.

That the country has been in similar situations is no cause for complacency. With the birth of the telegraph, the telephone, film, radio, and television, Tim Wu says in *The Master Switch: The Rise and Fall of Information Empires*, have come patent wars and a struggle for control among private interests and government. Although all of these technologies have their own story, in general the public fared better when government took the lead in creating a framework for growth.[32]

As for copyrights, it now stands that they are issued for the life of the author plus seventy years, and no renewal is required. This means that most works will not fall into the public domain until well over a century has passed. Although as an author myself I like the idea of never-ending royalties, century-long copyrights abuse the notion that such protection should be limited. In general, such "rights" are being abused.

In the preceding chapter, "Trust: How We Cooperate to Compete," I quote Bruce Scott of Harvard Business School as saying that capitalism depends on "the commons" not being abused. It is clear that commercial interests are now abusing the commons of intellectual property.

Clearly, events have gotten out of hand. In 2001 John Keogh, a patent lawyer in Australia, was issued a version of a patent for a "circular transportation facilitation device," in other words, a wheel.[33] This is in line with the increasing willingness of patent offices to issue patents for almost anything. Almost as far-fetched, the Patent Office famously allowed Amazon.com to patent the idea of ordering a book with one click of the mouse, forcing competitors like Barnes & Noble to make people order with two clicks. This is like allowing someone to patent the idea of hammering a nail with one swing of a hammer. On the separate arena of copyright enforcement, Robert S. Boynton, in the *New York Times Magazine* in 2004, tells of Girl Scouts being sued for singing songs around the campfire without paying royalties on the songs.

RIGHTS VERSUS POWER

The lengthening, broadening, and strengthening of rights associated with copyrights, trademarks, and patents tend to happen with all sorts of property. The state creates property, and by so doing, vests someone or a group of people with power, and thus the potential to win more power.

The *New York Times Magazine* on August 6, 2010, had a story by John Bowe that told of Devon Baker, an official from BMI, Broadcast Music Incorporated, one of the two principal associations of copyright holders for music, trolling the nation in a car leaning on bar and restaurant owners to pay for the popular music they play.[34] The story is sympathetic to BMI, perhaps because the author spent time traveling with BMI's representative, Ms. Baker, and it portrays the fees paid by restaurant and bar owners as the rightful due to BMI and its members, given that the bar owners are "profiting" from playing BMI songs. After all, a restaurant or nightclub makes money, and playing popular music makes it a more comfortable place.

But one could portray this in reverse. By broadcasting music, whether Beethoven or the Beatles, to a crowd, a restaurant owner is advertising that music, much like a radio station. How many people first hear music they like out in public somewhere? You could argue that BMI should pay a bar owner for advertising its product. Such a possibility is why record labels have sometimes illegally paid money to radio disc jockeys under the table to play their songs, even though the radio stations were also paying royalties to organizations like BMI. If restaurant owners, for example, had a lobby as strong as BMI or its sibling organization, ASCAP, then perhaps restaurants and bars would be receiving royalties, not paying them. The current arrangement of payments is indicative not of morality but of power, and who has it.

One of the leaders of the movement to contain and then roll back the use of intellectual property rights is Lawrence Lessig, a brainiac law professor who founded the Center for Internet and Society at Stanford Law School. His *The Future of Ideas* lays out the absurdities of what we have wrought:

> The argument of this book is that always and everywhere, free resources have been crucial to innovation and creativity; that without them, creativity is crippled. Thus, and especially in the digital age, the central question becomes not whether government or the market should control a resource, but whether a resource should be controlled at all. Just because control is possible, it doesn't follow that it is justified. Instead, in a free society, the burden of justification should fall on him who would defend systems of control.[35]

Following Lessig's lead, authors Adam Jaffe and Josh Lerner take aim at the patent system more directly in their 2005 book, *Innovation and Its Discontents: How Our Broken Patent System Is Endangering Innovation and Progress, and What to Do about It.* The title sums up the pair's perspective. People have tried, they say, to patent a peanut butter sandwich, and the Patent Office has almost let them.

In May of 2009 the American Civil Liberties Union came out against allowing patents on people's genes. This was not a foregone conclusion, given that some have argued that patents are natural rights to one's work, akin to a civil liberty.

"The government should not be granting private entities control over something as personal and basic to who we are as our genes," said Anthony D. Romero, executive director of the ACLU. "Moreover, granting patents that limit scientific research, learning and the free flow of information violates the First Amendment."[36]

In November of 2009, members of the US Supreme Court suggested, in the case of Bilski and Warsaw v. Kappos, that they were skeptical about continuing to allow patents of "business methods." Of course, what would be even better is if Congress addressed this type of patent in a public legislative revision. For the terms of intellectual property are clearly an important public issue.

PROGRESSIVE EVOLUTION

Government grants patents, trademarks, and copyrights to enhance public well-being. Shouldn't we regularly evaluate these institutions and ask how they are performing that function?

Other countries do. Canada, our neighbor to the north, adapted its copyright system a few years ago to suit the age where music can be passed around over the Internet at virtually no cost. Rather than try to stop such practices, Canada passed a law that put a tax on sales of blank compact discs, the proceeds of which were distributed to artists and record companies based on sales. Now, as conditions have changed, Canada is debating other modifications. Canada is functioning as a democracy, which means its citizens and legislators are constantly evaluating the structures of their society and changing them as needed.

William W. Fisher III, in his *Promises to Keep: Technology, Law and the Future of Enforcement*, says there are five general approaches to encouraging production of socially beneficial goods and rewarding their creators, of which copyrights and patents, which reward creators by giving them a state-conferred monopoly, are just one. For music, film, television, and other such easily reproduceable products in the digital age, Fisher suggests an American version of the Canadian system.

People would be free to copy music, film, and other works, but the creators would be compensated according to how much their creations are used.

Says Fisher:

> A creator who wished to collect revenue when his or her song or film was heard or watched would register it with the Copyright Office. With registration would come a unique file name, which would be used to track transmissions of digital copies of the work. The government would raise, through taxes, sufficient money to compensate registrants for making their work available to the public. . . . Once this system was in place, we would modify copyright law to eliminate most of the current prohibitions on unauthorized reproduction, distribution, adaptation and performance of audio and video recordings. Music and film would thus be available, legally, for free.[37]

I don't endorse Fisher's plan in its specifics, but do endorse a healthy and robust debate over the designs of this system vital to the health of our common wealth.

CONCLUSION

In the Glorious Revolution of 1688, in the American Revolution of 1776, the people brought to heel governments that had run amok with controls, monopolies, and taxes on products and services. We are in a similar situation today. Although not often portrayed as such, the ubiquity and increasing strengthening of patents and copyrights on software, written work, images, crops, genes, art, and even ideas are a threat to the rights of free association and communication necessary in a democracy and a free society. We need our own revolution, a nonviolent one of course, that can bring our systems of intellectual property back into the service of those they were originally meant to benefit: the public.

CHAPTER 7

LITTLE COMMONWEALTHS: CORPORATIONS
AND THE STATE THAT CREATES THEM

Another infirmity of a Common-wealth . . . [is] the great number of
Corporations; which are as it were many lesser Common-wealths in
the bowels of a greater, like wormes in the entrayles of a naturall
man. THOMAS HOBBES, *LEVIATHAN*, 1651

IN 2007 MAYOR MICHAEL BLOOMBERG of New York City began a carefully planned but ultimately futile campaign to get from the state legislature a seemingly small thing: authority over his streets. No, that goes too far. Simply the authority to charge a small fee to drivers who entered a certain zone of Manhattan below 59th Street, the central business district, at certain times of the day. He was trying to do something that was variously called "congestion pricing" or "traffic management." The idea was to charge drivers who entered the city at peak hours, and thus reduce street traffic to much more manageable levels, as well as make some money through the fees. The mayor was, in effect, acting like a capitalist in charging drivers for the right to do something of value, drive a personal automobile into the city's most precious, active, and, not incidentally, congested part. New York's Anglo counterpart, London, had implemented such a plan a few years previously, with great success, as had Stockholm. Manhattan, being an island with already limited access, could implement such a plan quite easily, but it needed state permission.

Bloomberg, a billionaire as well as mayor, deployed his lobbyists, his cash, his political favors, to no avail. The state legislature, that great father, decided it had no special reason to grant the mayor such authority. The proposal did not even come to a vote. Bloomberg, leader of the corporation called "The City of New York," had failed.

Meanwhile, other corporations located in Manhattan, from Alcoa to Time Warner to hundreds of other corporations great and small, proceeded about their business without asking their incorporators, sometimes the state of New York but often the state of Delaware, permission for much of anything. They bought, they sold, they pretty much did what they wanted as long as it was not expressly illegal.

So here's the question: why did New York City, a corporation created by a state government and housed in a big building called City Hall in Lower Manhattan, have to ask permission for something, while, say, Time Warner, a corporation housed in a big glass building on 59th Street by Central Park and also created by a state government, did not? And what does that say about corporations today?

Actually, let's back up one additional big step. Many of you—and really it's the main reason I'm starting this chapter with this anecdote—might be very surprised to learn that Time Warner and New York City are the same thing: state-created corporations. In fact, friends and acquaintances often look at me, dumbfounded, when I say this to them. The thought is nonsensical. That New York City, the embodiment of the public, of the democratic, has something in common with, indeed is the same thing as, say, Viacom or Colgate-Palmolive, the embodiment of the private, and the for-profit, simply defies reason at first. But it's true.

"There is no difference between Google and San Francisco," said Gerald Frug, a professor of law at Harvard who specializes in local government. They are both corporations—"bodies, empowered by government, to do stuff."

Let's say that again. There is no difference between Google and San Francisco. No difference between New York City and IBM. No difference between Albany and Acme Insurance. They are both, in each pair, corporations, empowered by government, to do stuff. Astonishing, given the difference in how we think of those respective pairs of things. We think of cities as these public creatures, controlled by us, their masters, through our politicians, at least in principle. We think of private corporations as controlled only by the boundaries of law, but not controlled by us, not created by us. But they are. That the average person does not know the status of the average city and average private company says a lot about the way we have let our power become veiled to us.

In this chapter, I offer a short history of corporations, and show that these creatures, which we usually think of as embodying the private, are in fact public. There are various analogies that can illustrate this relationship. Thomas Hobbes said the state was like a man's body, and corporations like worms within it, or parasites. Or the state could be said to be a planet, and corporations like moons, circling around it. Or the state could be said to be the parent, and the corporations children who have a lot of autonomy, but are on a leash that can be snapped taut. Or the state can be the hubris-filled scientist, and the corporation the Frankenstein monster he created that got away from his control.

Whatever the analogy, the first step in controlling our creations is recognizing them as ours. I tell how corporations began in medieval and Renaissance times as cities, universities, exploration groups, and road-building ventures, all granted power by a legislature or king. I tell how the nineteenth century would give birth to the "private" corporation, which would become distinct from the public one, and win great powers and autonomy for itself as the twentieth century approached. I do all this in the service of the idea of bringing corporations to heel, back to the service of their creators and masters, the public. Of contemporary markets, corporations are probably the single most important building block, so their form and the powers we the public give them should be designed very carefully.

THE BEGINNINGS

There once was a time when only a king or a legislature could create a company or corporation. It was a status not given easily, because it was a delegation of government power and immunity to a group of people outside government. It was "a little republic."[1] The word "corporation" comes from the Latin word "corpus," and means a body. A corporation is an artificial body. The form goes back to Roman times.

New York City is and essentially always has been a corporation, meaning it has a corporate charter, granted and written by a state. The city was first part of the Dutch West India Company, which was a corporation authorized by the Netherlands; then the city had its own corporate charter granted by Great Britain, which passed to the stewardship of New York state.

From medieval times to the mid-nineteenth century there was no clear distinction between a corporation such as the City of London, on the one hand, and, on the other, corporations such as the East India Company or the Virginia Company, authorized to explore and exploit Asia or the New World. Along the way, the purpose and form of the corporation have changed and evolved, even as one constant remained the same: it is a creature of the state.

The corporation, be it a city or a university, has often clashed with its parent, the state, as real human children do. We in the twenty-first century complain about the unruliness or excessive power of corporations, thinking of General Motors, Exxon, Microsoft, Bertelsmann, and lesser-known examples. But even in medieval and Renaissance times, when corporations were much smaller and more vigorously controlled than now, people worried that these free-floating institutions were insufficiently subordinated to a populace or a sovereign. Even the ancient Romans recommended "keeping the corporate form under lock and key," lest their child grow up and do ill to its parents.[2]

Thomas Hobbes, the sixteenth-century philosopher who put his faith in centralized government power, worried that corporations threatened the unity of the state:

> Another infirmity of a Common-wealth, is the immoderate greatnesse of a Town, when it is able to furnish out of its own Circuit, the number, and expence of a great Army: As also the great number of Corporations; which are as it were many lesser Common-wealths in the bowels of a greater, like wormes in the entrayles of a naturall man. To which may be added, the Liberty of Disputing against absolute Power, by pretenders to Politicall Prudence; which though bred for the most part in the Lees of the people; yet animated by False Doctrines, are perpetually medling with the Fundamentall Lawes, to the molestation of the Common-wealth . . .[3]

At a time when the state relied more explicitly on fear and violence as a means of control, officials worried that they could not torture these artificial bodies, or excommunicate them. "Corporations have neither bodies to be punished, nor souls to be condemned, they therefore do what they like," said Edward Thurlow (1731–1806) in the 1700s. A century earlier, the distinguished jurist and great advocate of the common law and of limits on the power of the monarchy, Sir Edward Coke (1552–1634), worried that corporations "cannot . . . be outlawed or excommunicated, for they have no souls."[4]

But while there were those who wanted greater control of the corporation, there was still a recognition that it was a creation of the state. The question was how much allegiance it should pay its creator.

THE CITY AS CORPORATION

Because its history illustrates the journey the corporation has taken, I want to look at how the city has evolved, from a quasi-independent creature to a vassal of the state.

With the dissolution of the Roman empire, cities and towns became more important as they emerged as power centers separate from the weakened or nonexistent central state. For example, the pope and the Holy Roman emperor would give special status to the four "maritime republics" of Italy—Amalfi, Pisa, Genoa, and Venice—that allowed them to raise armies and take other actions. Empowering a city as a corporation was often the legal vehicle used for such special status. Kings, popes, and legislatures would do the same to guilds, universities, and monasteries.

"One of the fundamental ideas of medieval law was that 'bodies corporate'—towns, universities, guilds—had a life beyond that of their members," said John Micklethwait and Adrian Wooldridge in *The Company: A Short History of a Revolutionary Idea.*[5]

Incorporated cities in Europe and Great Britain, like all corporations, had special privileges. Similar to the Church and the university, they had certain rights and powers that even the king could not violate or take away. In the case of cities, the reason the king would do this is that they were valuable to him. They furnished taxes and sometimes troops. They were also power centers, and could not easily be swept into his absolute royal dominion. As Fernand Braudel put it:

> The medieval city was the classic type of the closed town, a self-sufficient unit, an exclusive Lilliputian native land. Crossing its ramparts was like crossing one of the still serious frontiers in the world today. You were free to thumb your nose at your neighbour from the other side of the barrier. He could not touch you. The peasant who uprooted himself from his land and arrived in the town was immediately another man. He was free—or rather he had abandoned a known and hated servitude for another, not always guessing the extent of it beforehand. But this mattered little. If the town had adopted him, he could snap his fingers when his lord called for him.[6]

An important case occurred in 1682, when King Charles II, whose own powers were being threatened by a rebellious Parliament, sued the City of London and asserted his authority over the city he lived in, saying that he had an absolute right to dissolve its corporate status or rewrite it. Although he won the case, the Glorious Revolution occurred a mere six years later in 1688, and the new king, William of Orange from Holland, returned to the old conception of the autonomous corporation. London, and other corporations, were not completely subservient to the Crown. They had certain rights that only the Parliament could undo, with even then certain restrictions being in place.

This history of cities as independent power centers makes their present weakness all the more ironic. If the mayor of London in 1500 could watch Bloomberg's travails in 2007 and 2008, trying to get permission for a simple street charge, he would shake his head to see how low the city has sunk.

THE NEW WORLD: A CORPORATE VENTURE

While corporations existed before Christopher Columbus's discovery of the New World in 1492, the form leapt forward in power and structure with the push to conquer, explore, and develop the New World. Sending tiny ships out to the Americas, or around the horn of Africa to India, China, or Indonesia, "the East Indies," was simply too risky for a group of families cooperating together to try, or a few wealthy businessmen. The costs and risks were too high.

Through the vehicle of the corporation, several nations, particularly Holland and Great Britain, did several things to encourage exploration and the development of trade. One, they awarded limited liability, a rare thing in those days. Second, they awarded a monopoly on the particular trade route in question, be it for a limited period of years or essentially forever, as was done with the London East India Company. And they sometimes delivered funding—that is, start-up monies. Thus empowered, these corporate bodies went forth, often bearing the names that would be placed on the lands they discovered or explored. There were "East India," "Muscovy," "Hudson's Bay," "Africa," "Levant," "Virginia," and "Massachusetts."[7]

Although the Spanish and the Portuguese were the earliest explorers of the New World, the English and the Dutch pioneered the use of the corporation as a vehicle for exploration and colonization. They proved more successful. This was in part because failure was less costly for the state. Hundreds of prosperous Englishmen, who invested in the founding of Jamestown in 1607 through a corporation called the Virginia Company, lost their money, but the state itself was little harmed by it. Virginia the colony would not prosper until tobacco was grown and exported, decades later. (It is telling, but a subject for another day, that essentially drugs funded the exploration of the New World and made its first profits. Sugar. Tobacco. Rum.)

Holland in 1602 established the "Vereenigde Oost-Indische Compagnie," or the Dutch East India Company, often known by its initials, the VOC. Its Anglo counterpart was the English East India Company, founded in 1600. Both were very successful in their initial centuries of existence. Their mission was to trade with and control territories in what is now Indonesia, China, India, and other parts of Asia. The two companies controlled fleets of ships, bureaucrats, and soldiers. Although it struggled initially, the English East India Company, on its tenth voyage, made a return on investment of 148 percent on its capital of £46,092. Its second joint-stock offering raised a huge £1.6 million.[8] Eventually, its earnings accounted for about half of all of Great Britain's foreign trade.

After two centuries of robust growth, the Dutch and the English East India Companies diminished in power in the latter part of the eighteenth century. The Dutch East India went bankrupt and was dissolved in 1800. The English East India Company, in 1813, was deprived of its monopoly on trade, and it faded out of existence when its charter expired in 1874.

Paralleling their views on patents, "free market" advocates like the Scotsman Adam Smith disliked the English East India Company and corporations in general. Smith saw corporations correctly as little states, with special powers, artificially constraining trade. They were forms of mercantilism. Smith saw the limited liability company, correctly, as a subsidy to business. Smith also disliked that large corporations separated management from ownership. But corporations would only grow stronger in the centuries to come.

THE RISE OF THE PRIVATE CORPORATION: THE NINETEENTH CENTURY

The nineteenth century was when the corporation slipped beyond the grasp of its maker, the state. It was a century when the state began to distinguish between "private," "for profit" corporations and public corporations like cities. The latter would lose more and more of their independence, while the former would increasingly gain it. It was a century when eventually not only could anyone create a corporation, but it would automatically receive the special designation of "limited liability." It was a century in which courts would eventually recognize corporations as "persons," with virtually the same rights and privileges as those of flesh and blood. These changes did not happen all at once, but through a series of decisions in the chambers of national and state legislatures and courts.

When the century began in 1800, the corporation still was used for special projects of a public purpose, such as a canal, a dam, or a road. These corporations were similar to what we might think of as a housing or redevelopment authority, or bridge and tunnel authority.

States granted businesspeople special status to operate a limited liability company, with often monopoly rights to a particular product or service. Robert Fulton, for example, one of the developers of the steamship, was granted an exclusive right for steamship service along the Hudson. North Carolina granted permission in 1795 for anyone to create a corporation by right, as long as it was to build a canal. In 1799, Massachusetts gave "water companies" permission to incorporate by right. The Potomac Company, created to build the canal from Virginia through to Pennsylvania, had George Washington and Thomas Jefferson as executives.[9] This was a fascinating project that, if successful, might have made Richmond the economic capital of the new nation. But it failed for lack of capital.

A great canal through the Appalachian Mountains would have to wait until New York state put $8 million into its Erie Canal in 1817, which established New York City as the dominant manufacturing and commercial hub of the country.

The failed history of the James River canal is one reason Thomas Jefferson, when he was president, denied support for the Erie Canal, which the New York state delegation was seeking a decade before the state put its own money into it. This action, or lack of it, has sometimes been misinterpreted as Jefferson not liking or understanding canals, which was not the case. He denied his support on pragmatic grounds. He reasoned that if he and Washington could only scrape together a few hundred thousand dollars for the James canal, there was no way Congress would approve millions of dollars for the Erie Canal.

The great success of the Erie Canal in 1825 led to an explosion of canal-building by other states, who encouraged such projects with money and by making incorporation easier and easier. As corporations grew in number and size, their backers began to seek additional protections and power for them. In several important court cases it is clear that wealthy interests, usually of the Federalist party, were attempting to safeguard capital and give it more independence and power by strengthening the power and independence of the corporation.

In the famous case *Trustees of Dartmouth College v. Woodward* in 1819, Supreme Court Justice John Marshall, a noted Federalist, ruled that New Hampshire could not dissolve or significantly alter the corporate charter of Dartmouth College, even though it was created by a monarchy, Great Britain, that the United States had successfully fought a war against. This was a great victory for corporations. In the future, state legislatures would have to specifically say that a corporate charter was revocable, or would expire, which many afterward did. Although the case concerned a college, the court's logic would be applied to for-profit corporations such as railroad companies and banks.

RACE TO THE BOTTOM: THE SERVANT BECOMES MASTER

In the second quarter of the nineteenth century began a great race to liberalize corporate charters as US states competed for capital. This would eventually lead Great Britain to follow suit.

In 1830, Massachusetts made incorporation with limited liability easier, and stipulated that a newly chartered corporation did not have to be engaged in public works. In 1837, Connecticut followed with a similar law. But states still maintained control.

"As late as 1903, almost half the states limited the duration of corporate charters to between twenty and fifty years," say Micklethwait and Wooldridge. "Throughout the 19th century, legislatures revoked charters when the corporation wasn't deemed to be fulfilling its responsibilities."[10]

Imagine such a thing today. What if Washington state, for example, revoked Microsoft's corporate charter when, during the legal wars of the 1990s, the powerful software company failed to unbundle Internet Explorer from its Windows operating system?

In the nineteenth century the development of railroads, along with the Civil War in the United States, accelerated the creation of corporations and the accumulation of their powers. These great entities soon controlled much of the judicial and the legislative apparatus. I'll talk about the development of railroads more in a separate chapter.

In the same time period, Great Britain was changing and liberalizing its incorporation laws as nations competed for capital. The Joint Stock Companies Act of 1844, the Limited Liability Act of 1855, and the Com-

panies Act of 1862 launched the era of powerful, independent corporations. These made it possible in Great Britain for just about anyone
to start a company and have limited liability, an amazing thing in a
country where just a generation earlier, people were being thrown into
debtor's prison. These acts led to a mania of company starts and stock
speculation, which Gilbert and Sullivan and others wrote about in their
fictional works. Anthony Trollope caught the spirit of these times in
his amazing novel *The Way We Live Now*, published in 1875, whose
characters in London bid up the stock of a California railroad company,
which essentially exists only on paper, in ways remarkably similar to
the dot.com bubble of the 1990s.

The creation in this era of the limited liability stock company deserves special attention. The gestation and birth of these entities was
a subject of much debate. In 1854 in Great Britain, a year before the
passage of the Limited Liability Act, the *Economist* newspaper cam-
paigned against it. Such an invention, said the *Economist*, would
undermine traditional morality, which depended on people knowing
they could be thrown into prison or lose everything when they took on
a debt.[11]

Fast-forward a half-century or so. In 1911, the president of Columbia
University, Nicholas Murray Butler, declared it "the greatest single discovery of modern times . . . Even steam and electricity are far less important than the limited liability corporation, and they would have
been reduced to comparative impotence without it."[12] You'll notice
Butler says "discovery," an interesting if not quite accurate word. It's
clear from the context that what Butler probably means is an "invention," because he mentions steam and electricity in the same breath.
And indeed Butler is right. The limited liability corporation was a marvelous invention. But as with all tools, the ends toward which it would
be directed determined its merits.

CORPORATIONS AS PEOPLE

In the late nineteenth century all these trends—incorporation by right,
general granting of limited liability, the rise of private corporations,
and the enormous power of the railroads—culminated in the de facto
granting to corporations the status as "persons" under the Fourteenth
Amendment of the US Constitution, with just about the same rights
as you and I. The great, or infamous, moment came at the US Supreme
Court in 1886.

The saga of how corporations evolved into "persons" is told well by Thom Hartmann in his book *Unequal Protection: How Corporations Became "People"—and How You Can Fight Back*. Although he's not an academic scholar, Hartmann's blow-by-blow description of the 1886 case *Santa Clara County v. Southern Pacific Railroad* shows both what happened and the context of the times.

What the Supreme Court did in 1886 is actually a matter of some debate. In conventional legal histories, it is said that the court granted corporations the status of "persons," although this was a proclamation from the bench by Chief Justice Morrison Remick Waite and not an actual legal opinion. But Hartmann shows convincingly that the actual words about corporations being persons were inserted into the "headnotes" of the decision, based on oral comments by Waite, by J. C. Bancroft Davis, who held the then-prestigious job of court reporter. Once there, they became embedded into law, although Waite himself, who was ill and died relatively soon after the decision, might not have known that his loose remarks at the end of a trial became the law of the land. What is known is that the actual dispute in *Santa Clara County v. Southern Pacific Railroad* was not decided on the basis of corporate personhood, but on the more minor point of which municipality owned the fence along the railway.

The immense power of the railroads shines through in this and other histories. Railroads had by then entered every nook and cranny of government with their money, power, and influence. Almost every individual associated with the decision on the affirmative side, including both Waite and Davis, had some history of employment and service with the railroads.

Even so, the decision to grant corporations status as legal persons did not happen all at once, but was the result of a twenty-year campaign by the railroads and their political allies in the wake of the passage of the Fourteenth Amendment in 1868. During this two-decade campaign, corporations repeatedly attempted to have their corporate vehicle judged as "persons," only to be repeatedly told by courts essentially that that was ridiculous, everyone knows the Fourteenth Amendment was intended to ensure the rights of people, not corporations. Railroads lost four cases before the US Supreme Court on such a basis in 1877 alone.[13] There is great irony in the use of the Fourteenth Amendment, passed to ensure that freed slaves and other blacks were not denied their rights as citizens of the United States, to uphold the legal fiction of corporations as full people. African Americans would still not be allowed to vote, and be unable sit in public accommodations or go to school where they liked, for another century.

THE CONTEMPORARY CORPORATION AS PERSON

While it may now seem a cornerstone of law, acceptance of corporate personhood is still disputed, and not only among the political Left. Hartmann quotes Justice Hugo Black (1886–1971), appointed by President Franklin Roosevelt and considered liberal, and the late Chief Justice William Rehnquist (1924–2005), appointed by President Richard Nixon and considered conservative, as saying the acceptance of corporations as people was mistaken.

"I do not believe the word 'person' in the Fourteenth Amendment includes corporations," said Justice Hugo Black in 1938 in the case of *Connecticut General Life Insurance Company v. Johnson.* "Neither the history nor the language of the Fourteenth Amendment justifies the belief that corporations are included within its protection."[14]

Justice Rehnquist had similar views.

"It might reasonably be concluded that those properties [of corporations], so beneficial in the economic sphere, pose special dangers in the political sphere," said Rehnquist in 1978 in his dissent to *First National Bank of Boston v. Bellotti,* where the majority said Massachusetts could not restrict campaign spending by a corporation, in this case a bank, because the First Amendment applied to it.

> Indeed, the States might reasonably fear that the corporation would use its economic power to obtain further benefits beyond those already bestowed. I would think that any particular form of organization upon which the State confers special privileges or immunities different from those of natural persons would be subject to like regulation, whether the organization is a labor union, a partnership, a trade association, or a corporation.[15]

Despite Rehnquist's sentiments, as we come to our present era, we find the courts cementing the status of corporations as "persons." The January 21, 2010, ruling by the US Supreme Court in *Citizens United v. Federal Election Commission,* in a 5–4 decision, specifically said the state couldn't limit the speech—or expenditures on behalf of a candidate—of corporations any more than it could those of individuals.

"The Court has recognized that First Amendment protection extends to corporations," said Justice Anthony Kennedy writing for the majority, even while noting that many states had, dating well into the nineteenth century, prohibited corporations from backing political candidates.

> Under the rationale of these precedents, political speech does not lose First Amendment protection "simply because its source is a corporation." . . . The Court has thus rejected the argument that political speech of corporations or other associations should be treated differently under the First Amendment simply because such associations are not "natural persons."[16]

Might the courts begin to reverse themselves in recognizing corporations as persons? It's not inconceivable. After all, conservative heroes like Justice Rehnquist apparently disagreed with Justice Kennedy. It has been said that conservative judges like Justice John Roberts want to turn the clock back to the 1930s, before the empowering legislation and decisions of the New Deal. Perhaps it's also possible to turn the clock back to 1880.

My own view is that while granting corporations the status of "persons" was a mistake, allowing limited liability and incorporation by right was or could be a good thing. These latter devices unleashed a wave of entrepreneurial energy and investment. Not worrying about losing your house or your shirt makes one more of a risk taker economically, which on the whole is good for an economy. But the corporation should still be recognized for what it is: a tool, created by the state, with certain obligations and responsibilities toward the public and state that created it. If not, we come to a future predicted long before.

"Corporations, which should be the carefully restrained creatures of the law and the servants of the people, are fast becoming the people's masters," said President Grover Cleveland in his 1888 State of the Union Address.[17]

THE CITY LOSES ITS INDEPENDENCE

It's not coincidental that in the nineteenth century, while the private corporation was being created and empowered, the traditional public corporation, the city, was losing power and independence.

After the American Revolution, New York City initially was a "free

City of itself," an autonomous private corporation with absolute title to its own personal "estate," say Edwin Burrows and Mike Wallace in *Gotham: A History of New York City to 1998*.

"By increments, without anyone expressly intending it to happen," say Wallace and Burrows, "the corporation [of New York City] gradually came to be recognized as primarily an agent of the state, with its 'private' personality, so jealously guarded by earlier generations, remembered, if at all, as a relic of the rapidly receding colonial past."[18]

You can bump into this past, literally. At Madison Square Park there's an obelisk honoring General Williams Jenkins Worth (after whom the city of Fort Worth is named), a hero of the War of 1812 and others. It is one of the oldest surviving statues in the city. At the bottom it says: "By The Corporation of The City of New York / 1857 / Honor The Brave." It's one of the few times I have seen a public reference to the city's status as a corporation.

A series of writings that helped weaken the city came in the mid-nineteenth century, when Judge John Dillon, in articles that were part of an internal discussion among the courts, argued for an extremely limited view of the independent power of towns and cities. Although Dillon viewed himself as a reformer, he also wanted to restrict the ability of cities and towns to challenge the authority of the railroads by regulating them or, God forbid, starting municipally owned railroads. In what follows I have drawn principally on an article by Professor Gerald Frug of Harvard Law School.

"As both a state and federal judge, Dillon saw firsthand the problems engendered by municipal financing of railroads," said Frug. "He therefore advocated constitutional limitations and restriction of the franchise to taxpayers whenever any expenditure of money was at stake in order to prevent cities from engaging further in such transactions."

Dillon argued for his fellow judges "to require these corporations [meaning towns and cities], in all cases, to show a plain and clear grant for the authority they assume to exercise; to lean against constructive powers, and, with firm hands, to hold them and their officers within chartered limits."

Dillon's views did not go unchallenged. As Frug lays out in his seminal 1980 *Harvard Law Review* article, Judge Thomas M. Cooley argued that the right to set up and operate a local government was an absolute one, similar to the right, say, to print a newspaper or speak freely.

"In a concurring opinion in *People ex rel. Le Roy v. Hurlbut*, [Judge

Thomas] Cooley denied the existence of absolute state supremacy over cities. Relying on American colonial history and on the importance of political liberty in the definition of freedom, he argued that local government was a matter of 'absolute right,' a right protected by an implied restriction on the powers of the legislature under the state constitution. Amasa Eaton advanced the same thesis in a series of articles entitled *The Right to Local Self-Government*. Eaton canvassed English and American history to demonstrate that this 'right to local self-government' existed prior to state incorporations and could not be subjected to state restriction."[19]

As we look over the nineteenth century, we find it begins with US Chief Justice John Marshall, with the Dartmouth decision of 1819, giving private corporations special protection from state government. Toward the end of the century, we find courts doing just the opposite for cities, which are also corporations. Rather than protect them from arbitrary state power, the courts bound cities and their corporate form more tightly to state legislatures.

Now we have the irony of the powerful private corporation versus the restrained public one. Private corporations, like Google or IBM, are "persons," with certain rights that can't be dissolved or altered at will. Public corporations, though, like New York City, became vassals of the state, even as, in the case of New York City, its treasure continues to finance the very government that limits it.

THE MODERN CORPORATION

In the twentieth century, the corporation took different paths in different countries, which help us see the ways it could be redesigned to better suit our needs. In the next chapter, we explore some of those options.

CHAPTER 8

THE FUTURE OF CORPORATIONS

No nation is permitted to live in ignorance with impunity.
THOMAS JEFFERSON, 1821

IN 1787 IN THE MIDST of the Constitutional Convention in Philadelphia, James Madison, the lead writer of the document being assembled, had a great idea. He saw that the new country might need enterprises of a magnitude "so extensive that they would pass beyond the authority of a single state, and would do business in other states."[1] He also saw that such enterprises or corporations might threaten an emerging democracy, and so require a strong hand to not only establish them but control them. "To prevent businesses from eventually growing beyond the point of accountability to government," he believed that the federal government ought "to grant charters of incorporation in cases where the public good may require them, and the authority of a single State may be incompetent."[2]

In other words, Madison wanted a National Companies Act.

A National Companies Act? What is that? I've shown that corporations are political creations. In the United States, this usually means creation by an individual state, one of the fifty, and the corporation then does business across state lines. Wouldn't it be better to have a single national standard for corporations, so that they can compete fairly, and we could design the corporation to better suit national purposes? This is what most other countries do. Since Madison's time, there have been attempts to establish a National Companies Act. They have failed.

The discussion of just whether to have a National Companies Act, as well as what should be in it, is one point in a national conversation we should be having, which is, namely, how to design corporations better. Before we can start to have such a conversation, we first have to realize that it is within our power to have it. That's one of the purposes of this book.

In the global financial crisis of 2008–2010, banks and other private companies failed or faced bankruptcy on a massive scale. Governments were forced to step in to rescue these companies, and to pump money into economies, in order to stave off a global depression. The September 2008 bankruptcy of Lehman Brothers is usually seen as the kickoff of this financial panic.

One silver lining of the financial maelstrom was that it showed inarguably that banks and other corporations were creatures of states, of nations, not the wholly private actors they appeared to be most of the time. It was to their respective countries that AIG, Bank of America, Goldman Sachs, UBS, Hypo Real Estate (of Germany), and General Motors turned for succor, not private capital. Libertarian theorists had prompted Iceland to deregulate its major banks, which flew high briefly upon an updraft of global cash. But it was the country, the state, that was forced to nationalize Glitnir bank and assume responsibility for its debts.

In this crisis, you can see, like long extension cords going back to a wall socket, the essential state power that creates these companies and that they rely on. In the wake of the financial crisis there has been some rewriting of financial oversight rules nationally and globally. But particularly in the United States, we would do well to take advantage of this crisis, while it's still within memory, to rewrite, to redesign, the essential corporate architecture that creates and governs our corporate citizens.

"We cannot escape the conclusion that government has an important role, because in corporate governance, as in other spheres, it is the only power in the land which can strike a balance between the conflicting wishes of competing interests," says Jonathan P. Charkham in *Keeping Good Company: A Study of Corporate Governance in Five Countries*, which I have relied on in this chapter. "Furthermore, the framework within which these interests compete is one of governments' own making. Everywhere the company or corporation is a creature of statute not nature, designed to encourage the agglomeration and continuity of power that the sophistication of modern economies requires."[3]

CORPORATIONS ABROAD

In other advanced countries, we see that different nations construct the architecture of corporations differently. The corporations of some nations have strong chief executives; some have stronger boards, including double boards, that the chief executive officer, or CEO, reports to; some have more direct management by the state; and so on. The purpose of this architecture is to make society healthier, fairer, and more secure, not just to create profits for managers and shareholders. The variations in the way other countries design their corporations are similar to the variations in the design of their health-care systems. France, Germany, Sweden, Japan, Great Britain, and Italy vary tremendously in the design of their health-care systems. Great Britain employs doctors and nurses directly. Germany relies on private companies to provide health insurance. France pays private doctors through a system of national health insurance. These variations have roots in the histories of each country. But all have a similar end—to provide good health care to everyone at a reasonable cost.

"Everyone is to some extent imprisoned by their history, social, political and economic," says Charkham.

> The way we think and the assumptions we bring to bear are . . . the consequence of a long historical development which touches us throughout our lives without our understanding it. Only when we strike our shins on some iron protrusion of another system does the pain make us realize why we were so blind to it and why our imagination did not even contemplate the possibility of its existence.[4]

But our history does not imprison us. Our culture and history reflect more the choices we have made than the absence of choices. The history of the corporation itself shows this.

"In the nineteenth century, the company transformed itself from an instrument of government to a 'little republic' of its own, charged with running its own affairs and making its shareholders money," say Micklethwait and Wooldridge. "There can be little doubt that such an amoebic creature will continue to change shape dramatically in coming years."[5]

Widening our lens, we can see how cultures can change through the active intervention of the state. In the early 1960s, Copenhagen began a decade-long program of promoting a more open and public environment on its streets and sidewalks, converting parking lots into public plazas and promoting bicycling, walking, and sidewalk cafés. This effort continued, until now Copenhagen is one of the most livable and uplifting cities in the world, filled with people strolling, bicycling, and chatting.

But when this effort began, says Jahn Gehl, author of *Life between Buildings: Using Public Space* and one of the chief architects of this transformation, there were voices raised that planners like Gehl were attempting to turn dour Scandinavians into something they weren't. Scandinavians, critics said, were not Italians. They were not known for public strolling and outdoor cafés. They were known for being dour and uncommunicative, and stewing quietly inside tightly shut doors. But Scandinavians changed, as the context around them was changed. Now Copenhagen has some of the most public, gregarious people on earth.

For changes of this magnitude to occur here with corporations, there first must begin a discussion about the purpose of corporations. With the exception of Great Britain, countries other than the United States openly recognize that governments create and empower corporations for the broader social good. Beyond that, the corporate governing styles reflect their countries' priorities and histories.

In the United States, the CEO has much greater prominence, which reflects, in my view, our society's tendency to worship wealth and to promote a winner-take-all society. Our system favors that. We end up with Pennsylvania Railroad, Standard Oil, US Steel, General Motors, and Microsoft—organizations where power is put in the hands of one man or just a few people. This is ironic, because our global brand is individual freedom and liberty. But our system is designed to create huge concentrations of power, which tend to crush individuals and smaller companies. If we were to maximize individual choices, rather than the possibility of great individual power, we would design our corporate system and other economic structures differently.

Imagine if our Constitution included this line, which is from the German Constitution: "Property imposes duties. Its use should also serve the public weal" (Article 14[2]).[6]

Germany has a two-tier structure of corporate governance, the Vorstand and the Aufsichtsrat, that includes representatives from employees by law. The first board, more similar to our boards, is a management board that tracks the management of the company. The second board, the supervisory board, essentially supervises the first board and appoints it. It is made up of not only representatives of the company and shareholders, but of workers and other groups that have an interest in the company in question. This model ensures better, more informed management of the company, more scrutiny, than the American model.

You can see how the priorities of a company would be very different if half the members of a governing board, which is the case in some German companies, were worker representatives. For one thing, it might make better stuff. Germany in the last decade has vied with China as the largest exporter in the world. Unlike China, Germany does this while having one of the highest manufacturing wage and benefit rates in the world—$48 an hour in 2008.[7]

The country's corporate architecture and even its high wages are actually part of its competitive advantage. Having well-paid workers more integrated into a company, with worker representatives on a company's board, promotes a longer-term view of the company's health, rather than quick profits and quick exits.

Here's a startling difference: in the United States and Great Britain, information to the board flows through the CEO. In Germany, information to the CEO flows through the board, whose members get their information from a variety of sources, including labor representatives and independent financial analysts. German banks that have lent companies money often have seats on their boards. In general, the German system promotes cooperation, rather than competition, Charkham says.

France, with a tradition of a strong state and strong leadership, does not promote cooperation with its corporate architecture, like Germany or Japan. France's corporate system gives the CEO even more power than in the United States or Great Britain. But France also has heavy state oversight and direction. It is not uncommon for the national government to own a substantial share of a company.

"Obligation, family and consensus" are the values promoted through Japan's corporate architecture, Charkham says. You are obligated to your personal family, your company family, and even the wider grouping of companies, called Keiretsu, that Japan has and encourages. These groupings are sometimes formed around one big company, like Toyota or Hitachi. Or they can be grouped around a big bank, which would combine dissimilar industries.[8]

A striking difference between Japan and the United States is the level of egalitarianism promoted. The median annual pay rate for top executives at the two hundred largest American companies was

$9.6 million in 2008.[9] The CEOs of Japan's largest companies earned about a tenth of that.[10] Still a tidy sum, but much closer to the pay of the average worker.

WHY WE NEED A NATIONAL COMPANIES ACT

Of course, what most stands out when examining corporations in the United States, compared to those in other countries, is the lack of a common national architecture here. There is no "National Companies Act." In this country, states create most companies, with the company choosing where to incorporate. Often for large companies that is Delaware, which has a particularly lax corporate architecture. In 2008, "Over 50% of all publicly traded companies in the United States, including 60% of the Fortune 500 companies, have chosen Delaware as their place of incorporation."[11]

Commenting on this race to the bottom, which I talked about in Chapter 7, US Supreme Court Justice Louis Brandeis, in his dissenting opinion in the 1933 case *Liggett v. Lee,* said competition between the states is "not one of diligence but of laxity."

Madison proposed something akin to a National Companies Act, and he was not the last. The great crusader, and a Republican to boot, President Theodore Roosevelt took a stab at it. His successors Presidents Taft and Wilson also backed this effort.[12] From 1900 to the start of World War I in 1914, almost two dozen measures were introduced that attempted to establish national corporate charters. They reflected the tenor of the times. There were calls to control the great "Trusts," like US Steel or Standard Oil. Later, in response to the populist movements of the Depression in the 1930s, President Franklin Roosevelt took up the cause. But despite various attempts, no such bill passed Congress.[13]

TO COOPERATE OR COMPETE

The differences in the corporate structures of nations remind me once again that nations or societies are driven by very simple ideas that operate beneath the complex layers of their legal codes.

We in America operate under a very simple creed much of the time: Everyone gets a chance. Most Americans, I suspect, are comfortable with Microsoft founder Bill Gates being personally worth as much as the bottom 100 million Americans because they believe he got there by his own efforts. (Never mind that taxpayer dollars through federal defense research created most of the core structures of computers, from silicon chips to the Internet.) In my mind's eye, and I suspect many others', the United States is an open place where millions stream in to struggle, to work, and to get at least a small slice of the American dream.

Europe, Japan, and the rest of Asia share a different creed, despite their dramatically different cultures, which is this: If we work together, if we cooperate, we will all be better off. Cooperation, and its corollary, responsibility, are embedded in Western Europe and Asia more than here. This sort of cooperation has competitive advantages, something not often realized. For example, because competing companies in Germany often share information through industry associations, they may compete from a higher standard of quality. Germany's dominance in machine tools, chemicals, and industrial machinery is due in part to this. Similarly, because businesses in Germany cooperate more closely with schools and training regimes, they end up with better-educated workers, which again makes them more competitive. Because they give their workers more job security (as well as better wages), the workers feel more comfortable in learning specialized skills that in turn make the companies more competitive.

As our history shows, the move to have a common architecture for corporations has been around since the nation's founding and has periodically reappeared. A National Companies Act includes no guarantee that it will be a good one. And right now, there is a global race to the bottom as well as one here, although the dynamics here are different. But creating a common model for corporations seems an essential first step for getting a handle on our effective, but wayward, creations.

INFRASTRUCTURE:
THE MARKETS WE MAKE BY HAND

CHAPTER 9

FROM HIGHWAYS TO HEALTH CARE:
PROGRESS THROUGH INFRASTRUCTURE

I got a mule, her name is Sal
Fifteen miles on the Erie Canal.
THOMAS S. ALLEN, "LOW BRIDGE," 1905

IMAGINE YOURSELF IN 1835 in New York City, by far the largest city in the country and an engine of the state's and the nation's prosperity. Even so, this is still a primitive place. If you want a drink of water, you buy it from the "tea men" who carry it in barrels. But only those with money can afford this, so most people use one of the few public wells, which are polluted, or draw water directly from a dirty stream or pond. There are no sewers, so when you use the toilet, your waste goes into the ground, where it blends with the water you will later drink. The municipal water system would not open until 1842, and public sewer systems long after that. You walk dirty, muddy streets, many unpaved even by cobblestones, where roaming pigs function as trash disposers. When you walk the streets at night, you take your life in your hands because there is no police force (not established for good until 1857), only a motley collection of night watchmen and private security guards.

If you have a child, he or she goes to school only if you are wealthy. Public education for everyone, meaning simply elementary school, did not begin until the late nineteenth century. If you wanted a book to read, you had to buy it at high prices or pay a high fee to join a private member library. Public libraries, with books available to all citizens, would not exist at all until a few decades later and were not widespread until the early twentieth century.

This short history of services that were or were not available, ranging from a road to an education, is to illustrate a simple point: If you look at the way society and our nation have progressed, a simple rule is that they have progressed by converting private responsibilities to public responsibilities. The hallmark of an advanced economy is actually a larger public sector, or, in a word, more infrastructure of all types. I've used New York City as an example here, but every city in the country has gone through a similar path, from less public to more.

In this section of the book I look at how government makes places and markets through infrastructure investment. I look at how society appears to advance by, to borrow a phrasing from the late Sen. Daniel Patrick Moynihan, defining infrastructure upward. Infrastructure is a relatively new word in its current use, not my favorite really, and I'll talk about that shortly. But it serves to identify the gamut of types of investments that governments make that can create places and markets.

It is a premise of this book that market economies are made. They are designed. Laws, with their collection of dos and don'ts, are one way of doing this. But there is another way, and that is through government building, or helping to have built, physical infrastructure such as roads, bridges, train lines, sewers, parking lots, water lines, Internet connections, and so forth.

In this chapter, I show how society progresses by building infrastructure, and I give some examples of variations in doing this. I compare the Anglo-Saxon approach to infrastructure to the continental, or French, approach. I look at some of the fragmentation that we in the United States must grapple with.

WAGNER GOT IT WRONG

A nineteenth-century economist, Adolph Wagner, formulated a theory now called Wagner's Law, which predicts that as national economies grow, the share devoted to public spending tends to grow in absolute terms and percentage terms as well. But Wagner places most of the emphasis in explaining the reason for this on the public taste for more services, whether they be libraries, schools, parks, or what have you. Wagner has gotten a lot of attention in the first decade of the second millennium. The normally astute David Leonhardt of the *New York Times* even started a "Club Wagner," dedicated to raising taxes for public services that Leonhardt said it was clear Americans wanted, as the German economist Wagner said they would, as society grew richer.[1] Another *Times*man, or *Times*woman, put it this way: "Countries go through stages," said Gail Collins. "If they're lucky they start out poor and raw, and then they grow. The political challenge is to give the people government services that make their lives better without strangling economic development."[2]

I think Wagner, Leonhardt, and Collins got it backwards. The bigger an economy is, the more complex it is, the more state spending it requires on all types of "infrastructure" to keep it that way and grow it further. It's not an economy that supports infrastructure (meaning schools, roads, water systems, Social Security, fire protection, libraries, courts, and so on); it's infrastructure that supports an economy. Over time, we have progressed by converting more and more private responsibilities to public ones. This, is turn, allows the private sector to become more complex in a virtuous circle. A modern industrial economy could not function, for example, with an eighteenth-century school system, where most children received no education and those who did often stopped at adolescence. A national health-care system is increasingly a necessity for our economy. Businesses have more difficulty functioning if employees are sick and have no recourse for treatment. Generally speaking, the larger the economy on the basis of median per capita income, the larger the percentage of the economy government has. Even a parsimonious country like the United States has in modern times spent about 35 to 40 percent of its gross domestic product on state, local, and federal government. Before World War I, the figure was in single digits, in percentage terms. Other wealthy countries have gone through similar evolutions.[3]

SPEAKING PLAINLY

The word "infrastructure" itself is a new term and made its way into urban planning circles only in the 1980s. It was originally a military term, and like the word "logistics," an example of a military term migrating into public discourse.

"The emergence of 'infrastructure' as a generic concept and prominent item on the public agenda is a phenomenon of the eighties," Alan Altshuler, a Harvard University professor and former secretary of transportation for Massachusetts, wrote in a 1989 book review for the *Journal of Policy Analysis and Management*.[4]

So what does the term *infrastructure* really mean? The term comes from the Latin word "infra," meaning "beneath," combined with the word "structure." So infrastructure means the structure beneath. Nice. That captures the sentiment of infrastructure. Something that underpins something else.

The French appear to have introduced the word in the late nineteenth century as a railroad term. Then, in the 1950s, American and European military under NATO (the North Atlantic Treaty Organization) began using it to describe permanent military installations in Europe. Only in the 1970s and 1980s did the term start to apply to nonmilitary public works such as roads, bridges, and power lines.[5]

Herbert Muschamp, the late architecture critic for the *New York Times*, defined infrastructure as "an extruded form of social space in which the ideal of universal access is given both concrete and philosophical form."[6] What I like to say—and I think I'm saying the same thing as Muschamp, only in a simpler way—is that infrastructure is "the things we do in common." That is, it is those tasks or functions that we have opted to do collectively and cooperatively, rather than individually and competitively. There's something moving in that.

This book is really about infrastructure—physical, legal, educational, and other types of structures that the state puts in place or helps put in place, which, in turn, provide the foundations of markets. I use "infrastructure," but I like better the older-fashioned and simpler term: public works. It says that these are "works" that we the people, the "public," do together.

RAISING ALL BOATS

This shifting of responsibility from private to public, what I call defining infrastructure upward, usually only comes through a painful political gestation and birth. Whether they are for public education in the nineteenth century or health care in the twenty-first, these battles are long and hard. The battle to build a public water system in New York City, for example, went on for more than a half-century and involved villains like future vice president Aaron Burr, who sabotaged an early effort at a public water system and got the legislature to instead institute it as a private water system controlled by Burr and his cronies. After laying down a few wooden pipes, they put most of their energy into something an obscure few words in the bill had given them authorization for—starting a bank, the Manhattan Company, which is one of the ancestors of Chase Manhattan Bank. Meanwhile, the public would have to wait until 1842 to get clean, fresh water.[7]

ECONOMISTS VERSUS PUBLIC WORKS

Conventional economics doesn't factor infrastructure into its theories. The market is assumed to provide its own infrastructure. If it doesn't—and it doesn't—then conventional economics has a problem. Although this flaw is pretty obvious to anyone who has seen the Interstate Highway System or a public school, conventional economists tend to ignore this flaw and infrastructure because they don't fit theoretically. When they do look at infrastructure, they tend to estimate its benefits too narrowly. Such thinking has a long history.

In fighting about whether or not to build a new water system for Paris in 1854, Baron Haussmann, the architect of Paris's transformation from a medieval city to a modern one, was opposed by the chief engineer, at the time in charge of all public works, a certain Jules Dupuit, "famous as one of the originators of marginal theory and of cost-benefit analysis in economics; he was a committed believer in the Seine water."[8] Dupuit had calculations showing that the great expense of constructing pipes to carry and distribute water from the Champagne region, more than one hundred miles to the southeast of Paris, was not worth the benefits. Of course, Dupuit was wrong, by a factor of probably ten to one. Not only did universally available clean water drastically lower the rates of typhoid, cholera, and other diseases spread by dirty water, and all their associated costs, it made the city a much better place to do business. The replumbing of Paris, which included not only pipes for fresh water, but the city's now famous sewers, made a renaissance of the city and nation possible. Economists still have difficulty factoring in the transformative potential of good infrastructure.

One of the reasons this is not so clear to us is that we obscure the nature of government involvement with infrastructure by what I call the Anglo-Saxon approach, which uses the veil of private companies to conceal the state hand.

THE ANGLO-SAXON APPROACH TO INFRASTRUCTURE

If you took a pickax to a street in London or New York City, especially an older one, you would find beneath an amazing jumble of tubes and wires, some ancient and rusted, some new and shiny, some obviously unused or broken, some clearly working properly. Just whom all these pipes and lines belonged to would often be anyone's guess.

Now jet or take a fast train to Paris, and take a pickax to one of its streets. You would find Haussmann's spacious brick, which also houses modern-day fiber optic and telephone lines, as well as water pipes. Everything would be neatly labeled. Street signs underground would even tell you where you were. It would be very clear what everything was, and who owned what.[9]

Why such a difference, given that New York, London, and Paris are of similar size and importance, and that London and Paris are similar in each being a city with a long history stretching back thousands of years? The difference comes from their approaches to infrastructure, which reflect differences in their political economies.

In London and New York, private companies were and are encouraged to lay out water, gas, electrical, and other lines in the public streets. London actually had eight competing private water companies in the nineteenth century—such as the New Revie Company and the East London Water Works—which would sometimes lay out lines on the same street, often sabotaging each other's pipes.[10]

"Despite high death rates, fortunes were made out of the supply of poisonous waters," said J. C. Wylie in his book about sanitation, *The Wastes of Civilization.*[11]

London did not have a fully public water company until the twentieth century, when in 1902 the Metropolitan Water Board was created and the private companies were in effect nationalized. It took a generation of political work to make that happen.

New York City has a similar history with electricity and gas. Today Con Edison supplies electricity to most homes and businesses in New York City, and most citizens don't think much about the name. If they did, they would connect it, rightly, to Thomas Edison, the prolific inventor. But the full name of Con Edison is Consolidated Edison. The name goes back to the Consolidated Gas Company of New York, which was formed in 1884 out of six competing gas companies. The new Consolidated Gas Company would steadily buy out its many competitors, including the Edison Electric Company, and in 1936 it changed its name to Consolidated Edison. From then on, it has controlled most gas and electrical lines in the city, as well as the unique steam system.

The legacy of those days of ferocious competition is still underground. Now-defunct gas and electrical companies left miles of pipes and lines. They get in the way. And this is just one part of the underground legacy. Verizon and its predecessors, such as Bell Atlantic, NYNEX, and AT&T (attempting to tell a linear history here is quite difficult), laid the telephone cables that carry New Yorkers' voices. These, too, are private companies. Then there are private cable television companies, and the old pneumatic tube systems of the US postal system, as well as water and sewer lines laid and operated by the New York City Department of Environmental Protection, which is the formal title for the city's water department. All this makes for a crowded and messy environment underground.

THE POTHOLE TO THE POWER PLANT

This Anglo-Saxon approach is visible in a very immediate way: the pothole. Visitors to this country often comment on the poor state of our roads. One colleague from Germany commented that even a rich American city appeared "Third World" by German standards. The reasons for this are surprisingly complex. Most people probably blame city hall for a poor street, but the culprit is often, probably usually, a private utility company, such as a telephone, gas, or electric company. What we are seeing in a cracked or hole-filled street is a physical fragmentation that reflects the fragmentation of our political economy. When Verizon, for example, puts in a new phone cable, its crews tear up the street, and its crews then patch the street. And not surprisingly, its crews may not put as high a priority on repairing streets as they do on installing phone cables. Or even if Verizon does do a good job, it may not coordinate well with the city's transportation department, or vice versa. Sometimes a private utility company will tear up a road just after a public entity has repaved it. The smoother roads of our European brethren are a portrait of their more coherent hierarchy of government and private enterprise.

In France, state-trained civil servants, perhaps from the École Nationale D'Administration, plan projects that are staffed with engineers from the École Polytechnique, the state engineering school. These projects are planned systematically, so there is less duplication of effort or services. Everything plays well with everything else. The result is the both beautiful and efficient city of Paris, and country of France, which from an infrastructure viewpoint are among the best in the world. The coherence of France's bureaucracy has enabled it to build and run a national system of nuclear power plants, which now supplies more than three-quarters of the country's electricity and makes the country a net exporter of electricity. The country's elite team of civil servants stuck to this plan of nuclear power from its start in the late 1960s, as governments changed from Gaullist, to conservative democratic, to socialist, and so on.

Contrast that with Great Britain, whose Labour government in the roughly same time period backed construction of five nuclear power plants. All sorts of problems ensued, and the state ended up pouring an estimated £50 billion into the effort before selling the reactors at a huge loss. "If the Central Electricity Generating Board had been a commercial company the write-off would have represented by far the largest loss made by any company, anywhere, in business history," said John Kay in *The Truth about Markets*.[12] Such stories tempt one to conclude that cultural patterns can be determinative.

GOVERNMENT OF THE MANY

One pattern we picked up from the English is fractured government with overlapping and unclear lines of authority. It's telling that the actual City of London is still a tiny one-square-mile jurisdiction within the great metropolis that has resisted either being incorporated or incorporating others. As with our governments, in Great Britain courts play a larger role than in continental Europe or Japan. The United States is further fragmented by its federalist structure, where fifty states trade power and constitutional interpretations with a central government. Units of government in the United States lack a clear hierarchy beyond the textbook federal, state, local. From a European perspective, we are "medieval" in our lack of uniformity and common laws and controls.

Because our national government is less empowered, our local governments are powerful and resist subordinating themselves to regional or state authority. William Reinhardt, editor of *Public Works Financing*, says local governments in the United States are unique in generally being allowed to issue public debt, or bonds. In most other countries, that is reserved for the nation or province. There are about 1.2 million authorities in this country—water authorities, school boards, municipalities, and so on—authorized to issue public debt, Reinhardt says.

DOING INFRASTRUCTURE RIGHT

Infrastructure inspires me because it is a physical manifestation of our willingness to do something together, to be our brother's keeper. Because of this, it's appropriate that infrastructure be built with élan, with style, expressing physically some of the ideals it embodies.

But too often in this country, an air of grim utility pervades public works. It's not uncommon for managers to strip out a nice-looking feature of a bridge or building because "it looks expensive," even if it actually costs less and saves money. Saving the taxpayers money replaces the ideal of building a vital, beautiful public realm.

Still, we do have some beautiful public works. One example is the Washington, DC, Metro, the five-line, one-hundred-plus-mile system built in the 1970s and 1980s that knit the suburbs of the nation's capital together with the center city, and created new urban neighborhoods around its stations. It is beautiful and unique. With its barrel vaulting that wraps a platform dweller within an expansive tube of corrugated concrete, the basic components of the Metro system are some of the most distinctive in the world. Construction on the system began in 1969, and the first line opened in 1976, coinciding with the nation's bicentennial celebration. Although the physical construction of the system underneath a roughly two-centuries-old city was a tough engineering job, the political hurdles were, as usual, tougher. It meant bringing together the District of Columbia, the state of Maryland, and the state of Virginia, entities historically in conflict, as well as the federal government. They managed to design and build a heavy rail subway system at a time when, unlike today, train and transit use was dropping. How did this happen?

"The answer is to see Metro in the context of Kennedy-Johnson liberalism," said Zachary Schrag, author of *The Great Society Subway: A History of the Washington Metro.*

It was the embodiment of Great Society liberalism. It was about using the power of the federal government to take American wealth, and put it into grand public projects, not designed to serve the poor, not designed to serve the rich, but to serve everyone. And only if we understand it in those terms, we get a sense of what it's worth.

"I think it was a successful Great Society program," Schrag added. If at times Metro, with its expansive stations with numerous bells and whistles, seems almost grand in its design, it's because it was meant to be. "Metro was not designed to be the cheapest solution to the problem; it was designed to be the best solution to the problem. It was designed to do public works right. The point was not to do cheap; the point was to do good."[13]

We create the kind of markets we want. If we build elegant infrastructure, we have elegant markets.

A PINT IS A POUND THE WORLD ROUND

Infrastructure can mean not only roads and water pipes, it can mean systems of measurement and money that a nation depends on. In his masterful *Measuring America*, Andro Linklater tells the story of the many decades of work in the eighteenth and nineteenth centuries by government to create a standard system of measurement for the United States, primarily done so that land could be bought and sold. The task was Herculean, but was eventually completed. One of the principals was Thomas Jefferson—there he is again!—who personally designed a metric system of weight, volume, and length for the country, as well as the metric system of money we still use, the US dollar. There were also contributions from eccentric figures like Swiss immigrant Ferdinand Hassler, who, appointed multiple times by different presidents, would spend his life surveying the country and establishing standards, and was personally responsible for the weights and measures we all use today, as formalized in the American Customary System of Weights and Measures established in 1857.

At the time of the American Revolution, neither in the new United States, nor in Great Britain or in Europe, did there exist any common system of weights and measurement. Not only did terminology vary, but a gallon, barrel, or bushel, or a foot or a yard, varied in size and quantity from state to state and even from city to city. Money was equally a hodgepodge of pennies, pieces of eight, and pounds. Jefferson created and nearly succeeded in having Congress pass what was essentially a unified field theory of weights, measurement, and money that would have included a version of the new metric system under discussion in revolutionary France. The French decision in the 1790s to establish a meter by the nationalistic distance of one ten-millionth of the distance of a line from the North Pole through Paris to the Equator, rather than the original plan of the length of a pendulum's swing in a given time, undercut Jefferson's effort and similar efforts underway in Great Britain. But Jefferson did succeed in designing and pushing through the creation of the American dollar, instead of copying the British system of pounds, shillings, and so forth, which many had favored. Still, it took until after the Civil War for the decimal dollar to be truly accepted.

Future president John Quincy Adams in 1821, as secretary of state, told Congress of how "Even now at the end of 30 years, ask a tradesman or shopkeeper in any of our cities what is a dime or a mille, and the chances are four in five he will not understand your question. But go to New York and offer payment in the Spanish coin, the unit of the Spanish piece of eight, and the shop or market-man will take it for a shilling. Carry it to Boston or Richmond, and you should be told it is not a shilling but nine pence. Bring it to Philadelphia, Baltimore or the City of Washington, and you shall find it recognized for an eleven-penny bit; . . . And thus we have English denominations most absurdly and diversely applied to Spanish coins; while our own lawfully and established dime and mille remain, to the great masses of the people, among the hidden mysteries of political economy—state secrets."[14]

We can debate still, as they did in Jefferson's time, the merits of a meter versus the yard, the liter versus the quart. But without government's efforts a quart might still be a different size in San Francisco than in New York. Governments set standards.

CONCLUSION

While we have our history and structures that hinder and help us, people, governments, and cultures can change. The past reflects more choices made than the choices we can make. In the last decade there has been wider recognition of what infrastructure is and why it's important. Despite Americans' instinctual suspicion of government, there is room for government, either directly or through a supervising authority, to build and design better and more beautiful infrastructure that is available to all.

CHAPTER 10

MAKING PLACES

I am not your rolling wheels,
I am the highway.
AUDIOSLAVE, "I AM THE HIGHWAY," LYRICS BY CHRIS CORNELL, 2002

THE CLASSIC 1939 MOVIE *Gone with the Wind* memorably captures the burning of Atlanta by the Union army as Scarlet O'Hara and Rhett Butler escape through burning buildings in a horse-drawn carriage.

But despite its prominent role in movie history, few people may realize that the city was only a few years old at the time of the American Civil War. Atlanta was a railroad town, established by the Georgia legislature not long before the Civil War as the "Terminus"—the city's original name—and eventual connecting point to rail lines west. With fewer than ten thousand people before the war, it was still relatively small when it was burned to the ground by General William Sherman in 1864. But the city boomed afterward and in the first decades of the twentieth century. In more contemporary times, as the railroads were left behind, the city continued to grow in population, wealth, and unbelievable suburban sprawl as the intersecting point of three major interstates, I-20, I-85, and I-75, placed by the state of Georgia in cooperation with the federal government.

Cities—that is, urban centers—have been essential to markets, and indeed helped give birth to the very idea and practice of markets, many historians say, since a few traders made deals in the shadow of a temple in ancient Babylon.[1] This being the case, like markets themselves, few if any cities have emerged "naturally," based on a good harbor or river bend.

Cities usually emerge only when a political authority, be it the Dutch

West India Company or the Georgia state legislature, decides they will. My own birthplace of Norfolk, where my father and his mother were also born, was established when King Charles II of England, in 1680, ordered his underling Lord Culpepper, the governor of Virginia, to set up some towns, so that the king could more easily tax the trade coming off the docks of tobacco plantations that fronted on the James and other rivers.[2] This political will can make a town happen in a giant natural harbor like Norfolk, or in a difficult location like the swamps of Chicago.

Governments establish cities often by establishing transportation links, be they a port, a road, or a railroad. And different kinds of transportation make different kinds of cities, different sections of cities, and different neighborhoods—and different kinds of market economies. Big transportation decisions, like building a canal in the nineteenth century, an interstate in the twentieth, or a high-speed train line in the twenty-first, can create a new city or substantially enlarge an existing one. The Erie Canal altered global markets by allowing shipping to and from the Midwest. Smaller initiatives, like a new streetcar line or a new road, can create a new neighborhood or transform an existing one, as well as make a neighborhood grocery store viable or untenable.

HOW WE GET AROUND DETERMINES HOW WE LIVE

In physics there has been an ongoing debate as to whether electrons and other subatomic denizens are particles, occupying a particular point in space at a particular time, or waves, whose location can only be described approximately.

A similar ambiguity exists regarding transportation and its relationship to place. Our places, be they a village or a great city, are usually formed around some method of transportation, be it a ferry across a stream or a high-speed train to some other great metropolis. Yet while our places are formed around transportation links, our transportation links are formed around places. So these two entities, transportation and places, revolve around each other, and it's difficult to say which is the primary driver. Is transportation dependent on place, or more the contrary?

When I first started writing about urban planning and related subjects, I thought we had these things called cities, towns, and neighborhoods, and that we figured out how to get around and between them.

I eventually realized that we figure out how to get around, and that creates these things called cities, towns, and neighborhoods, as well as all their assorted kin like subdivisions, shopping malls, and office parks. We often build transportation to improve travel between places, be they two cities or two neighborhoods. But what usually happens is that the act of creating a transportation medium ends up creating a new place, a third place.

In a curious way, common conversations about cities mirror those about economic markets. City planners often assume, perhaps out of ignorance, that cities are naturally occurring organisms, which can be regulated but not controlled or designed. But cities, underneath the turmoil and bustle, have operating systems embedded in the infrastructure choices that governments make.

Government involvement with transportation is usually necessary to make it comprehensive and efficient. As one transportation planner said, "Transportation is a system. You can't have a little bit of transportation." And to get a system, you usually need government. To acquire the needed capital, to set standards, to take land and establish routes, needs powers that only government has. Although private companies sell automobiles, planes, trains, and ships, government usually builds or massively subsidizes the roads, airports, tracks, and ports.

When President Dwight D. Eisenhower signed legislation in 1956 to create the Interstate and Defense Highway System, he probably thought he was making it easier for Americans to travel between existing towns and cities. What the general did not realize was that he was also setting the nation on a course to create new cities, organized around those very same grade-separated, limited-access highways that now crisscross this land. He was signing the death warrant of downtown department stores and the birth notice of mega malls around the highway interchanges.

"The interstates were not planned to take on this role," said Robert Lang, director of the Metropolitan Institute at Virginia Tech in Alexandria. "The in-between spaces were thought of as just in-between spaces. At that time, the distances between, say, Seattle and Portland seemed very daunting, and the cities as very discrete." The idea that development could occur all along I-5 was simply not thought of.[3]

Interstates create places and market economies differently than railroads, which were the place-makers in the nineteenth century. Interstates have exits every few miles, which means, in the long run, you will get houses, offices, and shopping centers every few miles. Over time, these rivers of concrete take on personalities. There are songs written about driving along I-95, which, according to Lang, has more than 64 million people living within fifty miles of it. Lang said people in Oklahoma and Texas speak of I-35 as a "family freeway," because they visit relatives and friends along it so often.

Often minor policy decisions can shape places in big ways. New York City passed a law after the Civil War forbidding steam-driven locomotives, then the only kind, from passing below 42nd Street, a street well outside the core of the city. Steam locomotives sometimes blew up, and this was a prudent measure. So the New York Central railroad established its main terminus, Grand Central Terminal, at 42nd Street and Fourth Avenue. Freight and passengers were transferred there onto horse-drawn and later electric streetcars to go down into the center city. But as with the mountain coming to Muhammad, Grand Central grew in its importance, particularly after its overhaul in 1913, and the city grew toward and around Grand Central and Penn Station, finished in 1910 over on 33rd Street on the West Side. Robert Yaro of the Regional Plan Association calls Midtown Manhattan, which many now regard as the city and regional center, the original "edge city," because it emerged around a confluence of transportation links on the edge of town, just like Tyson's Corner outside Washington, DC, and other "edge cities" identified by Joel Garreau in his book of that name.

NOT ONE COLOR BUT MANY: MAKING BETTER PLACES

While we have a good track record of making places in this country through big transportation investments, we have a lousy track record of creating subtle and varied places. We tend to go to extremes in this country with our transportation investments. There's a parallel here with markets. The American- or Anglo-Saxon–style "free markets" tend to put too much power into too few hands, be they Microsoft's and Intel's in the twenty-first century or Cornelius Vanderbilt's and John Rockefeller's in the nineteenth. Both places and markets function better when we have a finer-grain set of decisions behind them. We have lurched historically from one extreme to another, first investing and then overinvesting in canals in the early nineteenth century, and then overinvesting in railroads, and then, in the twentieth century, overinvesting in roads and highways.

Lewis Mumford, like an all-seeing angry prophet, forecast the sprawl, inner-city decay, and auto-centric tyranny that would be produced by overinvesting in poorly located interstates, as laid out in the Federal-Aid Highway Act of 1956:

> When the American people, through their Congress, voted a little while ago for a twenty-six-billion-dollar highway program, the most charitable thing to assume about this action is that they hadn't the faintest notion of what they were doing. [Soon,] it will be too late to correct the damage to our cities and our countryside, not least to the efficient organization of industry and transportation, that this ill-conceived and preposterously unbalanced program will have wrought.[4]

PARKING IS DESTINY

Cars require spaces to put them when not in use, and this necessity determines the layout and feel of contemporary cities. Richard Meier, the classic modernist, completed in 2000 his $190 million federal courthouse on Long Island. It was built under the relatively new "Design Excellence Program" of the General Services Administration, which puts top architects in charge of new federal buildings. Meier's twelve-story tower of white, accompanied by a lopsided silolike cylinder that serves as a grand entrance, asserts itself against the island's low-rise world of shopping centers and subdivisions. In front of the building is a grand public plaza. It's a beautiful complex.

But by necessity a 1,600-space parking lot surrounds it. The parking, and the nearby highways, isolate the building to which they give access. Meier would like the courthouse to play an old role, that of community gathering space, but it will be an uphill battle. Unlike the courthouse of yore, no one will casually walk by it on his way to the drugstore. This isn't to say that Meier shouldn't have tried to make the building a public place, only that the transportation context will determine its use more than its controversial status as a modernist white box.

One of Meier's heroes, the Swiss architect and founder of modernism Le Corbusier, displayed a particularly dramatic example of miscalculating how transportation and building design mesh. Le Corbusier made architectural headlines in the 1920s with his Plan Voisin, which proposed tearing down old Paris and replacing it with soaring towers on parks interlaced with freeways. Le Corbusier loved cars, and showed freeways dotted with a few Model-T–style cars running between his towers.

Jonathan Barnett, a professor of city planning at the University of Pennsylvania, calculated that under standard formulas, each of Le Corbusier's tall towers would have had to be surrounded by 241 acres of surface parking lots. Instead of towers in the park, it would have been towers in the parking lots—which is what we got.[5]

Barnett's example got me to do the same calculations for the late World Trade Center and its twin towers. It turns out that the two towers, with fifty thousand workers and 10 million square feet of office space between them, would have needed more than 500 acres of surface parking lots under conventional developer formulas. If built as garages, they would have been more than two hundred stories, one for each of the towers. And then there's the freeway. You would have needed twenty-five lanes of freeways to carry all those workers there in the morning. Obviously, an impossibility. (But fortunately, most WTC workers rode the subways to their jobs.) The World Trade Center was a product of its environment.

MAKING PLACES AND MARKETS MORE CONSCIOUSLY

One thing leads to another. That's how most transportation improvements happen here. A lot of people want to cross a river; you build a bridge to replace the overcrowded ferry. A lot of cars are on a road; you expand the road into a highway. A lot of people want to fly somewhere; you build a bigger airport. And that's a legitimate way to plan transportation. We talk more about this in Chapter 14, about path dependence.

But there is another way to do it, and that is to build something to places where, currently, people are not traveling very much. You create demand through the very act of building a better way to get there. This is riskier than simply responding to demand, but the payoff is potentially bigger. Like the decisions we make that construct markets, we can make places (and markets) with our transportation decisions much more actively and consciously.

The biggest example historically of this is the construction of the Erie Canal in the early 1800s by New York state. Few people were trying to get from Albany to the tiny town of Buffalo, an almost impossible journey overland through dense forest, rivers, and rugged terrain. It was a planner's dream—in this case, a governor's—that if a canal were built, then passengers and cargo would want to travel to the Great Lakes, using the Erie Canal, which linked via the Hudson River to New

York City. And because it was just an unproven idea, many people derided the Erie Canal before and during its construction. But not after. Begun in 1817 at the urging of Gov. DeWitt Clinton, the 350-mile canal opened the entire upper Midwest to shipping, and cemented New York City's role as transportation hub for the nation, and as the country's greatest city.[6] It was built entirely with state funds. Historian Paul Johnson called it perhaps the greatest public works project in history in terms of its generation of wealth.

But you don't have to go back two centuries to find projects that anticipate demand and that use infrastructure as a tool for economic development and good place-making.

Spain, eyeing the fast trains in neighboring France, opted to build its first high-speed rail line in the 1990s between its capital city of Madrid and southern Seville, a beautiful city of Moorish architecture and flamenco dancers, but not so dynamic economically. At the time many Spaniards thought a more natural choice would have been between Madrid and Barcelona, the dynamic Catalan city that is one of the economic centers of Europe. Many businessmen already made that journey, and many wanted to do so quickly and more easily. I rode the new Seville line in 1994 shortly after it opened. It was marvelous, leaving from Madrid's cavernous and beautiful Atocha station. I went some 300 miles to the World's Fair in Seville at speeds of about 200 mph and returned that evening in time for dinner back in Madrid. But even I wondered at the wisdom of making Madrid–Seville the first line.

Flash forward seventeen years. Building the first line to Seville helped jump-start economically a poorer region of the country, Andalucía. It also helped win political support for the investment in high-speed rail, once the rest of the country saw how well it worked. Spain has expanded its network of high-speed lines, run by a public agency, RENFE, throughout the country, including to Barcelona. Now there are predictions that by 2020, a high-speed rail line will be within 31 miles of 90 percent of the country's population.[7]

It's not only transportation between cities that illustrates this principle. It's also transportation within a city or metropolitan area. In 1998, Paris completed its latest subway line, no. 14, the Meteor. This high-tech marvel, conductorless and with sliding glass doors, goes from the busy Left Bank across the Seine to the 13th arrondissement, still relatively undeveloped despite the presence of the new French National Library. Planners thought, correctly, that a way to drive metropolitan growth into an underutilized area was to build a fast subway line there—along with a new billion-dollar national library.

It should be understood that in both these examples, planners put the public's money into areas where there was less congestion, not more. And that's okay. Sometimes, the best thing to do with congestion is to ignore it. Congestion, whether it's on a train or a road, is not always the best indicator of where to invest precious transportation dollars. A wider set of markers should be used.

In 2005, former senator Ted Stevens of Alaska was derided for winning funding for his infamous "Bridge to Nowhere," which connected Gravina Island to the mainland via an enormous bridge. And maybe this was a boondoggle. I'm not close enough to Alaska to know. But just because there was nothing happening doesn't necessarily mean it was a bad idea. Sometimes, a bridge, road, or rail line to nowhere can create a somewhere.

There is a parallel here with market economies. Rather than just reacting to events, as transportation planners tend to do with traffic congestion, makers of, say, a patent system can construct one to reward creators or distribute intellectual property in ways that are not simply reacting to market pressures. We don't only have to enlarge what is there. We can light out for new territory, and make new places, and markets.

CHAPTER 11

THE GREAT NINETEENTH-CENTURY TRAIN ROBBERY

The time will come when people will travel in stages moved by steam engines from one city to another, almost as fast as birds can fly, 15 or 20 miles an hour. . . . A carriage will start from Washington in the morning, the passengers will breakfast at Baltimore, dine at Philadelphia, and sup in New York the same day.

OLIVER EVANS, AMERICAN INVENTOR,

FROM REMARKS DELIVERED IN 1813[1]

Railroad iron is a magician's rod, in its power to evoke the sleeping energies of land and water.

RALPH WALDO EMERSON, "THE YOUNG AMERICAN,"

AN ADDRESS TO THE MERCANTILE LIBRARY ASSOCIATION, 1844

ON MARCH 4, 1801, Thomas Jefferson took the oath of office as the nation's third president in what is now called the "Old Senate Chamber" of the US Capitol, then still under construction. He then turned to speak to the audience, reported to be more than a thousand people, crammed into the building. Historians have focused particularly on Jefferson's words "We are all Federalists, we are all Republicans"—an answer to the bruising election that brought him to office. But just afterward Jefferson said something pertinent to our discussions here. He said, basically, why argue so stridently, there's space aplenty in this big land, "with room enough for our descendants to the thousandth and thousandth generation." If taken literally, this would probably mean two thousand generations, or fifty thousand years.[2]

Even if Jefferson didn't mean that long, it seems he did mean it would take a really, really long time to fill up the wild continent they inhabited. After all, Columbus had "discovered" America in 1492, and in 1801, more than three hundred years later, the frontier was just a few hundred miles inland, basically on the other side of the Appalachian Mountains. Civilization was a long, thin band along the Atlantic and Gulf Coasts and their major rivers, where ships could easily reach. It was certainly reasonable for this president, who was also a learned scholar, scientist, and architect, to predict it would take many thousands of years to fill up the country, given how much was left after three hundred years.

But Mr. Jefferson would be proved wrong. It would take less than a century to fill up the country, for the edge of the frontier to move from Kentucky, where it was when Jefferson wrote, to the Rocky Mountains. How could this learned man have gotten it so wrong? In a word, infrastructure. Jefferson failed to foresee the construction and impact of the Erie Canal, begun in 1817, which opened up the Midwest to shipping and trade, and made New York City the dominant city of the nation. Jefferson failed to foresee railroads, those great iron horses that would also open up the country, even the driest parts distant from any navigable river, with a speed and violence unimaginable previously. In other words, he failed to see two transportation revolutions and the changes they would wreak.

These enormous changes, particularly from the railroads, would bring great benefits and costs. Before the century was through, the nation would have expended an enormous amount of blood and treasure to construct, by some estimates, more than 400,000 miles of railroad tracks crisscrossing the nation (of which only about 150,000 remain).[3] The construction of this national train network would help nearly wipe out the American Indian, whose encounter with white men Jefferson saw proceeding far more gently and slowly. The railroads helped spark the US Civil War, because railroads accelerated the land grab in the West, which was at the heart of the conflict between North and South. While hundreds of railroad companies were born and died, a few emerged triumphant. In 1891, the US military, all branches, employed 39,492 people. At the same time, the Pennsylvania Railroad employed 110,000.[4]

The drive to build railroads would create new forms of markets, both physically by creating and connecting new cities and lands, but even more important, by prompting leaders to change the political structure of the country to accommodate the drive to build railroads. The railroad mania would create the modern limited liability corporation and the huge corporation that spanned states. It would paradoxically—and this is important—help create the laissez-faire relationship between government and business, altering the very DNA of the nation, *because the necessity of government help for the private railroads in the form of lands, authority such as eminent domain, and cash led to government bending over backward to separate itself from the for-profit entity it was helping.* The political leaders would work to place government further from the hands of its citizens to keep them from taking control of the railroads that were receiving such enormous quantities of land, money, and power from those same citizens through their government. As one arm of government handed out huge sums of money and power to railroad companies, another arm, or sometimes even the same arm, restricted government's power to get something in return for that money. The efforts to build railroads would alter the country's governing structures as much as the Civil War did.

As we examine how government makes markets, no better example exists than the combined efforts of local, state, and federal governments to encourage and accommodate the railroads in the nineteenth century. And for this reason, even though the story is more than a century old, it is worth looking at. It is an example of how we create markets through physical infrastructure, and also the perils and pitfalls of doing so. It is primarily a cautionary tale. I tell the story not as an example to emulate, but to show how completely government is involved in the construction of markets, even when those markets are nominally led by private companies. The history of railroads contrasts with the history of roads, which takes place largely in the following century, the twentieth. Unlike the railroads, roads will be built almost entirely by the state.

THE STORY OF RAILROADS

The story of railroads began, oddly enough, with canals. Railroads began as a response to canals. New York state's publicly financed and conceived Erie Canal had been so successful that other states went on a frenzy of canal-building in an effort to compete.[5]

But some states and cities, for reasons of geography, were not able to construct canals, and they sought alternatives. One city and state found a new technology, first used in England to transport coal in mines, of moving cars along steel tracks. This led to the country's first railroad, the Baltimore and Ohio (B&O), familiar to players of the game Monopoly, a railroad funded by the state of Maryland and the city of Baltimore, in an effort to help the port city compete with New York City by giving Baltimore a way to have its goods and passengers reach the Midwest via an alternative to the Erie Canal. Maryland and Baltimore supplied and owned half of the $3 million in stock necessary to start the railroad, which ran from the harbor of Baltimore to the Ohio River. Construction began in 1828, and the railroad opened for business in May of 1830.[6]

This, arguably the first passenger railroad in the country, was the opening shot in what became a massive stampede by states and local governments to have railroads built through their lands. But only a few would choose to build these railroads themselves. This was because many states had lost money on the canals, which were not as successful as the Erie Canal. A political backlash set in, and when governments began encouraging railroads, the appetite for direct government ownership and control had declined. As we shall see, this was unfortunate.

Railroads were seductive in how thoroughly they changed the transportation game (although canals would actually stay quite competitive with railroads for much of the nineteenth century). For example, the railroad reduced a journey from Chicago to New York from three weeks to three days.[7] And in a frontier nation, building a rail line was the equivalent of harvesting new land. "The mechanized transportation system becomes, as it were, a producer of territories in the same way that mechanized agriculture becomes a producer of goods," said Wolfgang Schivelbusch in *The Railway Journey*.[8] The federal government soon joined the act with its support of the Illinois Central in 1850.

The sad thing was that unlike the B&O railroad, which at least had state and city officials on the board of directors, the vast majority of what would become hundreds of railroad companies were led and controlled and owned by private businessmen, even though government was supplying large quantities of the land, the capital, and legal powers including, but not limited to, eminent domain. As the country descended into the Civil War and then came out of it, the efforts to build the railroads only intensified, and with them the handing out of government power and treasure to private companies.

WAR CHANGES THINGS

Find a big change in society—the can opener, the car, the computer chip, the Internet, whatever—and it's striking how often it goes back to war. War mobilizes and resolves and brings government in to help on things, big time.

When the Civil War began, the Northern and ultimately victorious half of the country was led by a president, Abraham Lincoln, who rose to prominence as a successful railroad lawyer. His cases included representing largely Northern railroad companies in their efforts to gain the right to cross the rivers that bisected the country without interference from the largely Southern steamship companies. Lincoln's influence as president would be instrumental to the way railroads were built in this country. Not long after attaining office, and following the start of the war, Lincoln gained passage of the Pacific Railway Act of 1862, which set the country on a course to have tracks reach the ocean on the other side of the country, a project that has been rightfully compared to the mission to land a man on the moon announced by President John F. Kennedy in 1961. The act authorized extensive federal land grants— ten square miles on each side of the tracks outside of cities—as well as government funding through bonds, to railroad companies to further the goal of transcontinental coverage. This would be followed with the more generous and less rigorous Pacific Railway Act of 1864, which Richard White called "the worst act money could buy" because of the way it handed out public financial commitments with little control or possibility of return.[9] These monies were to build what White calls "the transcontinentals"—railroads that crossed the barren and spacious lands of Nevada, Montana, and other thinly populated areas. It was in the financing of these railroads that government largesse grew particularly indiscriminate.

Lincoln was an enthusiastic backer of government funding and construction of canals and railroads. He promoted them his entire life. As both president and a private attorney, he seemed to believe that the contribution to society outweighed any damage to a lone individual. In 1852 he won a case representing Alton & Sangamon Railroad before the Illinois Supreme Court that said the railroad did not have to compensate a property owner for taking his property, as long as the expected increase in value to the rest of the owner's property would exceed that of the land taken—an amazingly anti-property-rights argument.[10] The burden of proof lay on the property owner.

The Civil War turned the already existing torrent of government money and power for railroad companies into a flood. The historian Paul Johnson estimated that state and federal governments gave away $350 million in direct grants to railroad companies between 1861 and 1890, as well as anywhere from one-seventh to one-fifth of the total land area of the country for right-of-ways.[11] Johnson, in his *A History of the American People*, summarized the principal ways railroads were privileged, funded, or subsidized (pick your verb):

The railroads were subsidized and legally privileged in six ways. First, they got charters (rather like the original banks) from state legislatures, often—it was claimed—in return for free passes handed out to prominent state politicians. Second, they were given special banking privileges to raise money. Third, they got the right of "eminent domain," in effect the legal ability to make compulsory purchases. Fourth, they were given both state and federal tax exemptions. Fifth, they often secured monopoly protection against competitors. Sixth, further capital was raised by federal, state, county, and municipal subscriptions. In the thirty years after 1861, for instance, national bond loans totaled $64.6 million (all repaid). The rails received tariff remissions too.

But the most valuable form of government subsidy was undoubtedly the gift of federal lands, made on a prodigious scale. No other corporations in human history have been endowed in such a profligate manner by a paternal government—they were indeed treated as Eldest Sons. The rails got one-fourth of the states of Minnesota and Washington, one-fifth of Wisconsin, Iowa, Kansas, North Dakota, and Montana, one-seventh of Nebraska, one-eighth of California, and one-ninth of Louisiana. In all 242,000 square miles, a territory larger than Germany or France, was handed over. . . . In addition, individual states donated a total of 55 million acres, bore the cost of surveying in many cases, and contributed to the stock. In New York State alone, for instance, 294 cities, towns, and villages contributed $30 million, and fifty-one counties gave subsidies as well.[12]

It would nice to say that, in exchange for all this money and real estate, the country got a railroad system that served its citizens' interests, but that is not the case. It got a fragmented and incoherent system that served its private owners first, and sometimes ruined the citizens whose taxes had helped build it.

HEADS YOU LOSE, TAILS I WIN

The railroads were competing with each other to gain routes and lay tracks. Meanwhile, governments, state and local, were competing to get the railroads. This led to crazy situations where competing companies would lay tracks to the same jurisdiction, or where companies would lay track based on the payouts, either illicit bribes or publicly disclosed grants. Routes would proceed in snakelike fashion, which made sense if one mapped the bribes the companies were receiving from various towns.

"The lack of regulation and enforcement by government authorities meant substantial inefficiencies," said Charles Perrow in *Organizing America*.

Communities poured money into schemes that never produced (trains never ran, ties were untreated and rotted, wooden rather than iron tracks were laid and useless within a year, bridges collapsed). There was overbuilding to destroy rivals and gain market control, or for sheer fraud. Innovations that would promote safety were resisted. Without regulation, competing lines chose different track sizes, resulting in gross inefficiencies. There was wasteful duplication of lines for specu- lative and monopoly purposes, routes zigzagged as towns put up capital, and then the lines were abandoned.[13]

Richard White, in his masterful and damning *Railroaded: The Trans- continentals and the Making of Modern America*, makes the sobering point that the men who led these railroad companies succeeded in en- riching themselves but little else. They built poor railroads, and poor corporations. The corporations they built mostly went broke, losing their investors' money. And the tracks, trains, and stations were poorly constructed and placed as well.[14]

The budding discipline of economics was not unaware of this de- struction of private companies and often the public interest, and this recognition led to an interesting debate within the academy, which was recounted by Michael Perelman in *Railroading Economics: The Cre- ation of the Free Market Mythology*. Perelman says the huge capital and organizational requirements of railroads prompted economists, who were then ardently inventing and promoting the idea of a free market that worked akin to a natural system, to change their thinking about trusts and cartels. These economists concluded that government should actually encourage, rather than prohibit, the formation of trusts and cartels in railroading, to avoid what might be called the ruinous competition that was destroying railroad companies and leaving them undercapitalized. These cartels, though, should be regulated and con- trolled, they said. These economists "realized that a modern economy that followed the recommendations of conventional economic theory would court disaster," Perelman says.[15] As we shall see, there were other countries, chiefly Great Britain, that followed this advice. The United States unfortunately did not.

While private railroad companies ended up largely dominant, there

were a few state-owned or partially state-owned railroads, in addition
to the original B&O railroad in Maryland. North Carolina even today
has a state railroad company that dates back to the 1850s and is still
in use. It owns many of the main lines in the state, and charges Amtrak and freight railroads for the privilege of using them. Georgia had a
state rail system that worked well from 1836 to 1870, the Western and
Atlantic Railroad, which was involved in the creation of the city of
Atlanta.[16] As I've mentioned, the city was originally called "Terminus,"
because it was the end of the line. Then it was renamed "Marthasville,"
and finally "Atlanta."

There was considerable debate at the time as to whether private or
public interests should control the railroad. Said one newspaper editorial in muscular prose:

> A large corporation, like a mighty colossus, with one foot at Savannah
> and the other at Chattanooga, will bestride the state, whilst its iron
> fingers will be felt in every election and will direct the future legisla-
> tion of the State. No matter what guards and checks this legislature
> may throw around such a corporation, when they once get control of
> such immense resources they will elect a legislature to suit themselves
> and will break all these bands like cobwebs. We are willing to entrust
> the management of the road to the people, whether the Whigs or the
> Democrats are in power.[17]

Despite this nameless editor's words, his warning went unheeded.
Private railroads dominated government all the way to the Supreme
Court, and the few state-owned railroads proved the exception, not the
rule. Georgia's would be sold to private interests in 1870.

WHY WERE WE SO DUMB?

Given the inefficiencies and unfairness of letting private companies,
equipped with government money and power, run rampant over our
interests, it's pertinent to ask: why did we do it this way? Why were
there not more successful movements to establish public railroads, or
at least highly controlled private ones?

Although I've mentioned the backlash to canals, it's also true that
our national political system is not set up for coherency, not now and
certainly not in 1850. Our federal system has an independent federal
government (with an executive branch that does not grow out of a

legislative branch, as in a parliamentary system) only loosely linked to the governments of the fifty states, which in turn oversee thousands of separate municipalities. This constitutes a structural impediment to coherent national action. The one endeavor that is truly national is defense. It's the federal government's, and only the federal government's, job to make war. Consequently, many tasks only vaguely related to defense become defense projects, because Pentagon funding is an avenue for a national program. The 1956 National Interstate and Defense Highway Act, as it was often known, is a prominent example. The founders designed our government to make collective action difficult. They succeeded all too well.

Because collective action is so difficult, we Americans accept a variety of injustices and difficulties that would not fly elsewhere. They range from high fees at automatic teller machines—other countries quickly prohibited them—to the high costs of prescription drugs (not only don't we have a national health-care system, but our government forbids itself to bargain for better drug prices!).

HOW OTHER COUNTRIES DID IT, EVEN GREAT BRITAIN!

When you look at the great saga of the railroads in this country, one thing becomes clear: the United States did it differently. In France, Great Britain, and Germany, the state was more involved. It either owned the railroads directly, as in Germany (Prussia), directed them almost completely through nominally private companies (France), or regulated them strictly, while allowing private companies some freedom of action (Great Britain).

Great Britain, from which we gain our tendency to empower private companies for infrastructure development, encouraged the formation of cartels, groups of smaller railroad companies that would control traffic in a given area. These cartels were in turn highly regulated and controlled. "The British cartels fostered the cooperation that made extended runs possible without changing equipment, regulated track size, standardized equipment, and coordinated schedules from the start. (It took several decades to achieve this in the United States.) . . . The result was private capital, ownership, and management, which was coordinated by cartels and regulated by state agencies set up by parliament, and which was flexible and promoted regional development."[18] It also "protected the vitality and independence of individual firms as a source of industrial efficiency."[19]

In France, known both then and now for a strong, highly competent state sector responsible for infrastructure, the national Bureau of Roads and Bridges (Corps des Ponts et Chaussées) dictated where routes would go, where stations would go, what the track gauge would be, and so forth. Private companies had nominal ownership and title, and actually supplied much of the capital. But the state insured these private companies against any losses, and guaranteed them a return on their investment, while also setting a ceiling on it. The state led the way. "No railroads could be built, even on private land, without authorization by the state," said Perrow in *Organizing America*.

"There was never any doubt in France that this was the way to plan a rational and coherent network of railway lines," said Perrow. "Nor was there any question that the private interests building the firm were to be completely controlled by the state."[20]

Adolphe Thiers, minister of commerce and public works in the 1830s, who would go on to be the first president of France's Third Republic in 1871, said at the time in justifying state direction of the railroads:

If capitalists were left to their own devices, France would find itself with a mess of disjointed, poorly constructed stretches of track that would ill serve the nation . . . and squander the nation's resources on local projects without a view to constructing a national network.[21]

The irony of this remark is that it's as if Thiers were summarizing how the United States did build its network. Under the French model, a national rail system emerged quickly, with Paris at its center, and the towns along it were not at the mercy of a private railroad company that charged monopoly prices. Nor was there the chaos of bank deals and stock swindling that was the backdrop of American railroads. This centralized, coherent French approach continues today, and is brilliantly seen in the current TGV system—*trens a grand vittesse* (trains of great speed)—that was the first in Europe and has helped Paris remain an important city in Europe, given that now a European high-speed rail system is effectively centered on Paris.

Germany took a third way, with complete state ownership of the railroads, which it nationalized in 1879. This also worked.

The American way did not work efficiently or fairly. The country got a national system, but at a tremendous cost to the lives of both individuals and communities. What might have been if states and the federal government had done it the French or English way, which is more conceivable given our political economy, with government closely directing and supervising private companies? Without the huge independent private companies that emerged from the railroad era, we might not have gotten the US Supreme Court opinion that judged a private company "a person." We might have gotten state legislatures and a Congress more attuned to the interests of the electorate. We might have gotten a government that was more robust and capable, and thus able to take on new challenges in the twentieth century. But the time was not right for it. The one-two-three punch of the Civil War, manifest destiny, and a speculative bubble with largely foreign capital fueled the uniquely American way of constructing our railroads. And a poor way it was.

What is clear from railroad history is that if government is to mix with private enterprise, something unavoidable in most instances, then it should do so in ways that serve its citizens, and that mission should come first.

CHAPTER 12

A SOCIALIST PARADISE:
THE AMERICAN ROAD SYSTEM

Well if you ever plan to motor west,
Just take my way, that's the highway that's the best.
Get your kicks on Route Sixty-six.
Well it winds from Chicago to LA
More than two thousand miles all the way.
Get your kicks on Route Sixty-six.
"(GET YOUR KICKS ON) ROUTE 66," LYRICS BY BOBBY TROUP, 1946

THE SONG "ROUTE 66" IS HOMAGE to American individualism and the joys of the open road. Few may realize that it is also homage to American socialism, and the possibilities of individualism and freedom that such socialism permits. For Route 66, that winding ribbon of pre-interstate highway that runs from Chicago through Missouri, Oklahoma, Texas, New Mexico, Arizona, and into California, is a product of government action, its asphalt and right-of-way paid for by the various states on its path, with help from the federal government. It was not an easy task and is emblematic of the decades-long work to construct a national road network. It's also emblematic of the tortured relationship Americans have with government. Most important, it's an example of how individualism and government are not in conflict. In fact, the latter can empower the former.

FROM WAGONS TO TWO-WHEELERS

The history of Route 66 is entwined with the history of the early roads movement, which is, like all major chapters in American history, a fierce and internecine struggle among competing visions and interests, full of boosters, do-gooders, hucksters, and wheeler-dealers. It's a history that has largely been forgotten, overshadowed by the creation in the 1950s of the Interstate Highway System.

In the 1920s, though, the idea of a cross-country highway was a new one, or at least one long dormant. Under President Thomas Jefferson in 1805, Congress approved and funded the development of a National Road from Cumberland, Maryland, on the Potomac River, to Wheeling, West Virginia (then, of course, still in Virginia) on the Ohio River. It was designed to create a wagon road between the all-important river routes of the Potomac and the Ohio Rivers, where new settlers were coming. Even though the US Constitution states that Congress shall have authority to establish "post offices and post roads," the idea of an interstate road was still a new one, and Jefferson secured permission from the three states the road passed through, Virginia, Maryland, and Pennsylvania. Eventually plans were approved to build the road all the way to St. Louis on the Mississippi, but the road petered out a few miles short in the 1830s as first canals, and then railroads, undercut the road's raison d'être.

BICYCLING TO THE FHWA

A half-century later, a curious thing would bring roads back to a national agenda: the bicycle. In the 1880s and 1890s, the new "safety bicycle," with two wheels the same size driven by a chain, was all the rage. It was not just a toy. It was a personal transportation device of enormous efficiency and relative speed. But there was one problem. Bicycles travel poorly on muddy, bumpy, unpaved, or cobblestoned streets. The League of American Wheelmen, the major bicycle lobby, worked hard to improve roads, and in desperation, lobbied the federal government to get involved in road-building. This was unprecedented, because routine road-building, as opposed to a grand project like the National Road, had always been the responsibility of counties. But this Hail Mary pass worked. The federal government created the Office of Road Inquiry under the Agriculture Department. It eventually became the Bureau of Public Roads. After World War II it was renamed the Federal Highway Department and eventually became today's US Department of Transportation, of which the FHWA is the dominant part. So the mighty US-DOT, which oversees hundreds of billions of dollars annually, began with the humble Office of Road Inquiry within the Agricultural Department, begun at the urging of cyclists.[1] The bicycle craze lasted just long enough to pave sufficient roads so there were some around when cars began to be sold in larger numbers after 1900.

An unexpected group assisted the bicyclists and others in what became known as the "Good Roads" movement: the railroad companies. Several train companies donated trains and equipment so that officials from the Office of Road Inquiry could go around the country demonstrating paving techniques. The curious thing from a contemporary perspective is that train companies would help out what would become their doom, roads. For in just a few decades, the road network would start stealing traffic from train travel, and eventually passenger train companies would plunge into bankruptcy. But in the late nineteenth and early twentieth centuries, train companies were so dominant, with the automobile still essentially just a toy, that this was unimaginable. Train companies saw better roads as helping farmers and others get to the train station.

AN EMERGING FEDERAL BUREAUCRACY

As the bicycle craze receded and the nation headed toward World War I, two competing visions emerged as to how and whether the federal government should get involved with roads. One wanted Congress to focus on "farm-to-market roads," in essence city and regional roads, which would help farmers, in their wagons, get to the train station or to the city. This was the vision promoted by the Good Roads movement and its railroad allies. The other vision was that of actual intercity roads, which would help chiefly those in this new form of transportation, the automobile, get from one city to another.

The Federal-Aid Road Act of 1916 was a milestone for the second vision, that of intercity roads. The Act approved $75 million for highways, to be administered by the Office of Public Roads, the small agency still under the Department of Agriculture that would eventually grow into today's giant US Department of Transportation, with its own secretary who reports directly to the president. The Road Act of 1916 was the first of many appropriations by Congress over the next century. It was followed initially by the Federal-Aid Highway Act of 1921, which was more successful in getting pavement built between cities, and established the model of strong state DOTs guided by federal oversight. Congress now routinely approves every few years massive highway packages such as the Intermodal Surface Transportation Efficiency Act (ISTEA), or TEA-21. But in 1916 it was a novel and unprecedented use of federal power.

In typical American fashion, also in the early twentieth century, the private sector made some attempts to build roads for growing automobile traffic. This resulted, in 1913, in the Lincoln Highway, a cross-country highway from New York to California that was supported by a mixture of private contributions from the newly formed automobile industry and public ones. Championed by automaker and former bicycle maker Carl Fischer, a promoter extraordinaire who had begun lobbying for better roads during the bicycle era, the highway would link various existing roads and create new ones where before were only dirt and desert. Ultimately the group's private efforts would be superseded by state and federal governments, which created the millions of miles that we rely on today. The Lincoln Highway, although historical markers still indicate its path, became part of various numbered US highways across the country.[2]

It is telling to contrast the era of public road-building with the era of private railroad construction that had preceded it, and the era of public canal-building before that. Although private interests dabbled in building highways, ultimately state and federal governments paid for, built, and owned most roads, the opposite of what occurred with trains and tracks in the railroad era. The pendulum of government involvement swung from one end of the spectrum to another. As a policy it was pure socialism, and it would work wonderfully well, at least from the standpoint of getting Americans into cars and into a new transportation system. Unlike with the private railroad companies, the national highway network would not leave American citizens and businesses at the mercy of a single private company that might dominate a key trade route. Instead, a free road system, paid for almost entirely by tax dollars, created this network that would symbolize the freedom portrayed in the song "Route 66."

The particular moniker Route 66 came out of a fight in the 1920s between state interests to claim the catchiest labels from the federal government, which was putting in place a new numbered system to replace the hodgepodge of named highways, such as the Lincoln Highway, supported or conceived by private associations. A highway official came up with the plan, still in use today, for both US highways and the interstates to have even-numbered routes go east-west and odd-numbered routes go north-south.

As a prime highway through the nation's heartland, the catchy Route

66, pushed by Oklahoma promoter Cyrus Avery, entered the nation's lore through various popular references, as in the writing of John Steinbeck, who named it "Mother Road" in *Grapes of Wrath*. Songwriter Bobby Troup was driving the new national highway shortly after World War II and marveled at the diversity of the nation one drove through. He penned "(Get Your Kicks on) Route 66." It was one of many homages to the highway, including even a television show. The road itself was essentially a patchwork of existing roads, many of them unpaved, that were united by a numbering system that would alert travelers how to proceed.

THE ENGINEER AS POLICY MAKER

The story of the nation's early road system is the story as well of the bureaucracy that planned and built it. This brings into the story an engineer and master bureaucrat, Thomas H. MacDonald, who led the Bureau of Public Roads for thirty-four years, from 1919 to 1953. It was under MacDonald that the cornerstones of our road system were constructed, including the basic plan for the Interstate Highway System. As Bruce Seely tells so well in his *Building the American Highway System: Engineers as Policy Makers*, MacDonald embodies very well the seemingly neutral technocrat, who through his dispensing of facts to elected officials excels in setting a policy agenda.

MacDonald was the Haussmann of America's road system, the public administrator who had a vision and took the nation from a rail country to a car country via his national road system. But unlike Baron Haussmann, who eventually lost his post as prefect of the Seine, where he oversaw the overhaul of Paris in the 1850s, MacDonald operated with great subtlety, always staying in the background, always letting the politicians get the credit and presenting himself as the apolitical administrator. It was a good act, one imitated today in many sectors, but of course completely misleading. MacDonald was clearly not a neutral player but a great advocate for a national road system, although he retained a sense of balance. It helped that MacDonald was extremely good at his job. He did extensive research before advocating any policy. He was not a fan of indiscriminately paving everything in sight and believed the German Auto-bahns, for example, were ridiculously overbuilt.[3]

As is common, war played a role in setting the nation on a new transportation course. During World War I, trains backed up all the way from

New York to Washington, DC, as the train system was overloaded with men and materials on their way to be sent overseas. In desperation, the military began using motorized trucks on roads to transport men and equipment between cities, a novel idea at the time. This showed the utility of good roads and helped generate political support. The Great Depression of the 1930s also helped. Paving roads was a perfect way to put men to work. Route 66 was finally completely paved in 1938. The creation of this large system of roads was a great achievement, which we the public take for granted, as if these ribbons of asphalt going everywhere somehow created themselves. But even in the late 1920s, when millions of Ford Model T's and Model A's were on the "road," about 80 percent of the roads in this country were dirt and gravel.[4]

All this relates to markets, because building a new transportation system is about building a new market system of production and exchange. If you do it right, you make things faster and more efficient. And you need government to do it.

The era of this national road network, led by Thomas MacDonald, would be eclipsed by the creation of the Interstate Highway System (along routes, as it happens, almost entirely mapped out and recommended by MacDonald in 1947).[5] The creation of the Interstate Highway System, so strong and so flawed, merits its own story somewhere else. For now, let your attention stay on that casual road you might find on a trip outside town, one that passes through farm country, say, and which you take completely for granted. As you drive along it, thank your predecessors for building it.

DOWN THE MEMORY HOLE

With the establishment of our national road system, which was really done in three successive waves—the late nineteenth century and bicycles; the early twentieth century around early cars; and the postwar era around the interstates—the role of government in doing all this was largely forgotten. And with this amnesia, there has emerged in current times a strange, paradoxical creature—the antigovernment, pro-road lobbyist and commentator. It's as if someone were provegetable and antidirt at the same time. These commentators also sharply attack mass transit spending, particularly on trains. For some reason, they see a highway as an expression of the free market and of American individualism, and a rail line as an example of government meddling and creeping socialism. (Anyone who has ever tried to stand up to a state

DOT intent on building a highway could tell them differently.) As I have shown in this chapter, governments, not the free market, built our road system. The gas tax, which some commentators wrongly compare to a user fee, pays for less than half of the direct costs of roads currently, and far less than that historically.[6] A 2009 study by the Texas Department of Transportation that examined grade-separated highways in the state concluded that "there is not one road in Texas that pays for itself based on the tax system of today."[7] A typical example was a highway outside Houston that was projected to cost $1 billion over its forty-year life span and generate only $162 million in gas taxes.

Transportation is like education: it works best through heavy general funding that pays off down the road in a community's or nation's overall prosperity. Tellingly, Thomas H. MacDonald justified a free and open system of roads, without tolls, with almost identical logic. Our national road system would never have been built if every street were required to pay for itself. Transportation and education pay immense social and economic dividends in the long run, but are difficult to make profitable in the short run. That is why we have free public education, and why we have historically subsidized transportation. We do not require schools, highways, or airports to turn a profit. Neither should we trains. Governments at every level have put in trillions of dollars in roads over the last century. This system, open to all with a car, has created our automobile-based landscape of suburbs, single-family homes, office parks, megachurches, and shopping malls. Love it or hate it, it is the product of massive government spending.

For decades the United States has had difficulty establishing good intercity rail travel and has nothing comparable to the high-speed trains becoming common in Europe and Asia. We are having problems because we are trying to treat train travel differently than we have any other mode of transportation. Government has always subsidized transportation systems, often massively. When people make money on transportation, as car companies and airlines occasionally do, it's only because government is supplying one part of that system, the roads and the airports.

The pity is that we could have a network of fast, efficient high-speed trains. But this would require what every other form of transportation has required—massive government assistance. The idea that transportation is built by the free market is simply false. It requires too much money, too much investment, and too much time. If you're not convinced, just take any road and look at its history.

CHAPTER 13

WAITING FOR A TRAIN STATION

THE SCENE: about two dozen people, mostly men, sitting around a long conference table.

The place: inside one of several big office buildings sprinkled around Midtown Manhattan near 33rd Street.

The mission: to design a new central train station for the New York Region, to replace the aging and incomplete Penn Station, which despite its flaws serves as the largest transportation hub of any type in North America.

In 2007 and 2008, I was part of the scene I describe above as a hired consultant. I attended weekly meetings as an ad-hoc committee designed a train station. It would provide me a ringside seat to observe infrastructure development in this country.

I emerged with great respect for all the players, but even more convinced that our Anglo-Saxon method of infrastructure development is flawed. Even when confronted with an obvious public mission, a new train station for the largest transportation hub in North America, we turn to private enterprise and needlessly complicate what conceptually could be simple.

In this chapter I look in more detail at the attempt to design and build this particular piece of infrastructure. The effort to replace Pennsylvania Station and the circumstances surrounding it are unique. There are no other train stations in the country that handle half a million people a day, and probably won't be anytime soon. But in the mixture of public and private, in the layering of local, state, and federal governments, we do get a glimpse of the infrastructure process in this country. Constructing efficient and beautiful infrastructure is part of building efficient and beautiful markets. We in the United States are not very good at it. We in the main have uncoordinated and incomplete infrastructure systems, and these in turn trouble the paths of our markets and make them less than ideal.

HISTORY OF A HUB

Every weekday, roughly a thousand trains enter Pennsylvania Station at 33rd Street in New York City. More than 600,000 people board these trains.[1] Just for comparison, the nation's largest airport, in Atlanta, handles about 125,000 passengers a day on average, less than a third this number.[2] Penn Station is so big that streets are at Penn Station, not the other way around. The station actually stretches between Seventh and Eighth Avenues and between 31st and 33rd Streets and spills over beyond these streets in some places. This hub occupies a central place in the city's and region's economic life. More than 200,000 commuters come in from Long Island on the Long Island Railroad, going under the East River. Close to 200,000 people travel under the Hudson River from the towns of New Jersey through century-old tunnels. About 20,000 people come and go on long-distance trains operated by Amtrak, the nation's intercity train service. Many of these people will be among the 150,000 that get on the blue or the red line—also known as the A or the C, or the 1,2,3 trains—and make their way to points around Manhattan or the other boroughs. It's fair to say that if Penn Station stopped, so would the city.

All this activity takes place underground. Overtop the tracks, platforms, ticket booths, and hallways sit a tall office building, One Penn Plaza, and the round, pill-like, modernist arena of Madison Square Garden. Because of this barely a drop of sunshine leaks down into the station below, and to its throngs.

This was not always the case. The original Pennsylvania Station, glorious and monumental, was torn down by its corporate owner in the mid-1960s, a tragic event. It was at the time as if someone had torn down the US Capitol in Washington, DC. Built by Pennsylvania Railroad and opened in 1910, the station and its tunnels were a project that matched the size of the railroad, then one of the largest corporations in the world. The railroad was almost a nation unto itself, having acquired millions of acres of land from the US government in the nineteenth century and used its own powers of eminent domain, granted from the government, to lay out track routes. It was comparable to the East India companies of Holland and Great Britain.

The railroad would build two tunnels in the thick mud of the Hudson

River, an unprecedented engineering challenge. These would connect to the new Pennsylvania Station being carved out of bedrock, before going on under the East River to Long Island. Before this, city-bound trains terminated in giant ferry stations on the New Jersey coast, where passengers would transfer themselves and their baggage onto ferries. The new tunnels and station changed all that, and the station occupied a central point in New York City life. It's no accident that Macy's, a multistory behemoth that spans an entire block at 34th Street between Sixth and Seventh Avenues, one of the largest department stores in the world, was built right next door to Penn Station. It was built there for the same reason regional shopping malls build next to the biggest cloverleafs on the interstate.

Macy's still prospers next to Penn Station, as does the station itself, at least in terms of people and trains. This is a surprise. When the original Penn Station was torn down in the mid-1960s, passenger traffic was declining and Pennsylvania Railroad was struggling, its giant freight networks just barely profitable. The fabulous New York City station, the emblem of the company, had become a white elephant. There was an expectation that passenger traffic would continue to decline, and Penn Station would be needed less and less.

Significantly, this has not been the case. At the time that Penn Station was torn down, about 175,000 people a day, counting only those using commuter rail and long-distance trains but not subways, went through Penn Station. In 2009, it was 400,000 people a day, the increase due primarily to commuter traffic. These figures don't include the subway traffic, which has also grown significantly in the same period, also against many predictions. These statistics are a warning to those who consider technology as something that is inevitably hierarchical and progressive, one thing leading to another. Television does not necessarily lead to a diminishing of radio, the Internet does not lead to the end of regular television, and so forth. Cell phones do not inevitably kill landlines. Cars don't mean the end of bicycles. Technology affects other technologies, but in ways difficult to predict. Often the job of government in these transitional times is to preserve the older technology, lest corporate masters too quickly usher it off to a premature grave. For example, streetcar systems were ripped out of cities all over the country, in the expectation that diesel-driven buses as a replacement were better. Today, cities yearn for these systems, and the rare city that has kept its streetcars, like Toronto or Melbourne, has significant advantages.

But back to the old, grand Penn Station. Although it took four years to do it, the original Beaux Arts palace with fluted Corinthian columns, modeled on the enormous Baths of Caracalla in ancient Rome, was torn down, the job being completed in 1967. (The station of stone and pillars actually had a steel-frame skeleton, which was concealed underneath the granite. Only in the great train hall, which had a soaring ceiling of steel and glass, with accompanying spiderlike steel columns, was this core architecture visible. I was not alone in thinking of this as the most beautiful part of the station, more so than the lavish, classically styled adjacent halls and exterior.) "One entered the city like a god; one scuttles in now like a rat," said architect Vincent Scully in an oft-quoted line. Architects and city lovers have been lamenting that station's destruction ever since.

One of those was the late Sen. Daniel Patrick Moynihan. A lover of architecture and urban design, Moynihan wanted people to enter his beloved city as kings again. How to do it? Right across Eighth Avenue from Penn Station was the mammoth Farley Post Office, which occupied a section of real estate as vast as the original Penn Station. It also looked a great deal like the original Penn Station, for good reasons. It was designed by the same architecture firm, McKim, Mead and White, and was built as a companion to Penn Station. At the time the original Penn Station opened in 1910, the vast majority of mail in the country traveled by railroad. So the US Post Office in 1910 needed a companion to the glorious new station. Alexander Cassatt, the head in the 1900s of Pennsylvania Railroad, who was leading the effort to build the tunnels and station, sold the US Post Office the property, which already had the tracks underneath it for the mail cars and trains.[3]

Sen. Moynihan, as head of the Senate Finance Committee, managed to get funding to convert Farley Post Office into a train station. His staff had a design all set. But after using his muscle to get funding for the effort, Moynihan died in 2003, his station still unbuilt. Despite the presence of actual money to build the station, various political interests, ranging from the US Post Office to various city, state, and private interests, were not so keen on Moynihan's vision. The plan was reworked, going through multiple iterations in an attempt to make it better (one interpretation) or satisfy various commercial interests (another interpretation).

As the plans changed, an idea surfaced that seemed to make a lot of sense: Why not actually tear down Madison Square Garden, which sits over a central part of the present Penn Station, and build a new Penn

Station? The location made sense logistically because of the position of the platforms and tracks. Madison Square Garden, or MSG, could build a new arena over the Farley Post Office building, which, given the Corinthian columns ringing the structure, would make MSG appear like the Roman Colosseum. And there would still be enough room left to make the front half or third of the old post office into a new train hall to accompany a new Penn Station across Eighth Avenue.

AROUND THE TABLE

This was the plan on the table when I entered the picture in 2007. For the next year and a half, I sat in at generally weekly meetings around large conference tables. The meetings showed the ability of diverse groups to work together cooperatively. Week after week, these people from several railroads, states, and for-profit and nonprofit entities worked together on such things as how wide the hallways would be, where the restrooms would be, where the police departments would be. Representatives included those from private developers The Venture, which would build the station and operate retail within it, and Madison Square Garden, which wanted a new home for its concerts and sports spectaculars overtop the Farley Post Office. Also present were the architects The Venture had hired to design the new station from Skidmore, Owings and Merrill, one of the top firms in the world. The architectural team was led by Vishaan Chakrabarti, a former top city planner. Then there were the public railroads, which included Amtrak, the Metropolitan Transportation Authority and its arms, New York City Transit and Long Island Railroad, and New Jersey Transit. Then there were the governmental institutions, including the Port Authority of New York and New Jersey, the Moynihan Station Development Corporation, which was an arm of the New York State Empire Development Corporation, and, of course, the New York City Planning Department and the New York City Transportation Department.

Sometimes these meetings were inside a battered-up old conference room inside Penn Station itself, below ground. Sometimes they were in a conference room of Parsons Brinckerhoff, the enormous engineering firm. Sometimes they were at some of the nearby offices of Long Island Railroad. Often they were at Amtrak headquarters, in a conference room inside its offices on Ninth Avenue overlooking the open West Side rail yards that lead into Penn Station. The meetings were a generally male affair, which reflects transportation planning. Many of the

men were engineers and dressed like them: white shirts, 1950s hair-
cuts. The men and sometimes women dressed more fashionably were
either architects there to give presentations, the leader of the meetings Alex Washburn, who is also an architect, or representatives from
ARUP, the artsy structural engineering firm based in London, whose
members, even the engineers, display flair in their personal dress.

Washburn, a former aide to Sen. Moynihan who had helped conceive of the original proposal and who was now chief urban designer for
the city under the Planning Department, acted as a kind of ringleader
and master of ceremonies. He blew a train whistle to call the meetings
to order, and then led the participants through the design decisions.
Sometimes he acted as architecture teacher, showing great train stations from around the world and leading the class through a historical
overview of the evolution of civic design.

Overall it was a great example of collaborative design, but in the end
it was mostly for naught. As the group, which included some pretty
high-level folk, worked, some even higher-level folk made decisions, or
failed to make decisions, that would largely kill the project. The resig-
nation of Gov. Eliott Spitzer in March 2008 because of a sex scandal
reduced support for the project, since Spitzer was seen as a champion
of it. Then the Dolan family, which owned Madison Square Garden,
decided not to cooperate in moving its arena across Eighth Avenue. Instead, the family would renovate the present Madison Square Garden.
As of 2010, a much smaller project was proceeding in stages, with some
work set to begin on the old Farley Post Office.

In all it was a portrait of how extraordinarily difficult it is to get
anything done in the American system of government and business.
No one was in charge here. There were multiple levels of government
and quasi-government agencies present here. Then there were the real
estate companies, which were almost in charge. They were the ones
paying the architects to make the fancy models. But the government
agencies had to sign off on their work, and through that requirement
these agencies exercised some kind of control. But why were these private companies sort of in charge in the first place? We had a process
where we had "persuaded" the private developers to build a train station, and then we attempted to hang our public purposes off their profit
motives like appendages on a mobile. And then we wonder why these
public purposes get lost?

The basic plan with Moynihan Station was that a private developer, in this case a consortium called The Venture, which combined

two existing big developers, Related Companies and Vornado Realty Trust, led by the confusingly similarly named Stephen Ross and Steven Roth, would actually pay to build what in the end would be a publicly owned station. In return for paying to design and have built the station (whose total cost was an estimated $3.2 billion), The Venture would get the rights to build more than 5.4 million square feet of office and other commercial space, or about as much as the entire downtown of a medium-sized city. The "rights" for this much space were taken from the existing "air rights" above Madison Square Garden, combined with some new "density bonuses." But most of this new development would not be built above the new Moynihan Station. Instead, it would be built "off-site," on available spaces in surrounding blocks.

Confused yet? Designing and building a multibillion-dollar train station in the heart of a busy city aren't easy; but the way to do so is pretty clear. Have government buy the land, design and build the station, and open the doors. In this case, the federal government, through Amtrak, actually already owns the tracks and tunnels and existing station, because it ended up with them when it took over the Penn Central (the railroad's new name after merging with New York Central Railroad), which filed for bankruptcy in 1970. Have the federal government use eminent domain to push Madison Square Garden off the site so a new train station can be built. If building the largest transportation hub in North America is not an appropriate occasion for exercising eminent domain, what is? With cases like *Kelo v. the City of New London*, the courts and the public have struggled with whether it was appropriate for government to seize land to use for private purposes, in that case, a private, for-profit company. But with Penn Station, government would be seizing land to use for a public purpose, a train station, which is similar to a bridge, a road, or a school. Surely not even the Dolans would argue this was an inappropriate or illegal use of eminent domain.

Instead of this simple, straightforward method, we ended up with a strange, behind-the-back attempt to flip the ball into the net via having private developers design, build, and pay for the station. Why? Well, for one, to avoid seeking additional billions in public funding, which would have been necessary to build the more ambitious plan. But it's more than that. There is these days a turning to the private commercial sector to do the job of the public sector. But the private interests look after their own business more than the public's.

This unwillingness of the public sector to take responsibility means that less often are created the kind of places that have the magic al-

chemy that is present when public and private purposes mesh in a har-
monious way to yield the "polis" the Greeks spoke of.

I came up with various mottoes while watching the proceedings.
One, inspired by watching as Amtrak tried to back out of moving into
Moynihan West, the old post office building, was: "A public agency,
when faced with a strategic juncture, will always pick the most short-
sighted choice, even for its own interests."

Another was that endless patience is necessary to be involved in a
big infrastructure project, at least in the United States. Alex Washburn,
at one point, after the entire enterprise had been socked in the gut by
some news or other, reminded people why they were there.

"Why does this project refuse to die after fifteen years?" Washburn
asked. Because "there is a clear civic vision. Its civic heart is what keeps
it going. It's partly an atonement for tearing down the original Penn
Station, it's partly the vision of the senator, it's partly a lot of things.
For a lot of reasons this project refuses to die."

Early on in the design process, Washburn laid out seven principles
that he got participants to agree on for the station design.

1. Ceiling heights, volumes, and sequence of public space
2. Abundance of natural light
3. Connectivity to adjacent infrastructure
4. Clarity of pedestrian pathways and ease of passenger movements
5. Standards of architectural detail
6. Power of civic expression in the design of both interior public space
   and exterior portals
7. Degree to which nature and green building standards are incorporated into station

They are great principles for civic design. And you need a government
to do them.

CHAPTER 14

WHAT WE DID BEFORE:
PATH DEPENDENCE AND MARKETS

Life must be lived forward but understood backwards.
SØREN KIERKEGAARD, 1843

I'M WRITING THIS BOOK in a different language. My tongue doesn't speak this different language. My fingers do. It's called Dvorak. "Dvorak" (pronounced duh-VOR-ak) is the more efficient keyboard layout designed by efficiency expert August Dvorak in the 1930s. With Dvorak, the letters are laid out to correspond, roughly, with their frequency of use: All five vowels, for example, repose under the left hand. Five common consonants rest under the right hand. Your fingers stay put more and cover less ground. You type faster and more comfortably.

I switched to Dvorak around 1997, because I thought it might help with some medical problems with my wrists and hands brought on by too much typing and scribbling. (It did help.) Once I had switched, I found Dvorak so markedly better than QWERTY that an obvious question presented itself: why doesn't everyone use it? The reason is something called "path dependence," which I want to examine in this chapter. It's the tendency of habits and processes to persist. Or, said another way, people keep on doing one thing, despite some disadvantages, because people before them have been doing it and it takes effort to switch. You can find examples of this everywhere, once you start looking. It is closely related to, but not exactly the same as, "standards" and their influence on how we do things. Standards range from the type of cassettes used in VCRs to the threading of lightbulbs to the dimensions of a letter-size sheet of 8½-by-11-inch paper to the half-dozen differing cell phone technologies, such as GSM, used in Europe, and CDMA, used by some American phone companies. Finally, I look at a phenomenon that I haven't cooked up a good name for, but might be called the slow fade, which is the way developers of one mode of technology or infrastructure are influenced by another, often unconsciously.

What do path dependence, standards, and the slow fade have to do with the design of markets? They all show that our options are not unlimited. While markets are designed, we cannot easily replace whole systems. We tend to adapt, rather than create anew. In this chapter I explore these phenomena, as well as those who try to deny their existence.

THE HISTORY OF HUNT-AND-PECK: QWERTY

The history of how QWERTY came to be, and with it a vivid example of the phenomenon of path dependence, is told very well by Jared Diamond, anthropologist and author of the now-classic *Guns, Germs and Steel*. Diamond, in "The Curse of QWERTY: O Typewriter? Quit Your Torture!," first published in *Discover Magazine* in 1997, shows how the placement of keys under QWERTY does not fit the logic of the English language and the physiology of our bodies. Here is an excerpt:

> When you prepare to type, you rest your fingers on QWERTY's second-from-the-bottom row, called the home row. Obviously, the more typing you can do without having to move your fingers from the home row, the faster you'll be able to type, the fewer errors you'll make, and the less you'll strain your fingers. Confirming that straightforward prediction, motion-picture studies prove that typing is fastest on the home row and slowest on the bottom row.
>
> You might then naively expect that the QWERTY keyboard was designed so that most typing is done on the home row. You would be wrong. Only 32 percent of strokes are on the home row; most strokes (52 percent) are on the upper row; and a full 16 percent are on the bottom row, which you should be avoiding like the plague. Not more than 100 English words can be typed without leaving the home row. The reason for this disaster is simple: QWERTY perversely puts the most common English letters on other rows. The home row of nine letters includes two of the least used (J and K) but none of the three most frequently used (E, T, and O, which are relegated to the upper row) and only one of the five vowels (A), even though 40 percent of all letters in a typical English text are vowels.[1]

Diamond goes on meticulously, showing himself to be not only a great anthropologist, but a great journalist as well. After showing the weaknesses of QWERTY, Diamond then explains why the flaws were built into the design. Basically, the first typewriters were designed to be slow to avoid jamming the machine. Second, the QWERTY keyboard really was designed to allow you to type the word "typewriter" on the upper keyboard alone. Try it right now, you'll see. This was considered good marketing. Diamond gives the inventor a name—Christopher Sholes—and places his invention into the whole context of typewriter invention in the late nineteenth and early twentieth centuries. Then Diamond shows how QWERTY, which was just one of several early typewriter layouts, achieved dominance. It was basically a story of how the QWERTY layout piggybacked on Sholes's other, more useful innovations, such as having an inked ribbon, in being adopted first by Remington, and then by Underwood, the leading typewriter manufacturers. It's a bit like reading the history of the early computer industry, where the adoption of certain standards by IBM, like the MS-DOS system, led to its computers quickly defining industry standards, even though IBM eventually lost control of its chosen child.

After showing how the QWERTY keyboard proliferated via Remington's and Underwood's support, Diamond shows how August Dvorak, a "distant cousin of the famous Czech composer," invented in the early twentieth century the alternate keyboard system, which he named after himself. First introduced in 1932, it made some initial inroads, despite QWERTY's dominance in an era when using a different keyboard layout meant lugging your own typewriter everywhere. Dvorak typists started sweeping typewriter speed competitions. The navy, faced with the need to have thousands of trained typists at the start of World War II, actually studied having its typists learn Dvorak. It actually ordered thousands of Dvorak typewriters.

"They never got them," Diamond says dramatically. "The Treasury Department vetoed the Navy purchase order, probably for the same reason that has blocked acceptance of all improved, non-QWERTY keyboards for the last 80 years: the commitment to QWERTY of tens of millions of typists, teachers, salespeople, office managers, and manufacturers."

And here Diamond starts to go into path dependence, although he never uses that term.

"QWERTY's saga illustrates a much broader phenomenon: how commitment shapes the history of technology and culture, often selecting which innovations become entrenched and which are rejected."[2]

THE WAY OF ECONOMISTS

It's telling that some economists, although hardly all,[3] question whether path dependence really exists. That they do so shows how economics can be as much an ideology as a science. The reason some economists argue against path dependence, I believe, is that it would mean that the so-called "free market" does not always arrive at the optimal solution. It would mean that history matters.

In a study called "The Fable of the Keys" (admittedly a nice title), economists Stan J. Liebowitz and Stephen E. Margolis attempt to show that Dvorak is *not* necessarily better than QWERTY.[4] The subtext seems to be demolishing path dependence as a phenomenon. They focus with particular intensity on the study done by the navy that Jared Diamond refers to.

"The Navy study concludes that training in Dvorak is much more effective than retraining in Qwerty," say Liebowitz and Margolis.

> But the experimental design leaves too many questions for this to be an acceptable finding. Do these results hold for typists with normal typing skills or only for those far below average? Were the results for the first group just a regression to the mean for a group of underperforming typists? How much did the Navy studies underestimate the value of increased Qwerty retraining due to the inconsistent measurement? Were the two groups given similar training? Were the Qwerty typewriters overhauled, as were the Dvorak typewriters? There are many possible biases in this study. All, suspiciously, seem to be in favor of the Dvorak design.[5]

Their rhetoric has a strained quality. Why are Liebowitz and Margolis even examining this question? Because it shakes their faith that conventional market competition produces the best outcome. It's significant that their study was published in *The Journal of Law and Economics*, which has been the bible for those who believe economics so much like a natural science that it can be applied to law, with policies and court rulings derived from it. One of the sponsors of the study was the Independent Institute, which promotes its ideal of free markets with minimal government involvement. Liebowitz was a fellow at the Institute.[6] *Reason Magazine*, a journal of Libertarian advocacy, published the study of Liebowitz and Margolis.

TRAVELING IN OUR ANCESTORS' SHOES; OR CARRIAGES

Photos from New York City from the late 1940s show that horse-drawn wagons bearing fruit, junk, or milk were still quite common, even as automobiles also crowded the streets. Photos from 1910 depict horse-drawn streetcars mixing with the electric streetcars. Transportation eras do not neatly switch from one to another, but slide into one another, with long transitions over many decades. In that transition, different modes influence each other, and often the newer mode mimics the older mode it is replacing.

I'm sure this phenomenon exists in other fields as well, from clothing to computers. It's a variation on path dependence. Some interesting examples can be seen in the history of transportation.

As Wolfgang Schivelbusch details in *The Railway Journey*, the passenger areas of trains for many decades in the United States resembled the interiors of steamboats or the long canal boats that floated along the Erie and other waterways. These ships and boats were the dominant mode of transportation from the 1820s on into the 1850s, and it was natural for trains to copy them even though one glided on water and the other on rails.[7] This led to long, open compartments in train cars. Seats were either on benches on the sides or in rows.

Trains in Europe, in contrast, imitated the stagecoaches that ran on the far more extensive network of highways that were then available in Europe. This led to the classic small European compartment, with its door onto a hallway or to the exterior of the train, where four to eight passengers sit in a small, intimate room similar to that of the stagecoach.

"In other words, the riverboat became for the American railroad train what the stagecoach had been for the European: a means and form of travel that was representative of the period before the introduction of railroads, and thus one upon which the railroad modeled itself," says Schivelbusch.

Schivelbusch even quotes an early railroad train designer from 1829 who proposed to build a "Land Barge," which "to the Traveler will furnish an idea of all the convenience and comfort which belongs to the best steam boats." An accompanying illustration looks a bit like the compartment of a steamboat placed upon a flatbed carriage and hauled by a locomotive engine. Schivelbusch cites commentators of the era speaking of the discomfort of Europeans traveling in the wide, open compartments of American trains, and of Americans uncomfortable with the, to them, claustrophobic and overly intimate compartments of European trains.[8]

Similar tendencies and patterns can be spotted in other transportation eras. Cars in the early 1900s, even production ones like the Ford Model T, resembled carriages with motors. They sat up high, as if the drivers still had to see over some horses. It took a few decades for Studebakers and Buicks to sink lower to the ground, a more stable and functional arrangement. (Today, though, we seem to have gone back to the future, with drivers of contemporary SUVs towering over their neighbors, as if they still had horses in front of them.) Robert Moses, the great and infamous master builder of the twentieth century, designed his parkways thinking that people would use their cars the same way they had carriages: for long, leisurely drives in the country. Thus, he was surprised when traffic jammed along his new parkways as people used cars simply as a means to get from here to there.

Luxury and status set standards in ways that go beyond the practical. Just as a peacock's feathers may impede its hunting abilities but help it win a mate, so there are more important things in determining mechanical design than efficiency, comfort, or ease of use. When I look at the development of air travel in the twentieth century, and high-speed rail travel in the late twentieth and early twenty-first, what I see is a conversation between the dominant luxury modes of each era, with the less dominant mode attempting to copy the more dominant mode.

The last time I rode the Eurostar high-speed train in Europe between Brussels and Paris, around 2003, I was shocked to find conductors dressed like airline stewardesses, who proudly served meals on trays in one's lap! I had noticed a similar phenomenon on the Spanish AVE high-speed train between Madrid and Seville that began in 1994. To me this was absurd. One of the pleasures of train travel is, or was, dining at a table with others in a pleasant, relaxed fashion. You can walk around, and not dine pinned to a chair, with food and drink always about to spill into your lap. That Europeans would consciously imitate the inconveniences of plane travel shows how they associate air travel with high status, even in a land with good train service. You see similar things happen on our side of the ocean, where at times Amtrak, our national train company, seems bent on copying the inconveniences of air travel. Thus, tickets on Amtrak look like airplane tickets, and Amtrak offers the train equivalent of frequent flier miles. Amtrak's Acela trains, its highest-speed ones along the Northeast corridor, have sleek, airplanelike interiors, with cramped, closed luggage racks overhead. You could have plentiful luggage compartments at the end of each car, or in a separate baggage car, but this would not be planelike.

All of this is ironic, because if you look further back in time, you will find the airlines in their infancy imitating train travel, setting patterns that continue to the present day. Why, for example, did airlines ever serve full meals on what were comparatively short journeys that lasted a few hours rather than a few days? Airlines in the 1920s and 1930s served meals because that's what passengers experienced on the luxury trains that set the standards for luxury travel then. Airlines were trying to "brand" their travel mode as a high-status one. At that time, meals on trains were particularly lavish because companies used them as loss leaders to lure passengers. Companies with competing lines would serve elaborate full meals of duck and quail on fine china, all at enormous losses.

"To attract passengers away from competing lines, railroads swallowed their food service losses and specialized in gastronomical delicacies," said John Stilgoe in his classic book on trains, *Metropolitan Corridor*. These delicacies included regional favorites such as grouse, salmon, antelope steak, Maine lobster, haddock, oysters, and terrapin stew! Train companies, Stilgoe says, were "happy if they earned fifty cents on every dollar expended," because the good food bonded passengers' palates and bellies to the train lines.[9]

Moving from the interior of trains and airplanes to their stations, you'll find that early airports resembled train stations in many respects. You can see this in Berlin's famous Tempelhof, which was built in the 1920s and 1930s. Travelers walked from their airplanes into a gorgeous, spacious hall filled with benches, just like in the grand train terminals of the time. From there they could exit via the terminal's front door into the city itself. The airport, in effect, backed up to the city of Berlin, making possible a truly urban airport, something that would cease to be possible as air travel expanded, along with its space requirements.

You see this pattern of transition the more you look for it. Bicycle seats are still often called "saddles," because bicycle designers copied horse saddles when bicycles became popular in the 1880s. People "rode" a bicycle just as they "rode" a horse. The interior of early buses resembled the streetcars they replaced.

THE RISE OF THE INTERNET;
THE DECLINE OF PATH DEPENDENCE

That I am typing this book in Dvorak is proof that path dependence is no longer as strong as it used to be, at least in some areas. The reason is the rise of the Internet and the related telecommunications and computer revolutions. I did not have to go out and buy a special typewriter with its keys placed differently; I had only to open the keyboard layout menu on my Apple computer and switch it to Dvorak. The keys on my laptop still show the QWERTY layout, but as a touch typist, I am not bothered much. It's still an inconvenience when I visit a library and use a computer invariably set to QWERTY there, or when I use a computer at someone else's home, but otherwise it's pretty easy. I don't have to lug a special computer into the office where I work in Manhattan; I just make the switch there as well. Boosted by these possibilities, thousands of people around the country are switching to Dvorak. Dvorak has also inspired a dozen or so websites that promulgate its virtues. Its prominent users and backers include Nathan Myhrvold, formerly a top executive with Microsoft. I interviewed him way back in 1998, when I wrote an article about Dvorak for *Salon Magazine*.

"I'm the Johnny Appleseed of Dvorak," said Myhrvold, who noted he was instrumental in getting Dvorak into the Microsoft operating systems. "Because of Windows, there are 100 million people with access to Dvorak. I'm actually surprised there hasn't been more of a revolution" toward it. In what may say something about the single-mindedness of Microsoft's technology officer, Myhrvold has never touch-typed in any other system. "When I was a little kid, I read an article about Dvorak. I was outraged that there was a better way to type, and that it wasn't being used. I vowed to never learn another system. And I didn't."[10]

What is true for Dvorak and QWERTY is also true in other arenas. The Internet and associated technologies make the worlds they create closer to the frictionless, perfect information world that the free market economists envision. We are still a long way away from there, but we are closer. Evidence is that seldom have major companies and major systems risen and fallen so quickly. The biggest examples are in the field of computers and telecommunications, where so many of the systems do not involve physical hardware, but computer code. Netscape, using a system developed by the US government named "Apache," seemed to establish dominance on the Internet with its browser. Then Internet Explorer, showing the potence of market power, pushed it out. Now, as of this writing, Internet Explorer is threatened by several other competing browsers, including Firefox. Yahoo seemed to establish dominance as a search engine. Google, with a better one, pushed it aside, if not out. The corporation Wang Laboratories, which at its height employed forty thousand people and had revenues of $3 billion, filed for bankruptcy in 1992 and simply disappeared.[11]

But while the Internet and computers in general have diminished friction in the market, they have not eliminated it. Path dependence still matters. In some areas, like software, it has increased. I write this book in Microsoft Word despite not liking the program. I have little choice, though. Word's file format is the lingua franca of word processing, and it's simply too convenient to be able to exchange files easily with other people. And in fact, my publisher demands the manuscript be submitted in Microsoft Word. And what we Americans in particular should remember is that fluidity in a market is not always a good thing. We humans need stability to live, to raise families. A future where one's job is even more uncertain than it is today is not always a good one.

CHAPTER 15

POLICE AND PRISONS:
FREEDOM, SECURITY, AND DEMOCRACY

You gotta go for what you know
Make everybody see, in order to fight the powers that be
Lemme hear you say . . .
Fight the power
LYRICS BY PUBLIC ENEMY

IF YOU STROLL BY a police station in New York City, you might notice a pair of green lights out front, one on each side of the main door. These green lights are links to a past stretching 350 years back. They show once again that history and life are a series of currents, leaving some trace of themselves even as they mutate into forms difficult to predict from their beginnings.

It was in 1658 that Peter Stuyvesant, the seminal mayor of New Amsterdam, established the eight-member "Rattle Watch." It was first largely volunteer and then became a paid detail of strolling watchmen, paid a small sum to keep an eye on the growing, bustling town. Their charge was to catch "pirates and vagabonds" and "robbers," by whatever means they thought appropriate. To alert citizens of their presence, they carried a green lantern over their shoulder on a pole like a hobo's stick. This patrol force would eventually grow into the thirty-five-thousand-strong New York City Police Force, under not the Dutch or the English, but a city called New York in a nation called the United States of America, but the green lantern would remain.[1] Police stations in this city of 8 million people that has evolved from New Amsterdam still have green lanterns by their doors.

In this chapter I look at police and prisons. The cop strolling his beat and the jail cell are as much a part of our economic infrastructure as a water system, a sewer system, or a road. In the case of police, they are, like water and sewers, relatively recent. While laws creating property are old, police are not, not as a professional, extensive force. They are yet another example of how a modern, advanced capitalist economy depends on a more extensive array of government services to function.

From a historical perspective, it's clear that prisons and a paid, professional police force were part of the great growth of infrastructure, including water and sewer systems, electricity and gas, roads and train lines, and public education, that came about in the nineteenth century. That was when cities were transformed from essentially oversized villages, with wells and cesspits, into machines, with systems of transportation, communication, power, policing, and educating their citizens. As with the now-accepted public water systems, and the systems of public education, the development of a paid police force necessitated a psychological stretch on the part of the populace and city leaders. Why should government take on a task that had largely been handled privately? What did it mean if government took this on? Those were the kind of questions asked when both the city's water system and police force were started. Along with police would soon come more prisons. Over the course of the nineteenth century and into the twentieth century, jail cells would change from temporary holding places for criminals awaiting trial into permanent homes for thousands and eventually millions of people, mostly men.

FROM LONDON TO NEW YORK

As with so many things, probably because it was industrializing first, London led the way in developing a model for a paid professional police force in the nineteenth century. New York and other cities around the globe would copy it. In the growing city of London, which had passed the 1 million mark around 1800, crime and security were a growing concern. Prior to this, like New York, London and other English towns had a system of parish constables and watchmen that dates back to King Henry VIII, who set up the system of parishes in 1536.[2]

After several large riots in the 1820s due to unemployment and falling wages, Parliament empowered Sir Robert Peel to come up with a plan. Peel set up a commission in 1828, which ended up establishing the London Metropolitan Police force. Peel had the new police force report directly to him as home secretary, which angered some people who started calling the police "bobbies," derisively, in reference to Peel's first name.[3] Whom police report to is a key decision. They are an armed force, and so potentially a corrupter of the state as well as a protector of it. Peel established many of the basics of what we think of police as doing. Chief among them was that police would focus primarily on preventing crime, rather than investigating crime and finding culprits after the fact. Another feature was that the police would not be part of the military, but would be organized in a quasi-military manner, with a hierarchical chain of command and military-like titles.

FROM GREEN LANTERNS TO THE FORCE IN BLUE

In the early nineteenth century the biggest and most prosperous city in the new nation of the United States would eventually copy London and start a professional police force. But before it did, it would have to wrestle with the idea of whether having armed, uniformed men walking among its residents was consistent with the ideals of a democratic republic, where citizens were masters of the state, not its servants. While this is New York's story, cities around the country underwent similar changes.

Policing, as opposed to, say, a public water system, is in a special category, because it involves more openly the use of force, even lethal force. While building a road or a train line also involves substantial use of state coercion, it does not usually involve physical harm, at least not legally. And unlike a national army, a police force is being used on a city or nation's own citizens, a disquieting thing in a democracy.

In New York City, citizens and their leaders were not comfortable with a paid police force for a long, long time. Over several centuries they would go back and forth, creating one only to disband it soon after. It was not until 1857 that the state created the "Metropolitan Police," a fully paid police force that has continued to this day.

The previously mentioned Rattle Watch under the Dutch continued after the English conquered the town in 1665, but the English shifted it back to a volunteer basis. Then, in 1734, the English-led city established a twelve-man paid force of watchmen. Less than a decade later, it was terminated and replaced with volunteers. The ratio of watchmen to citizens was 1:800, a ratio that would stay surprisingly consistent for another century, and then gradually increase.[4] Today, New York City's force of 35,000 to its 8 million population is a ratio of about 1:200.

These early watchmen in the 1700s were not what we would consider policemen. They carried minimal if any weapons, and they had minimal training. They would walk about with their lanterns and call out the hour and the weather. If they saw something amiss, they would attempt to do something, but they were not a trained police force.

The pressure to establish a professional police force grew in the early nineteenth century, as the economy and population of New York City exploded with the great wealth and business opportunities created by New York state's construction and completion of the Erie Canal in 1825, with social and political problems to match.

Civil unrest was a big part of the picture. Riots occurred both regularly and unpredictably. They included the anti-abolition riot in 1834, which was sparked against those preaching the end of slavery, and the riot over the price of flour in 1837. This prompted calls for a paid police force to keep the peace, but there was substantial resistance. In 1836, city leaders specifically rejected a proposal to establish a London-style professional police force as a "threat to democracy." In a population that had within memory thrown off the paid occupation force of the English, there was a reluctance to let paid, uniformed men carrying weapons patrol among them. There was a fear that these servants would become masters.

After a few more riots and a spectacular crime or two, in 1844 the governor of New York signed the New York Municipal Police Act. It did not last. The paid police force was disbanded a year later. In 1857 the state created the "Metropolitan Police" force, and this time it stuck. But initially the officers did not wear uniforms or carry weapons, only badges to identify themselves. This gradually changed. The Draft Riots of 1863, one of the largest and worst occasions of civil unrest in the nation's history, would result in the deaths of hundreds of people, including three police officers. The riots were a huge boost to the idea of a paid police force, as well as a more militarized government. The state and city would build more than fifty huge armories all around the city, stacked with weapons and large enough for drills of citizen militias. They were built specifically to guard against other occurrences of civil unrest, which did occur nevertheless.

BEHIND BARS

While people have been held in captivity for thousands of years, prisons as large places with thousands and thousands of inmates mostly began after the industrial revolution. For better and for worse, holding a substantial part of the population in captivity is part of our modern political economy, particularly in the United States. Prisons in the modern sense are an invention, like the police force, of the nineteenth century. And of course they occurred early in London.

Before this time, a jail or a prison was typically somewhere you held a person accused of a crime before either execution, a trial, or a disciplinary act such as flogging. There were also debtor's prisons, for this was a category separate from prisons for violent criminals. The idea of being held in captivity as a kind of punishment was itself a new idea, and a reformist idea, pushed by Jeremy Bentham, the great secular philosopher/economist/social reformer and founder of the philosophy of utilitarianism, which espoused the greatest good for the greatest number. Bentham actually invented a design for a prison, the Panopticon, which was a circular building around a central guard tower that allowed a guard to watch many prisoners without their being aware of when they were being watched.

Before the modern prison, if flogging or execution were not judged the appropriate punishment, then the accused or condemned were often sent to distant lands, to live out their lives somewhere else in usually unpleasant circumstances. Australia was founded as a prison colony in 1787 by Great Britain, largely in response to the American Revolution, which had ended North America's serving as a place to dump English pickpockets and vagrants and Irish prisoners of war.

The contemporary United States has one of the highest incarceration rates in the world. According to the International Centre for Prison Studies at the University of Essex, the United States has 2.3 million people in prison or in jail.[5] Our rate of incarceration per 100,000 people is 743, which is several times higher than it was a generation ago. It appears to be the highest among advanced, democratic nations.

The high prison population is caused partly by having an Anglo-Saxon economy, meaning that property owners have lots of government-given rights and privileges, and those who don't have few. In some strange way, having a million or two people in prison is part of the functioning of our economy. One can speculate about what its purpose is, but you can't remove 2 million people from the labor force without some effect.

CONCLUSION

Whatever one thinks about them, police and prisons and the whole apparatus of the coercive state are a part of modern markets. This apparatus ranges from the policeman walking the beat to the officers of the Federal Bureau of Investigation, from the local jail cell to the industrial-scale prisons. Having a uniformed officer close at hand if trouble emerges is a great privilege. On the other hand, the locking away of great portions of our citizenry is not consistent with an equitable democratic society. Ways should be found to reduce our prison population without increasing crime. What is certainly true is that police and prisons are part of government's use of force, an aspect of government that is both essential and disquieting.

CHAPTER 16

WHY DON'T YOU MAKE ME?
GOVERNMENT AND FORCE

It is not wisdom, but Authority that makes a law.
THOMAS HOBBES, *BEHEMOTH, A HISTORY OF THE
ENGLISH CIVIL WAR,* 1668

*For by art is created that great "Leviathan" called a "Common-
wealth" or "State," which is but an Artificiall Man, though
of greater stature and strength than the Naturall, for whose
protection and defence it was intended.*
THOMAS HOBBES, *LEVIATHAN,* 1651

*God hath certainly appointed government to restrain the partiality
and violence of men.*
JOHN LOCKE, *SECOND TREATISE ON GOVERNMENT,* 1689

LOSE YOUR CAR TO A THIEF and government is your friend. Park your
car in front of a fire hydrant and government is your enemy. Mundane
events like this illustrate the dual nature of that thing which is so much
a part of our lives, government. This book is about how government
creates and shapes and designs markets. Given that, it makes sense to
explore what government is, how it functions, and in particular one
central aspect of government, its use of force. How central is force to
government? That's a question that has occupied people's thoughts
probably since the first government was instituted.

Markets, where people buy and sell things without coercion, are an
example and embodiment of freedom to many people. Our common
reference to a "free market" only reinforces this combining of the concepts of markets and freedom. But even the loosest of markets is in-
separable from the use of force, in the sense that you need an authority

that rules out force by market participants. Government has a monopoly on legal violence and coercion.

Government is, among other things, "a system of authority." It can, when it needs to, make you do stuff. The rationale for the frequent analogy of government as father or household leader is easy to see. Like a parent, government nurtures, disciplines, persuades, and coaxes; it can take you in or turn you out. It can be the friend you turn to when no one else will have you, or the stern authority that pursues you without mercy. Whether a government is a dictatorship, a democracy, an autocracy, or a theocracy affects its character, but not this essential parental nature of government. There are different styles of parenting, and so it is with government. In a democracy, the goal is for us to be our own best parents—to raise ourselves and our society to be productive, happy, peaceful, and creative.

In this chapter I look at the elements of force or coercion that are inherent in government, whether coming through the use of a jail cell, an army, a policeman, or a hangman's noose. I look at how others have regarded government, including its use of force and coercion. After that I look at government's role in the development of trade, and how force is usually part of that equation. Commerce grows from the barrel of a gun. And I look at our special relationship with government here in America.

GOVERNMENT AS FORCE

The ancient Romans had a saying: To make a road straight, you often need to make someone's neck crooked. This chilling refrain vividly sums up an obvious fact: Building a road is a manifestation of power, particularly state power. Carving a road across multiple jurisdictions and property lines can be done only by an institution that can override the wishes of any one individual or groups of them.

I bring up roads because they are an obvious function of government, one that scarcely even the most committed Libertarian believes "the market" could produce by itself. Yet this basic function of government requires a large and often heavy-handed assertion of state authority and prerogative.

It's probably correct to see the operations of government as being on a continuum between force and cooperation, with their place on that continuum depending on the moment and the context. Those northern European countries like Denmark, Holland, Norway, Iceland, and Finland seem for the most part to work primarily through an agreement to agree, working things out through democratic processes based on the will of the majority, and with relatively little turning to the dark side of the force, which is force itself. These countries have low prison populations, astronomically low compared to the United States. The more homogenous populations of these countries probably do figure into making it possible to live with few overt expressions of force. At the other end of the spectrum are Iran, North Korea, and various other countries where the threat of force is implicit on a more regular basis.

Paradoxically, our very suspicion and fear of government in the United States seem to have pushed government here into a more forceful, clumsy, and at times brutal relationship to its populace. Here in New York City, it has not been uncommon for someone to be locked up in jail for a few days after a minor crime like drinking in public or jumping a turnstile. As the writer Malcolm Gladwell said in a 2010 *New Yorker* article, we are comfortable having government jail someone for drunk driving but not teaching the driver to drink with restraint.

MARKETS AND FORCE

The relationship of markets to force can be seen when the arm of that force collapses. To have sophisticated markets you need sophisticated government. Large-scale markets and their supporting institutions collapsed with the Roman empire around AD 500. People stopped buying and selling things, because there was no one to create a money system, no one to enforce a contract. People stopped making stuff, because there was no way to sell it. The wonderful Roman roads remained, some fifty thousand miles of them,[1] and even many of the aqueducts kept carrying water to cities from Segovia to Rome itself. But without the presence of armies and a government to guarantee contracts, to create a money supply, and to ensure some safety along those roads, large-scale trade as such collapsed.

"Little economic progress was made in Europe during the thousand years which followed the fall of the western Roman Empire," said John Mills in *A Critical History of Economics*. "The collapse of organized civil authority, and its replacement by warlord government, meant that contracts could no longer be enforced. . . . Even pottery ceased to be produced in England after about 400 AD. In these circumstances, economic relations, based mostly round subsistence agriculture, were largely non-market orientated."[2]

In such circumstances both the rich and poor were equally tied to the land. If you were a feudal lord, you could not leave your property and, say, move to London, because your property could not be sold for money. Nor were "rents" paid that were transportable in the form of money. You were as tied to the land as the feudal serfs who worked it for you.

Money and trade are products of the state, as is the market itself. A market is a place, either actual or conceptual, where people meet to exchange goods and services for prices set by bargaining. But of course, for there to be prices, there needs to be money, and for there to be money, there needs to be a state, or a bank, which, in turn, depends for its existence on the state. And for people to meet without robbing each other, there needs to be a police force, and for there to be a police force, there needs to be a state. And so on. To buy and sell, you need something to buy and sell with, whether it be gold, cigarettes, or dollar bills.

"From the evolutionary standpoint, money is the father of private property," says Max Weber in his *General Economic History*.[3] The more abstract the medium of money, the stronger the state. James Buchan, in his wonderful book about money and markets, *Frozen Desire*, compares the issuance of paper currency to the ability of "women to sunbathe naked in public parks." Each only can occur with the presence of a strong, confident, and stable state.[4]

GOVERNMENT: MY ENEMY, MY FRIEND

Government ensures our freedom, but uses force to do so. So here we get to the paradox of Americans' relationship to government. We want our personal freedom, and we don't want government to intrude upon it, but we also want government to guarantee that personal freedom for us.

In general, we here in the United States take a wrong turn when we see government primarily as something to be protected from, rather than something to empower us. Americans have often impaled themselves on these twin horns, government is necessary to ensure freedom, but we want protection from government itself. There's a similar schizophrenia with markets. We often see ourselves as standing apart from our own government, even as we are proud of being perhaps the world's oldest existing democracy, which means therefore that government is an extension and reflection of us. We have sections of our

Constitution that protect our freedom to do things without government interference, which helps obscure that perhaps our most essential freedom is the ability to participate *in* government.

This schizophrenia is seen in the writings of President Barack Obama, the former professor of constitutional law, who although labeled a liberal or leftist, has ingested the conservative view of government as something from which we need protection:

> And yet for all our disagreements we would be hard pressed to find
> a conservative or liberal in America today, whether Republican or
> Democrat, academic or layman, who doesn't subscribe to the basic set
> of individual liberties identified by the Founders and enshrined in our
> Constitution and our common law: the right to speak our mind; the
> right to worship how and if we wish; the right to peaceably assemble to
> petition our governments; the right to own, buy, and sell property and
> not have it taken without fair compensation; the right to be free from
> unreasonable searches and seizures; the right not to be detained by the
> state without due process; the right to a fair and speedy trial; and the
> right to make our own determinations, with minimal restriction, re-
> garding family life and the way we raise our own children.[5]

Obama focuses on what scholars dub "negative liberties," meaning what government can't do to us, rather than what it can do for us or how we can be creators of government. Obama doesn't talk enough about having the freedom to participate *in* government, to come together as a populace and to make change, democratically, peacefully. This is not just a flaw in Obama's thinking, but in our Constitution. Its focus on ensuring "negative liberties" distracts citizens from the fact that government can be a tool for change, for action, for freedom—freedom from want, from fear, from a lack of possibilities, from distress.

I cannot help but wonder if Obama's delineation of negative freedoms and what appears to be, judging from his economic policies, a doctrinaire view of markets is due to his longtime residency in Chicago and employment at the University of Chicago, the epicenter of the free market economists and their views on the world. Is Obama a "Chicago Boy"? His employment in his first administration of Lawrence Sumner and Timothy Geithner, and the distancing of more nuanced economists such as Paul Krugman, Paul Volcker, and Joseph Stiglitz, would seem to say so.

MY FRIENDS HOBBES AND LOCKE

Much of the work of the famous philosophers Thomas Hobbes (1588–1679) and John Locke (1632–1704) was on the nature of government and on the use of force in particular, and the work of the two men has come to represent two opposing viewpoints on what government is and its legitimacy. Both men wrote in England largely in the seventeenth century, but about two generations apart, with Locke beginning his career as Hobbes, an old man, ended his. Both wrote during the turbulent times of the English Civil War from about 1625 and leading up to the Glorious Revolution in 1688, the bulk of the seventeenth century, which did so much to establish the nature and structure of English government.

Hobbes was most famous for his line that in a "state of nature," life would be "nasty, brutish, and short." Here's the full quote:

> In such condition there is no place for industry, because the fruit thereof is uncertain: and consequently no culture of the earth; no navigation, nor use of the commodities that may be imported by sea; no commodious building; no instruments of moving and removing such things as require much force; no knowledge of the face of the earth; no account of time; no arts; no letters; no society; and which is worst of all, continual fear, and danger of violent death; and the life of man, solitary, poor, nasty, brutish, and short.[6]

This was so true, Hobbes said, that even absolute tyranny was better than no government at all.

Locke had a different point of view. He maintained that in a state of nature, things like property would occur naturally, and that government was only needed to ensure these "natural rights." Government was simply tidying up around the edges, or making sure you got what you already had.

Both men wrote in the context of their times. Hobbes was a backer of the absolute monarchy of Charles I and his successors. Locke was a backer of Parliament and the limited monarchy that would come with the Glorious Revolution of 1688, and which Locke's advocacy helped bring about. Both men in essence created philosophies to justify their existing predispositions.

Between the two, I side with Hobbes's logic, if not his support of absolute monarchy. Locke's theories have a disquieting tendency to rely on God. Locke's chain of logic with regard to property goes something like this: God created the earth and gave it to Adam; therefore, Adam has dominion over the earth, meaning property. God exists to ensure that Man keeps dominion over the earth through owning it via property, and government exists by the grace of God to ensure this as well. Says Locke:

> Whether we consider natural reason, which tells us, that men, being once born, have a right to their preservation, and consequently to meat and drink, and such other things as nature affords for their subsistence: or revelation, which gives us an account of those grants God made of the world to Adam, and to Noah, and his sons, it is very clear, that God, as king David says, Psal. cxv. 16. has given the earth to the children of men; given it to mankind in common. But this being supposed, it seems to some a very great difficulty, how any one should ever come to have a property in any thing . . .

Earlier, Locke says simply, "God hath certainly appointed government to restrain the partiality and violence of men."[7]

Locke reminds me of a slippery political operator, adept at "spinning" whatever argument gave his side the most advantage. Certainly Locke's private life suggests a contrast between his words and deeds. Although he spoke of the natural rights of man, he was a stockholder in the Royal Africa Company, the leading importer of slaves, whose initials "RAC" were branded on the chests of the slaves it caught and imported from Africa.[8] Locke also helped set up the colonies in South Carolina and the West Indies, where slavery was foundational. At one point in the *Second Treatise*, Locke even talks of Man naturally being able to own slaves:

> But there is another sort of servants, which by a peculiar name we call slaves, who being captives taken in a just war, are by the right of nature subjected to the absolute dominion and arbitrary power of their masters. These men having, as I say, forfeited their lives, and with it their liberties, and lost their estates; and being in the state of slavery, not capable of any property, cannot in that state be considered as any part of civil society; the chief end whereof is the preservation of property.[9]

Our country grows from Locke more than Hobbes. The idea of "natural rights" is deeply embedded in our spiritual and constitutional DNA. When Thomas Jefferson, a huge Locke fan, says in the Declaration of Independence that "We hold these Truths to be self-evident, that all Men are created equal, that they are endowed by their Creator with certain unalienable Rights, that among these are Life, Liberty and the Pursuit of Happiness," he is saying that there are natural laws that trump those of King George III.

In January of 2003, President George Bush stood before Congress assembled in the Capitol and, in the context of discussing the imminent war with Iraq, stated that "The liberty we prize is not America's gift to the world; it is God's gift to humanity." What Bush had done with his rhetoric was signal which side he stood on in a centuries-old debate about where the justification for liberty, and thus law, comes from.

I'm not the first to spot Locke's thin logic. In 1791, the philosopher Jeremy Bentham derided Locke's "idea of natural rights held independently from the state as 'nonsense upon stilts.' . . . The only meaningful rights men possessed were those the state chose to enforce, he [Bentham] argued."[10]

Theodore Plucknett points out that in arguing for natural law enforced by God, Locke was not necessarily arguing a modern point of view. It was in many ways a return to a medieval form of logic.

> Where Hobbes had considered law to be the command of the State, Locke returned to the notion of natural law—a conception which was easily reconciled with the medieval view of law as the will of God. Where Hobbes had made law the tool of the State, Locke regarded it as the guardian of liberty.[11]

This book is a continuation of that argument between Hobbes and Locke. As perhaps Hobbes might approve of, I argue that no real markets exist without a government to make them and enforce them. Most economists are explicitly or implicitly Lockean, arguing that markets exist in a state of nature, and government exists only to regulate them or tidy them up, but that the markets would exist without any government at all.

In the last century conventional economists have implicitly sided with Locke in stating that capitalism functioned pretty much by itself, subject only to natural laws of supply and demand. But the history of Russia and its satellite countries after the fall of the Soviet Union in

1990 was an awakening for many economists. They had thought that, without the heavy hand of a Brezhnev or Stalin, a natural paradise of capitalism would bloom. But what bloomed was a criminal paradise of Mafioso types who made life hell for the average person and enriched themselves by taking control of markets in a very direct way. The country did not stabilize until the strong leader Vladimir Putin was elected to office. Putin was Hobbes's man. Meanwhile economists, while still often hostile to governments, entertained the notion that markets depended on governments, and not the reverse.

The war of the United States in Iraq in the first decade of the second millennium can be viewed as a test of Hobbes and Locke. When the United States invaded Iraq in the spring of 2003 to remove the Iraqi dictator Saddam Hussein, defense secretary Donald Rumsfeld appeared to expect, based on the few troops he left in Iraq, a functioning capitalist and democratic state to quickly emerge, once Hussein was removed. Instead, just as in Russia, except worse, what emerged was killing and looting. As Hobbes would have predicted, absent Hussein's evil but strong controlling hand, chaos and violence erupted. And quite quickly, as Hobbes again would have predicted, this prompted average Iraqis to view Hussein in a more positive light. Iraqis may have hated Hussein, but many began to say they preferred him in power to having their daughters raped and their cars hijacked, things that happened with impunity after Hussein was toppled and the American military failed to impose order. It's hard to swallow, but the average Iraqi was safer under an evil dictator.

But although I think Locke's theory of natural rights is generally "nonsense upon stilts," I sympathize with his point of view, even if it strikes me as absurd in its general logic. My sympathy comes from a spiritual place. Man should have an inherent dignity. I believe in the rights of Man. I believe in human rights, as in the right to be free of torture and coercion. It's just that I see these rights as being, not God-given, but Man-given, by all of us, to each other. And government can be the means.

THE NONVIOLENT GOVERNMENT

Are there alternatives to government possessing and using force? I see some, even though I don't see them as practical.

Historically, the philosophy of anarchism has posed an alternative to government as cudgel. While anarchists endorse the absence of government, they don't endorse an absence of organization. In anarcho-syndicalism, worker collective councils organize society and get tasks done, from disposing of trash to building houses.

Instead of having no government, what if we had government that did not use violence as one of its tools? I've long admired Gandhian and Quaker-style nonviolence, and I wonder if government could function through such means. What if when someone stole something, instead of having a police officer respond with a gun, you had a team of people surround him and accompany him night and day, until he returned the item? What if they smothered him with words? I taught at a Quaker school before becoming a journalist, and when there was a conflict between individuals, whether students or faculty, the standard solution for dealing with it was to form a committee, where you had to sit and listen to each other while a mediator looked on. Believe me, it's a powerful dissuader to conflict. Even the most violent criminal might be dissuaded if he knew he would be greeted by committee members who would smother him with words. Another tactic would be to have government withdraw its services, from police protection to contract enforcement, when a citizen violated one of its precepts.

CONCLUSION

For the near- or even long-term future, I see no alternative to government, and I see no alternative to government possessing and using force at times. But to turn a phrase and put it to another use, while some may say, "that government is best that governs least," I would say, "that government is best that uses force and violence the least." I recall President Obama citing President John F. Kennedy's words when Obama accepted the Nobel Peace Prize in 2009. He was talking about foreign policy and the use of war as its instrument, but his words can be applied to government and the use of force in any capacity, even in enforcing a speeding ticket:

> So part of our challenge is reconciling these two seemingly irreconcilable truths—that war is sometimes necessary, and war at some level is an expression of human folly. Concretely, we must direct our effort to the task that President Kennedy called for long ago. "Let us focus," he said, "on a more practical, more attainable peace, based not on a sudden revolution in human nature but on a gradual evolution in human institutions."[12]

SEEDING THE FIELDS:
THE MARKETS WE MAKE IN OUR MINDS

CHAPTER 17

COMMON TONGUE, COMMON CULTURE, COMMON MARKETS

As you sow, so shall you reap.
TRADITIONAL SAYING, OFTEN ATTRIBUTED TO THE BIBLE

IT'S BIG GOVERNMENT moving into sectors that should belong to the Church or the family. It's an intrusion of government upon the marketplace. It's redistributive taxation.

The arguments above are not about instituting a national healthcare system, not from the debate about Medicare or Medicaid in the 1960s, not about establishing the Social Security system in the 1930s, although the rhetoric is the same. These arguments are from those who opposed the establishment of public education in the early and mid-nineteenth century.

Although we take the right of everyone to receive a public education for granted, as well as the related laws that *require* all children to attend school, these twin pillars were not easily built. The nation struggled mightily for more than a half-century from its founding in 1776 to establish the right of everyone to receive an education. For many decades, it was recognized more in word than by deed, but public education eventually became widespread around the middle of the nineteenth century, although its enactment was not accomplished all at once, but state by state.

I bring it up here for two reasons. First, it's an example of how the things we take for granted, like clean water or public education, were the products of long, hard political battles that took decades—or longer. As we fight our own battles today, it's good to remember this. It can dispel the notion that anything is easy.

The second and more important reason I bring it up is that it relates to the core concept of this book, the establishment of markets. Governments design markets by giving us property rights and inventing the patent system. But there's another way governments design markets, which is to design and build the structures inside our heads, the way we think and talk. Though this may sound Frankensteinian, government does it in ways that, as with patents or a road system, become obvious once you look at them.

In the remainder of this chapter, I'm going to look at two principal ways government does this: schooling and language, which are closely connected to each other. We take for granted in this country that most of us are educated to at least a basic degree, and most of us speak English, and that the English we speak is the same in Anchorage, Albuquerque, and Oahu, with the exception of a few regional words and phrases.

This did not happen "naturally," to use an imprecise word. This happened because we as a country made it happen, through decades of largely political work, as we used our government to establish a common tongue, a common stored set of facts. Government plowed the fields in our heads. This common education and language are the mental equivalent of a national road system. They are an infrastructure of the mind, and a primary step toward building a nation, as well as having a market economy constructed on a national basis. It's true that, compared with other countries, the United States more often chose the route of a public/private partnership in these matters, but government still played an indispensable role.

In very brief form, given how rich this history is, I'll lay out how we achieved a common language and culture. I'll touch on familiar names like Noah Webster, and less familiar ones like Horace Mann, and forgotten but crucially important laws, like the Free School Act that Pennsylvania passed in 1834. I'll talk about how these processes of establishing common language and education happened in other countries, and how we could do it better here.

COMMON TONGUE, COMMON MIND

Scratch almost anything foundational in this country and you find Thomas Jefferson. Education is no exception. In 1779, with the Battle of Yorktown still two years away and the war not yet won, Jefferson, the governor of Virginia, introduced into the House of Burgesses a plan to do something unprecedented: give most Virginia children some education, by right. His plan divided the state into districts a few miles across, each of which would be required to have a public school to which admission would be free for three years. Under a sort of pyramid plan, the top students would then be eligible to go on to further education at state expense, with the very top students of those classes going on to the College of William and Mary in Williamsburg. By contemporary standards, this was a meager public education plan, guaranteeing only three years. And of course it was not available to the children of slaves. But by the standards of the late eighteenth century, it was radical. It died in the state legislature, without even a vote.

In a few years, with the revolution won, the nation would be on fire with plans and ideas for more universal education. The revolution had been won under the banner of universal standards and rights, including those embracing education. There was tension between those like Jefferson, who saw themselves as part of the drive for the universal rights of Man that would lead to the French Revolution, and those like John Adams, Alexander Hamilton, and George Washington, who wished to replace the British masters with a native elite, with less emphasis on democracy and popular suffrage. This would lead to the formation of the Republican Party, led by Jefferson and the predecessor of today's Democratic Party, and the more elitist and centrist Federalists. Their partisan battles produced great rhetoric about providing education for everyone. The obstacles were formidable. It meant asking dominant institutions, particularly the Church, which traditionally had run many schools, to play different roles. The drive to establish common education became wrapped up with establishing a more secular society. Most of all, early advocates of universal education wanted it to be a vehicle to teach future citizens about the ideals and workings of their new experiment: a democratic and republican nation.

"Institutionalized education had before this time been regarded as a responsibility either of the church or of the family, and in its upper reaches it was available only to the privileged classes," said Stuart Noble in *A History of American Education*. "Now, with the recognition of citizenship as a goal, public education became a responsibility of the state."[1]

But for the first few decades, the drive to spread public education was one more of word than deed. True, in the Northwest Ordinance of 1787, which created a system for giving away the land northwest of the Ohio River in the unsettled territory that would become Ohio, Indiana, Illinois, and other states, there was a provision setting up a system for establishing and funding public education in the new lands of the West.

Based on a report by Thomas Jefferson, the act, among the many, many things it did, reserved "lot 16" of each six-mile-square township, which had thirty-six lots, for public education. This was something. The Congress of the states under the Articles of Confederation passed this ordinance, and it was reaffirmed by the US Congress after the passing of a new Constitution. But as the revolutionary fires cooled, so did the will to actually achieve substantive progress on the goal of free public education.

It was significant that Pennsylvania in 1776 wrote a new constitution that guaranteed everyone a right to a public education. But in a few years, this ardor had diminished. In 1790, the constitution was rewritten to establish public schools only for the poor, and then only if it essentially was not too much trouble. The language read: "The legislature shall, as soon as conveniently may be, provide by law for the establishment of schools throughout the state, in such a manner that the poor may be taught gratis." Quakers, Lutherans, and other religious orders had opposed public education at taxpayer expense, by and large. Even this constitutional provision was largely unenforced. No free schools for the poor opened until 1818. Pennsylvania would enact a groundbreaking public education law for everyone, the Free School Act, in 1834, one of the first in the country. But it was controversial. Many German Americans, who were a large segment of Pennsylvania's population, opposed state-supported education in English. The passing of the act cost Democrats the governorship of the state, and under the next administration there was a drive to repeal the act. It is said to have been saved by a rousing speech by legislator Thaddeus Stevens, who had actually been elected as part of the anti-public-school wave. Stevens effectively reversed positions, and chided his fellow legislators for recently voting money without argument to improve the breeding of hogs, but being less willing to spend money to improve the breed of man.

"If an elective republic is to endure for any great length of time, every elector must have sufficient information, not only to accumulate wealth and take care of his pecuniary concerns, but to direct wisely the Legislatures, the Ambassadors, and the Executive of the nation," Stevens said. "If, then, the permanency of our government depends upon such knowledge, it is the duty of government to see that the means of information be diffused to every citizen. This is a sufficient answer to those who deem education a private and not a public duty—

who argue that they are willing to educate their own children, but not their neighbor's children."[2]

As the speech above foreshadows, the drive to establish public education was similar in tone and logic to campaigns for other universal services, such as health care. In the 1800s, as now, words were cheap, but as soon as proposals to actually fund schools came up, then opposition was evident in numerous quarters. Church leaders often opposed "common schools," because their own religious schools were threatened. Citizens opposed new taxes, then as now. Significantly, according to Noble, the ultimately successful drive to establish public schools for everyone came not from a class uprising—the poor and working classes were too busy for political work apparently—but from a mass do-gooder movement.

It "was essentially romantic in character," Noble said. "It was a manifestation of that broader humanitarian movement that comprised also prison reform, the abolition of slavery, and the care of the defective and feeble-minded in state supported asylums. . . . it was a middle-class movement supported by clergymen, teachers, patriots [etc.] . . . the movement as a whole was a middle-class humanitarian crusade rather than a proletarian uprising."[3]

Even more so than Pennsylvania, Massachusetts was a leader, and Horace Mann gets much of the credit. A future congressman, candidate for governor, and president of Antioch College, Mann by all accounts tirelessly promoted public education from his essentially ceremonial post as Massachusetts secretary of education from 1837 to 1848. The state's education department was the first such in the country. Often called "the father of American public education," Mann helped lead a national movement to establish "common schools." It was not easy.

In 1852, Massachusetts took the drive to establish public schools even further by passing a law requiring parents to send their children to either a public school or an acceptable religious school. The Massachusetts law was mild. It required only that a child be in school three months a year, and not necessarily contiguous months. There were few provisions for enforcement. But no wonder this was controversial, this bedrock law that we accept with little question now. The state was literally entering the family's home, and escorting the child out the door and into a classroom.

"Compulsory schooling was bitterly opposed by many people who argued that it deprived parents of their inalienable rights, that it was not necessary in order to secure attendance, that it was an uncalled-for assumption of powers by the state governments, that it was inimical to the spirit of free democratic institutions, and that it was an obstacle to the employment of child labor" is how two authors summarized arguments against public education at the time.[4]

It is striking to me how this rhetoric against compulsory public education is almost identical to the rhetoric against national health care, and previously, against the establishment of Social Security. The arguments we engage in today about the role of the state are very old ones.

Other states followed Massachusetts only slowly. It was not until 1918 that every state in the union had a public education attendance law.

The movement to establish public education for everyone continued and continues. The Morrill Act of 1862, which created land-grant colleges in the West and helped make higher education more affordable, was a milestone. The GI Bill of 1944 was a huge achievement. Still, the US system of higher education today is much like its system of health care: expensive and inaccessible to much of the population. There are undeniable points of excellence. Universities like Harvard, Stanford, Yale, and Rice are world-class. But this obscures the fact that we are one of the few advanced countries that does not guarantee a right to higher education. In countries like France or Germany, the difficult thing is getting into a good college and then graduating, not paying for it.

These things evolve, though. Just as in early 1852 it was a significant achievement for Massachusetts to require students to be in school for three months a year, today it would be a significant thing to make higher education or even vocational education more accessible. I would favor a system where all students would have a right to go to any college they could win admission to, with the tuition paid by government.

CONTENT MATTERS: ON LANGUAGE AND DEMOCRACY

Imagine being so successful at your job that your surname becomes like the word "aspirin," moving from the private into the public domain. That's what happened to Noah Webster. He wrote the first real dictionary of the American English language, and there are now many "Webster's dictionaries," published by many companies. The phrase has come to mean essentially any dictionary of the American English language, although Merriam-Webster traces back to Noah Webster's original work.

While the drive to establish schooling for everyone was difficult, almost as difficult was the question of what schools should teach. Education was engaged with the effort to establish a democracy, and there was great awareness of the fact. From this emerged the idea that this new nation should speak a common language, and share a similar set of knowledge—and values.

Here Noah Webster, who did not just concern himself with dictionaries, enters the picture. His first crusade was, essentially, establishing a national curriculum and a pedagogy for elementary schools. This resulted in what came to be known as Webster's "blue-back speller," named for its characteristic cover. Although called a speller, it actually taught children to read, using the then-common method of having the children spell out words and then pronounce them.

Webster was a classic American type, the kind of person who today would probably lead an Internet startup company while contemplating a run for governor. Tireless, unflagging, long-lived, Webster worked from his youth during the American Revolution to the 1840s, when he was an old man in his eighties, to shape what Americans would learn, how they would learn it, and the language they would speak. He was a fan of the new democracy, but he was entrepreneurial, helping drive through copyright laws so he could be assured of gaining royalties from his many books. And make royalties he would. His blue-back speller, first called the *Elementary Spelling Book* and part of the three-volume, chunkily titled *Grammatical Institute of the English Language*, is estimated to have sold 80 to 100 million copies. His *An American Dictionary of the English Language*, published in 1828 after twenty years of work, with more than seventy thousand entries, was not only the first real dictionary of the American English language, but one of the first dictionaries of English, period. It would be the bible of words, the resolver of disputes, the touchstone of knowledge, into the twentieth century.

All this relates to market economies, because it helps our markets to have us all speak the same language. This did not happen naturally or easily. Webster's competition for elementary school classrooms was the British *A New Guide to the English Tongue*, by Thomas Dilworth, first printed in 1747.[5] American publishers loved Dilworth, because they could print his book for free, given that international copyright law did not exist. (This situation would last through much of the nineteenth century, and would infuriate authors, like Charles Dickens, who saw little to no income from their best-selling books here. It is quite ironic, given how loudly we complain now that China, the emerging nation of the twenty-first century as we were in the nineteenth, does the same thing with our DVDs and software.) Webster would make his new book, on which royalties did have to be paid, the new standard through his own tireless promotion. He is sometimes called the father of the copyright, because he managed to get the new state of Connecticut to pass a copyright law before his influential spelling book was published. This, is turn, became an influence on the one passed by Congress.

Webster firmly believed that a common base of knowledge and learning was the glue that would bind Americans as their new nation became a coherent one. The citizens in this democracy (although suffrage even for all white men would be a long way away) would need to know how to read and write, and would need a common base of assumptions about how their republic functioned.

"As soon as he opens his lips, he should rehearse the history of his own country," said Webster in 1788 in an early tract called "On Education of the Youth in America."

> He should lisp the praise of liberty, and of those illustrative heroes and statesmen, who have fought a revolution in her favor.
>
> When I speak of a diffusion of knowledge, I do not mean merely a knowledge of spelling books, and the New-Testament. An acquaintance with ethics, and with the general principles of law, commerce, money and government, is necessary for the yeomanry of a republican state.[6]

He was hardly alone in believing this, but he was almost certainly the most effective and influential leader of this movement.

Webster understood that part of establishing a universal education was establishing *a universal language*. Both in England and the United States, people not only spoke a variety of tongues in their own home and often in public, they spoke English different ways and spelled it and wrote it differently as well. The Englishman David Simpson, in his lively *The Politics of American English*, noted that Thomas Jefferson, unquestionably a learned man, followed very loose rules of writing and spelling in his handwritten draft of the Declaration of Independence, composed in 1776. He spelled "payment," "wholesome," and "soldiers," "paiment," "wholsome," and "souldiers." He spelled "honour" in what would become the classic British spelling, but spelled "tenor" in American fashion. His publishers would change many of these, but not all. Simpson calls the situation with regard to spelling at this time "moderate chaos."[7]

L'ACADÉMIE AMERICAIN?

Some, like future president John Adams, wanted to establish the American equivalent of the French Academy, L'Académie française, which semi-officially establishes correct spelling, grammar, and usage for the French language. In a letter in 1780, Adams, who was aware of the French Academy and its efforts, recommended forming an American Academy that would consciously unify and promote the English language. Said Adams:

> The honor of forming the first public institution for refining, correcting, improving, and ascertaining the English language, I hope is reserved for congress; they have every motive that can possibly influence a public assembly to undertake it. It will have a happy effect upon the union of the states to have a public standard for all persons in every part of the continent to appeal to, both for the signification and pronunciation of the language.[8]

This was not to be, and it's interesting to ask whether it would have succeeded. In general, the United States has frowned on official bodies that say what is and isn't correct in matters that are essentially cultural. But the country's leaders often find other means to do the same thing. Webster's "blue-back speller" and then his dictionary would come to have the same authority as a pronouncement from the French Academy. In a few generations no longer would an educated man or woman in the United States write and spell in an indeterminate fashion.

As the decades passed, with the beginnings of universal public education, with compulsory school attendance, with widely used elementary textbooks and a common dictionary, the furrows plowed inside young students' heads became remarkably similar. They would learn to spell and write and speak in a common fashion, and their heads would be stuffed with similar bodies of knowledge constituting a set of facts and stories about how democracy worked.

It was a remarkable achievement, and it is part of the design of markets. For a nation to function coherently economically, it helps tremendously if citizens speak and write a common language, and this is only done politically.

E. D. Hirsch, in his underrated and often-misunderstood book *Cultural Literacy*, speaks of how a common language and a common culture are necessary for both an economy and a nation to function effectively. It is—and this is what many liberals miss—a *democratic* (with a small "d") achievement to build a common language and culture and body of knowledge that are accessible to all. Many liberals, with their emphasis on multiculturalism and allowing or even encouraging a polyglot of languages and teaching, are undermining a goal they probably would embrace, which is a more egalitarian nation, both economically and politically. Hirsch shows that a common culture is a constructed thing, the work of political and other elites, but that once constructed, it is akin to a language (another constructed thing put into place by elites), which includes elements of both high and low culture, and which cannot be arbitrarily changed. If we abandon teaching this common culture, which includes everything from George Washington and the cherry tree to what is DNA, we abandon being a nation to some degree. We also abandon the ideal of inclusiveness, because having a common culture is a boon most of all to immigrants and others trying to make their way into society.

The old blue-back spelling book of Noah Webster consciously included stories about the founding fathers and parables about how civics works in order to teach children about their democracy at the same time as teaching them to read. As Hirsch points out, this contrasts with the new "educational formalism," which regards reading and writing as merely skills to be taught, and ignores that these are skills that cannot be practiced without content on which to use them. If you read the words "The Gettysburg Address," they have no meaning unless you can call up from memory a short narrative of what the Gettysburg address is, who wrote it, and why.

"Current schoolbooks in language arts pay little systematic attention to conveying a body of culturally significant information from grade to grade. Their 'developmental' approach contrasts sharply with textbooks from earlier decades, which consciously aimed to impart cultural literacy," says Hirsch in *Cultural Literacy*.[9]

THE QUIET REVOLUTION IN QUEBEC AND ITS IMPLICATIONS

Conventional economists generally don't take into account factors like language when they discuss supply and demand, and the meeting in a clearing of a willing buyer and seller. But language is part of the operating system of an economy, and who controls language is part of determining who has wealth and power in a society. The history of Quebec, including current social developments, demonstrates this.

Jocelyn Proulx is a middle-age man and a native of Quebec who lives with his family in Levis, across from Quebec City near where the English launched their successful surprise attack in 1759 that would result in the handing over of New France to Great Britain. He talks in a memoir about how his father worked for the Canadian National Railways and was denied access to higher-paying and higher-status jobs because he spoke little English and lacked an English surname. He remembers as a young boy his father, after a week of hard labor, lying on the couch trying to learn English and botching the job.

"Even if he would have recited Shakespeare with a perfect accent, my father could never be Foreman, because at the Canadian National Railways, the boss had to have an English name," Proulx said. "In this Crown Corporation with roots back to the Loyalists idea of 'Uniting this country against the U.S. threat,' the roles were strictly defined. If you were Black, you would be porter or busboy. Immigrants or French people were manual workers. Any white collar was mandatory of British origin. This was a natural order of things."[10]

Then things changed.

In the 1960s and 1970s, Quebec underwent the "Quiet Revolution," where nationalists like René Lévesque, a future premier of Quebec, advocated sovereignty for the French-speaking nation. While they would fail in their efforts for complete independence, they would succeed in enacting laws like the famous (and still infamous to some) Bill 101, passed in 1977, which essentially required that all children attend French public schools and that not only public, but commercial, signs be written only in French. (Such a law requiring commercial speech to be in one language would almost certainly be unconstitutional in the United States, because it would have violated freedom of speech.) In Quebec province these laws led to considerable turmoil, as many English-speaking residents and companies moved to Toronto and other parts of Canada. Dire economic consequences were predicted for Quebec. But the nationalists persisted. And power gradually shifted from a wealthy English-speaking elite to a French-speaking one. Now, Quebec is the richest, most populous, and most economically powerful part of Canada, but it is French speakers who generally control its direction. And the French majority is no longer downtrodden, comparable to Shiites in Sunni-led Iraq. And as the French majority has gained power, it has become less militant. Fewer Quebec nationalists now advocate full independence. One can even walk into a bar and order a beer in English and receive it. That was not the case in 1975, I was told.

The point is that the economic implications of Quebec's revolution are not on the radar screen of conventional economists, at least not that I have seen. The way that language functions as a sort of money, with the dominant language being a tool of commerce, goes unrecognized. I'm a fan of Quebec's Quiet Revolution, despite my misgivings about stifling expression, because I think it's fair that a majority gets recognition and support for its language and culture, and that this downtrodden majority gets political and economic power. Achieving that through language is part of the battle. Quebec's story is the flip side of our own. Our efforts two hundred years ago to forge a common language and culture helped prevent the emergence of some minority/ majority that spoke a different language and was somehow kept out of the economic mainstream. The current efforts of multiculturalists to promote many languages, even in official proceedings, risk creating a regime of economic exclusion, which I'm sure is not what they desire.

HOW FRANCE BECAME FRENCH

We can compare how the United States, led by individuals such as Noah Webster, Thomas Jefferson, and Horace Mann, forged a common culture and language with how the French did it. Many people may not realize that France, seen as culturally unified, was until recently a polyglot nation held together by a thin glue of language, laws, and leaders of the elite.

In the 1780s at the time of the French Revolution, when Thomas Jefferson was ambassador to France, only about 3 million of France's 20 million citizens, or 15 percent, could actually speak French. Most people spoke local languages, from Provençal to Breton to Basque. Over the next century and a half, the French government, by turns republican or autocratic, put enormous effort into making its citizens "French." It built up a common language, through the French Academy. It mandated what would be taught in school. It wrested control of the schools away from the Catholic Church. But still as late as 1890, about 7.5 million of the country's 30 million citizens, or roughly a quarter, spoke no French. In Eugen Weber's book *My France: Politics, Culture, Myth*, a certain Batista Bonnet tells the story of serving in the country's army for six years, including being wounded in the Franco-Prussian

War in 1870, and emerging still not speaking much French. When he wanted to stay in Paris and work, he had to take private French lessons. French was the language of the state and the upper class, and for many citizens, it was a language one only spoke on the job or for official duties.[11]

The effort France put into unifying its country linguistically paid off. One should not discount what was lost in this effort, and I say this as someone who appreciates smaller languages and cultures such as Basque. What should be recognized is that the achievement of a universal common language of French, with an accompanying culture to some degree, was an achievement *of the political Left*. The common man was wresting away a language of the elite and making it his own. An elite culture and economy were being opened to him. It is in this spirit that the French effort to maintain a unified culture and language, an effort often laughed at in the United States, should be seen.

But where did this common language come from initially, in France and other countries? Hirsch, in the kind of great synthesis that a great scholar can do, shows in *Cultural Literacy* that these mother tongues most likely came out of the great cities of Europe—London, Paris, and others—as they were forming. They were not the languages of the upper class simply transferred to the masses. Says Hirsch:

> Dialects rubbed up against each other in the public streets and halls of London. The great city was a meeting place for public interactions of all sorts. There, people of all types—artisans, trades people and aristocrats—were attracted by the magnetism of London's money, amusement, and excitement. . . . The local London dialect actually disappeared and was gradually replaced by something that had never existed before—an amalgam that had no singular identifiable parent. . . . King and courtier had to learn the common London speech; it formed the upper-class speech of the court, not vice versa.[12]

Hirsch cites a well-known quote about the Italian language, that the lingua franca of Italy was *lingua Toscana in bocce romana*, or "Tuscan speech in Roman mouth."

"The great cities forged the beginnings of the common, classless languages of all the great European nations," Hirsch says.

> Neither in origin nor in subsequent history have national languages been inherently class languages. It is true that after national dictio-

naries were formulated, the standard languages were more likely to be acquired by people who were rich enough to be educated than by poor people. But the distinction is one of schooling, which we have made universal, not of economic or social class. . . . It is, therefore, a very odd cliché that connects literate national culture with elitism, since it is the least elitist or exclusive culture that exists in any modern nation.[13]

Defenders of having an array of languages spoken without the promotion of a common one are unwittingly attacking the ideal of a common nation that is accessible to all its citizens. Those nations that are multilingual, like Canada or Belgium, are hardly models of stability. The exceptions like Switzerland tend to be very small, and to have put immense effort into promoting multifluency, meaning fluency in two or more languages, with a common culture to match. Hardly an easy task.

We should therefore understand that well-meaning linguistic pluralism, which would encourage rather than discourage competing languages within our borders, is much different from Jeffersonian pluralism, which has encouraged a diversity of traditions, values, and opinions. Toleration of diversity is at the root of our society, but encouragement of multilingualism is contrary to our traditions and extremely unrealistic.[14]

All of this gets back to markets. Part of having an accessible and open market, meaning anyone can participate, is having an accessible and easily learned culture and language. It is not the only requirement, but it is one. Conservatives, or market-fundamentalists, should realize that they need government and its institutions like schools to plow these fields in our heads, so a common ecology can flourish.

We are so conditioned to think about markets as getting rid of controls and barriers. But markets and society as a whole are also about creating commonalities. Markets and society work better when people speak the same language, when they have similar education levels, when they have similar values. These things do not appear by magic. So to have better-functioning markets, we actually need a more proactive state.

Liberals in the United States tend to view efforts to make a common culture or language as "fascist." But mandating standards is one of the jobs of a democracy. Requiring people to speak English, to have certain standards of civic knowledge, and having classes to help people reach these standards empower them to be full citizens. A society open to all can only be achieved by some universal standards. Common culture and language actually enhance the role of the individual. I am reminded of how from the creation of a national highway network, something only achieved through great state action and the subject of Chapter 12, emerged the mythic American driver who explores the country on his own, Jack Kerouac–style.

COMMON CULTURE, COMMON LUNCH

One can go beyond language and basic education into areas like health, artistic appreciation, and food. All nations do this to a degree. France, as usual, goes further than most. Visit a French public school at lunch-time and you'll find a strange sight: rows of students and teachers at long tables, eating family-style meals, for a good two hours. Students are taught how to eat and what to eat.

"At one school, students were served a choice of salads—mâche with smoked duck and fava beans, or mâche with smoked salmon and asparagus—followed by guinea fowl with roasted potatoes and carrots and steamed broccoli," says Deborah Madison, author of *The Greens Cookbook*, after a visit in 2007 to study French public schools and their lunches.

> For dessert, there was a choice of ripe, red-throughout strawberries or *clafoutis*. A pungent washed-rind cheese was offered, along with French bread and water. Yes, the kids took and ate the cheese. . . .
>
> About two hours are given for lunch, a portion of which is used for very loud and active exercise. Second, they were civilized. Food was served on heated plates; real silverware and glasses—not plastic—were used; and the lunchrooms were pretty and comfortable for the kids.[15]

This would be the visual equivalent of seeing Martians on the moon to American parents, accustomed to seeing crowded cafeterias with kids hastily sitting down, if at all, at Formica tables and gulping down sloppy joes in nineteen minutes. True story: My lunch period at First Colonial High School in Virginia Beach in 1977 lasted nineteen minutes, beginning, if memory serves correctly, at 10:40 a.m. Flash forward to 2011 in Brooklyn. The lunch period for my son's kindergarten class in public school started at 10:40 a.m. and lasted for twenty-five minutes. Some things don't change.

In France, teaching children *how to be French* includes teaching them how to eat and what to eat. The state is intruding into the children's mouths, and down into their palates and belly. Here in the United States, we accept that the state may have some responsibility for seeing that children are properly fed, but might blanch at training them in table manners and culinary habits. This is a mistake. We face an epidemic of childhood and adult obesity, and part of the reason is our reluctance to intrude into the American stomach. In our own American way, we can and should assert ourselves.

What France achieves with this more proactive exercise in acculturation is a more rapid assimilation of new citizens. French President Nicolas Sarkozy may be the essence of Frenchness with his penchant for drama and taste in beautiful women. But he got his un-French-sounding name from his father, Pál István Ernő Sárközy de Nagy-Bócsa, who was Hungarian and managed to make it to France in the turmoil after World War II. That his son could so quickly rise to the top says a lot about how well France creates Frenchmen. Immigrate to France, and the state will teach you how to speak, how to eat, and how to behave. In one short generation, a child will be French, even if his mother was Spanish and his father Polish. It's true that France and the whole of Europe have had difficulty integrating North Africans and other Muslim populations. But this misses the fact that they have tried and with many of the newcomers have done a very good job of it.

THE MARKETS WE BUILD ABROAD

CHAPTER 18

BY YOUR BOOTSTRAPS:
DEVELOPING COUNTRIES AND MARKETS

IN 1957, SOUTH KOREA had a per capita income of less than $100 per year, on par with some of the poorest countries on earth. Its per capita income was below that of the West African country (and former British colony) of Ghana.[1]

A half-century later, a blip of time historically, South Korea is a First World country. The United States buys South Korea's cars and computers. The cities of South Korea gleam. Seoul, the capital, has gone through almost every cycle of urban development, from garden cities to high-rise apartments to freeways through the middle of the city to tearing them down, in rapid sequence, like a movie speeded up. The nation has a high-speed rail system. Meanwhile North Korea, a Communist dictatorship, has grass growing in its streets, literally and figuratively. Its population is stunted in size because of low food intake. It is a Fourth World country.

What accounted for South Korea's rapid rise in fortune? Make no mistake about it, it was markets. It was trade. Comparing the fate of the two Koreas since World War II is certainly evidence of that. After a bloody civil war, one part, South Korea, went the way of markets. The other, North Korea, went the way of a type of Communism that not only had a command economy, but resembled a medieval police state. Neither North nor South Korea was a democracy at first, but only South Korea staked its future on trade. But South Korea did not conform to rhetoric about open free markets, and this was crucial to its success. I'll tell that story here.

I have shown how markets are constructed at a local, state, and national level, through a variety of types of infrastructure, be they legal, a set of laws; physical, a set of physical infrastructure such as roads and bridges; constabulary, both internal and external, such as municipal police and a national army; and mental, or intrapersonal, a set of institutions, such as language and education, that build the intrapersonal facilities that function in a market.

International markets have all these things, only they function across national borders. It's easy to fall into the trap of thinking about international trade and commerce as the most liberated kind of trade and commerce, where a buyer and seller meet on a plain or at port's edge and exchange baubles or gold bullion in a direct, unmediated way.

But actually just the opposite is true. A thick web of laws and physical infrastructure supports and creates international commerce. We don't see or hear much about these laws and infrastructure. Joe Citizen is aware of laws against speeding or stealing that carton of milk from the local store. But it's doubtful he knows about how the Universal Postal Union makes it possible for him to mail a letter to a high school buddy who has moved to France. Be that as it may, these laws and treaties, as well as physical infrastructure, have played important roles in those poorer nations that have developed successfully and those that haven't. And they are open to being crafted and designed, just as they are in designing other markets.

South Korea went the way of markets, but it did not go the way of the free market. It consistently ignored the advice of the United States, even while taking US financial and military aid. The state decided which markets to participate in and how. It *designed* how its industries would relate to world markets. Ultimately, South Korea lifted itself out of poverty by systematically violating the "rules" offered by Washington and detouring from "the Washington consensus," as it was called in the first decade of the second millennium. South Korea played favorites with its industries; it kept its currency value artificially low; it restricted the inflow of capital funds; it allowed outside investment on its own terms. By violating the Washington consensus, it got rich.

This story is one that has been acted out in not just South Korea, but a slew of Asian countries, sometimes called "the Asian Tigers." They include Taiwan, Singapore, and Malaysia. They include Japan. What I'm attacking is the idea that simply constructing markets can be enough to lift a nation out of poverty. I know of no examples of that. Douglas North, who was awarded the Nobel Prize for his work recognizing the institutional basis for capitalism, said as much:

There is no mystery why the field of development has failed to develop during the five decades since the end of the Second World War. Neo-

classical theory is simply an inappropriate tool to analyze and prescribe policies that will induce development. It is concerned with the
operations of markets, not with how markets develop.[2]

GETTING THE PRICES WRONG

In the wake of the Korean civil war in 1953, South Korea, like its Communist neighbor North Korea, was a smoking rubble. As its leaders
contemplated a path upward, the most many international observers
expected or hoped for was for this country of peasants to become a kind
of economic appendage to Japan.

But Korean leaders had other ideas. Relying on state initiatives,
they first used American money that was given as foreign aid and that
sloshed through the economy through the presence of American military bases, and second, mobilized their armed forces to function as
quasi-industrial development companies to funnel credit and resources
into particular economic sectors.

"This industrial success is not something that the elder George
Kennan or our good Fabian Beatrice Webb would ever have predicted,"
says Bruce Cumings in his wonderful book, *Korea's Place in the Sun: A
Modern History*, which I have relied on in this chapter.

> Nor was it something any Japanese or American predicted before 1960
> or so. But it happened, making for a sharp break, another rupture,
> both in Korean history and in our understanding of it. As it happened,
> much of our understanding of what it takes to build a strong capitalist
> system was thrown into question, Western conceits get mirrored back
> to ourselves, and pundits scratch around for something to explain it:
> must've been a miracle.[3]

And in the decade and a half since Cumings's words were published,
South Korea has continued to follow this basic model, which I might call
neomercantilism, that almost every country that has risen to wealth
has followed. The state leads the country in development, selecting
various industries to favor, and subsidizing them in various ways direct
and indirect, such as providing access to capital at lower interest rates
and access to workers educated at state expense, and through currency
manipulation to keep prices "right"—for the exporter. These policies
depend on having an elite that can exercise control. Here's Cumings
again:

Here is one of the secrets of finance most of us would rather not think about: giving a conscious minority a grip on our jugular. The highly conscious agents of the miracle on the Han were state bureaucrats willing to hand out something for something: no-cost money if you put it to good use, building up another industrial prodigy. Policy loans for export performance, they were called, and they showed that sometimes there is a free lunch in capitalist economics.[4]

The military, both South Korea's and America's, played a part in this transformation. South Korea's huge military—600,000 in 1953—consumed half the country's budget.[5] Yet rather than hinder the economy, it helped the state mobilize resources. The American military presence helped the country through all the American dollars going into the bases there, and then out into stores and South Korean factories. But American military spending alone was not sufficient to take a Third World nation to First World.

One of the architects of South Korea's growth was Syngman Rhee, born in 1875, who led South Korea as president as an old man from 1948 to 1960, when he went into exile in Hawaii for various misdeeds. Rhee was a strongman. It is a troubling fact that successful developing countries tend not to be democracies, or at least not full democracies. A strongman or some autocratic faction tends to lead them, be it the Communist Party in present-day China or the ruling families of the Republic of Venice in the twelfth century.

Whatever word you use, corruption was rampant in South Korea at every level. Rhee looted millions for himself, as did officials high and low.[6] Corruption is, like the absence of democracy, commonplace in economic development. The standard knock against developing countries is that their corrupt governments are to blame for their low growth rates and endemic poverty. But often corruption seems to be a prerequisite for growth.

As Cumings explains, South Korea's development occurred using American capital but without American guidance. Virtually no one thought South Korea could become an independent, industrial, modern state.[7] But South Korea had other ideas. Its leaders used the money the United States was pouring into the country, a very large sum when considered against the very low per capita income of about $100 a year, to build industry and a modern state. (Cumings says that from 1945 to 1965, the United States put $12 billion into the country.) The country took capital where it could get it. In the 1970s, South Korea took huge loans from international banks laden with petrodollars from OPEC, which had become wealthy from jacking up prices. Mexico, Brazil, and other Latin American countries would squander these loans. Not South Korea. It grew into even more of an economic powerhouse.

Here's how the South Korean model worked in its formative years. I'm a Korean who wants to make television sets. Maybe I'm the brother-in-law of a key finance minister, to add in a dollop of "corruption." The state will arrange to have a friendly bank lend my new company $10 million at 10 percent a year, below the market interest rate of 20 percent. The state will also guarantee the loan to the bank. The state will arrange to have surplus American cement delivered to my door, and then help me set up distribution channels abroad, including in the United States. The state will also provide me with workers, well trained and disciplined, fresh, perhaps, from the army or public schools. A pretty nice deal. But it's not all give. The state, even if my brother-in-law is there, will also set production and sales targets, and if I don't meet them, I'm likely not to get any more loans or state help. But because the state finance minister is my brother-in-law, I'm also not likely to let him down. This was "the Korean model."[8]

It's a model that Western experts have not squared themselves with, despite its clear track record. You can see this discomfort in the tone of a book called *The East Asian Miracle: Economic Growth and Public Policy*, published by the World Bank. The authors speak in embarrassed tones. Could it be because the stories of South Korea and other successful Asian countries violate everything the World Bank had been recommending for several decades? This little book examines the high economic growth rate of eight countries, Hong Kong, South Korea, Singapore, Taiwan, China, Indonesia, Malaysia, and Thailand.

> In most of these economies, in one form or another, the government intervened—systematically and through multiple channels—to foster development, and in some cases the development of specific industries. Policy interventions took many forms: targeting and subsidizing credit to selected industries, keeping deposit rates low and maintaining ceilings on borrowing rates to increase profits and retained earnings, protecting domestic import substitutes, subsidizing declining industries, establishing and financially supporting government banks, making public investments in applied research, establishing firm- and industry-specific export targets, developing export marketing institutions, and sharing information widely between public and private sectors. Some industries were promoted, while others were not.

Then the authors go on to say: "At least some of these interventions violate the dictum of establishing for the private sector a level playing field, a neutral incentives regime."[9]

In other words, they get the prices wrong. Shocking. This book sounds at times like an atheist commenting on a successful faith healing. It couldn't have happened, but it did. The book goes on to discuss how the success of the East Asian nations violates the "neoclassical model," the adherents of which basically are left with arguing that South Korea and like-minded countries succeeded in spite of the state efforts, not because of them.

The state as the architect of growth, and an arena for making economic choices, contradicts the standard discourse on globalization, which portrays it as a force that must be adapted to, rather than one that can be shaped to one's advantage. The worst commentator in this regard is Thomas Friedman of the *New York Times*, who in his columns and books has a strange myopia about political choices, despite his extensive reporting on global trade. In his *The World Is Flat*, Friedman focuses on ten "flatteners," such as outsourcing and particular types of software, which equalize commerce among nations. Most of these have underlying political components, but Friedman leaves those out.[10]

MANY MODELS

South Korea copied Japan, but it also ignored Japan. South Korea did not guarantee workers lifetime job tenure, which worked so well in Japan. In South Korea, the big firms and groups of firms, chaebols, were started and are still mostly held by family groups. Not so in Japan. The chaebols included companies like Samsung, Lucky-Goldstar, and Daewoo begun by Kim Woo Choong in 1967 that grew and dominated industries.[11] But Cumings talks about how this also worked on a smaller scale, like a small, family-run fish store.

State-directed neomercantilism, family-centered or not, has long been a path to success. Venice, an empire built on trade made possible through military might, was a state-led trading machine.

"The Venetian travelling to the Levant on business was likely to go on a state-built galley, commanded by a captain chosen by the state, within a convoy organized by the state, and when he reached Alexandria or Acre he might well be ordered to join other Venetians in a joint, state-organized purchase of cotton or pepper. The advantage of the last system was that the prices would be kept lower if Venetians were not competing against each other," says Daniel Waley in *The Italian City-Republics*.[12]

Whether it be Venice in the eighth through fifteenth centuries, Holland in the sixteenth, Great Britain in the eighteenth and nineteenth, the United States in the twentieth, or Japan in the twentieth, all these nations have triumphed economically not through the free market, but in finding ways to leverage the market and compete in it on their own terms. In the twentieth century, the record of the Asian Tigers, and, more recently, the record of China, have given us a fairly straightforward model for neomercantilist economic development.

The basic recipe is as follows: First, induce savings among citizens, even among the poorest. Second, make this pool of capital available to selected industries at advantageous terms. This subsidization of production should also include investing in the education of the people, particularly in the elementary and secondary grades.

This strategy runs a heavy risk: the state is actively involved in "picking winners," even if this is just in a general sense like types of industry. But the state is always involved in picking winners, even or especially in the United States. Most significant developments in the American economy can be traced to some form of state action. For example, both the computer boom and the Internet were founded on government funding of research and development, with the Internet itself a direct government creation. Other big developments in the economy—like radio, airplanes, and railroads—were all funded by state aid and subsidies. The corporation RCA was originally a joint creation of the US military and private industry. The secretary of the navy sat on its board. People forget that even the car could not have triumphed without the commitment of the state to building roads.

Any study of the post–World War II boom ends up basically being a study of the US military and its investments. It was military research that funded the development of the silicon chip, the Internet, and a thousand other basic components of the computer and telecommunications revolutions. Perhaps we should thank the Soviet Union for fueling the no-holds-barred arms race, since so much of the research and development ended up creating the architecture of private, enhanced commerce, through industrial titans. California, whose Silicon Valley was home to Apple Computer, and Washington state, home today of Microsoft, were little more than vassals of the defense industry for decades. A substantial number of articles and books were written worrying about California's overreliance on defense spending. But this defense spending would generate spin-offs in ways that could not be predicted. Satellites, which we rely on for everything from Global Positioning Systems to mundane interactions, were developed to spy on the Russians. The Boeing 747, which helped propel postwar travel overseas, is little more than a tanker with seats put into it. The military had developed this plane, with a huge fuel capacity, to be able to refuel B-52s on their way to drop nuclear bombs on Moscow and St. Petersburg, and then return. Boeing turned this plane into one of the most profitable passenger airplanes ever. The Boeing 747's unique jet engines have a similar history. It isn't for nothing that Airbus, the European consortium producing planes that are a rival to Boeing's, complains about Boeing's military work giving it a substantial subsidy for its commercial aviation work.[13] The Internet, of course, was developed by DARPA, the Defense Department's resourceful research arm, to create a communication system that would still function during a nuclear war.

The big lesson for developing nations is that there is a different strategy for poorer nations than for rich ones. They should resist adopting developed countries' standards. Every country in every decade needs to find its own way. Nations need to be entrepreneurial, looking for opportunities in the global marketplace that they can fine-tune their political economy to exploit.

I'm hardly alone in recognizing this export-oriented, state-led model. In *Bad Samaritans: The Myth of Free Trade and the Secret History of Capitalism*, Ha-Joon Chang, a South Korean, argues, as I just did, that state-led capitalism works. He recounts his own boyhood in South Korea, still poverty-stricken even as a glistening phoenix was emerging. Chang notes in his book that South Korea was really copying both the nineteenth-century United States, which had high tariffs to protect its industry, and Great Britain before that. These nations lowered their tariffs and other trade barriers only after achieving dominance in various industries.

Latin America is discovering state-led capitalism. In the 1970s, Chile, at the request of its dictator Augusto Pinochet, was invaded by Los Chicago Boys, led by free market champion Milton Friedman, who crafted an open-market policy for the long, narrow country along the Pacific. This appeared to work initially, but then led to a crash in the late 1980s and 1990s. After 2000, Chile began climbing to prosperity again by having the state, against all the principles of Milton Friedman, direct industry and trade. Chile regulated the flow of foreign capital, increased spending on education and health, raised taxes on corporations, raised minimum wages and strengthened labor laws, and devalued its currency to boost exports. It invested in new industries like salmon fishing and essentially primed the pump for many industries.

"While many Latin American countries have whittled government's role in business affairs, Chile has gone largely in the other direction," says Jon Jeter of the *Washington Post*. "Not only has it wielded influence in getting to market its key exports, from table grapes to goat cheese to sofas, but it also has used more legislation, regulation and taxes to tame a feral free-market system that failed to deliver in the 1970s and '80s."[14]

Joseph Stiglitz, a Nobel Prize–winning economist, writes about the domination of the free market model in international development circles, despite the clear evidence it doesn't work. "Decisions [at the International Monetary Fund] were made on the basis of what seemed a curious blend of ideology and bad economics, dogma that sometimes seemed to be thinly veiling special interests," says Stiglitz in *Globalization and Its Discontents*, published in 2002. "Alternative opinions were not sought. Open, frank discussion was discouraged." The policies recommended often led to hunger and riots, and if they worked at all, they mostly helped the rich.

He notes that the IMF was founded, as part of the Bretton Woods agreements recommended by John Maynard Keynes, as a contra-market institution, one to work in ways the market in a grand sense often didn't. But it has slowly mutated into a market follower, not leader. "Keynes would be rolling over in his grave were he to see what has happened to his child," Stiglitz says.[15]

KOREA VERSUS VIETNAM

The post–World War II histories of Vietnam and Korea illustrate the unpredictability of national development and should be a dose of humility to those who find it easy to judge the mistakes of their predecessors. Vietnam's and Korea's stories and fates are so similar, yet so different. After World War II, both Vietnam and Korea endured civil wars and revolutions that would divide the countries into a Communist-led North and an autocratic, capitalist South. Luckily for Korea, war was halted there in 1953 in a ceasefire. Vietnam endured decades of American-led war before the Communist North triumphed in 1975.

Given the history of Korea and its Communist North, you would expect Vietnam, where the Communists won control of the whole country, to also be a pariah state, or at least miserably poor. But this is not so. Vietnam, still nominally Communist but really a developing capitalist nation, is rising, and in its own way copying capitalist South Korea. Vietnam is even planning its own system of high-speed, intercity trains. And while it's not a democracy, it's not a totalitarian dungeon.

I think about this when I'm critical of the fire and bloodshed the United States unleashed on Vietnam from the 1950s until 1975, when our collective firepower of bombs and troops nearly razed a country. This was a grievous error, but it's also true that hindsight is 20/20. Korea benefited from our intervention, while Vietnam didn't. Perhaps the lesson here is to look at the nature of autocrats and dictators and founding fathers. Ho Chi Minh, Vietnam's founding father, while perhaps no George Washington, had a better, less selfish vision for Vietnam than Kim Il-sung and his son Kim Jong-il have had for Korea. Meanwhile, if we look to the Right end of the political spectrum, we can also find autocratic governments with greater and lesser degrees of success.

THE EUROPEAN UNION VERSUS NAFTA

The discussion of the economic policies of successful developing countries leads one to consider the practices of the European Union versus the United States. The EU, although it was founded in many ways as a kind of United States of Europe, has worked out a more equitable and successful model of free trade. This is true even accounting for the financial turmoil of 2011 that has left the fate of the common currency, the euro, in doubt. Even if the EU has to take a step backward, even if it has moved too fast to incorporate new countries into its union, it has still taken many steps forward. Long-term, countries like Spain have benefited markedly from their EU membership. When a poorer country like Spain in 1980 or Estonia joins the EU now, it can expect a steady stream of direct cash and policies that work to lift its wages and incomes up to the standards of those in France or Germany. It's a very different model than the North American Free Trade Agreement, which essentially throws open the door for trade among Mexico, the United States, and Canada with little direct help from the richer countries to the poorer one. Many are starting to see the mistake in this.

"For 15 years, policy experts have suggested that, instead of seeking a trade arrangement aimed solely at benefiting U.S. companies in the short run, the United States should do for Mexico what the European Union did first for Spain, Portugal, and Greece and is now seeking to do for Eastern Europe: use development aid and temporary protections to upgrade dramatically its economy and infrastructure, particularly its educational system, thereby making Mexico more attractive to Mexicans," says John Judis. "Princeton sociologist Douglas Massey has argued that 'if the money devoted to U.S. border enforcement were instead channeled into structural adjustment in Mexico, as was done by the EU for Spain, unauthorized migration would likely disappear as a significant demographic and political issue in North America.' And that would ease pressures on American workers."[16]

What Western Europe and the European Union have pioneered is a different conception of the free market, one that resembles more a club you join, with certain explicit rules, than something that is symbolized by an absence of restraints.

In an amusing way, the European Union resembles Apple Computer, with its coordination of suppliers and parts; and the United States resembles Microsoft Corporation, with its at first seemingly admirable openness that produces a tyranny of the few over the many. Like Apple's Macintosh or its iPhone or iPad, the political economies of the EU are more tightly regulated, with only certain inputs and outputs permitted. There is repressiveness to this, but the final product is more equitable and fair.

The United States and its conception of free trade belong to the Microsoft/Windows/Intel universe. At first glance, this universe appears freer, because anyone can play. Anyone can produce software for Windows computers. There is no gatekeeper. But Windows and Intel computer products are notorious for not playing well with each other, as well as being susceptible to viruses. Even worse, Microsoft and Intel function as giants in this environment, crushing smaller companies when they decide to, as Microsoft did with the Netscape browser and the media player produced by RealPlayer.

CONCLUSION

The stories in recent times of countries like South Korea and Japan, as well as the stories of Great Britain, Venice, and the United States in centuries past, show that at no time can the fate of a nation or its people be consigned to "the market," especially when that market economy is one of trade among nations. For whether a nation is developing or advanced, it must continually develop and manage its relationship to global trade. To do otherwise is to court failure.

CHAPTER 19

LAST NIGHT UPON THE STAIRS:
INTERNATIONAL LAW

It's a small world after all
It's a small world after all
It's a small world after all
It's a small, small world
RICHARD M. SHERMAN AND ROBERT B. SHERMAN, DISNEY TUNESMITHS

IN 1717, A WEALTHY YOUNG PLANTATION OWNER, Stede Bonnet, in the English colony of Barbados, decided to try his hand at something less gentlemanly than supervising slaves and growing sugarcane: piracy. Bonnet bought a ship, equipped it with ruffians, and went a-pirating along the eastern seaboard of North America. He soon met up with another famous pirate, one Edward Teach, or "Blackbeard." The two teamed up for a while, before separating. A few months later, Bonnet and his crew were captured in the Cape Fear river of South Carolina after a fierce battle. In December of 1718, Bonnet was hanged in Charleston. Thus ended the life of "the gentleman pirate."

In 1863, as the Civil War raged across two countries that were no longer These United States, fifteen postmasters from Europe and what remained of America met in Paris at the Paris Postal Conference. It was the start of fifteen long years of meetings about how to deliver mail simply and easily across national borders. As with setting up Internet protocols, cell phone systems, or whether the titles on books are read right-to-left or conversely, transnational mail delivery was a complicated business, with both parochial and common interests to be satisfied and safeguarded. The many meetings in various capital cities of Europe led in 1878 to the Universal Postal Union, which was the postal equivalent of a universal standard. It allowed mail to be sent all over the world without separate treaties or duties. Considered one of the most successful treaties in history, it included, by 1914, when China was admitted, almost every independent country in the world. The United Nations now administers it, and it is still in effect.

Question: what does mailing letters across borders have to do with piracy? The answer is that both activities depended on international law, and show its importance. International trade has expanded exponentially in recent decades, an activity depending on something that is little discussed, international law. In this chapter I show the foundations of this immense but largely unseen edifice, which makes so much of our daily lives possible. I'm going to talk about piracy and postal practices, and then sketch out the immense mountain of international law. It's a structure that has grown up over the centuries, with now largely forgotten—but still essential—treaties like the Universal Postal Union playing important roles. In the design of markets, international law has become essential. It would help us design better markets if we were more aware of the role this body of law plays.

In the past decade or two there has been a lot of writing about globalization, about how interconnected we are through the great growth in international trade. Usually this trade is depicted as a force of nature, like the tides or the weather, something that can be dealt with but not controlled. But the international markets that have arisen have done so not only because of the webs of physical infrastructure such as underwater cables and satellites above in the heavens, but also because of webs of legal infrastructure, the laws and treaties that make it possible for trade between nations to be as commonplace as it is today.

Both piracy and postal practices show this.

"BEYOND THE LINE"

Let's look at pirates first, because we think of them as being outside the law. But the golden age of piracy between 1500 and 1800, when legendary figures like Blackbeard and Captain Kidd were on the stage, was actually produced by law.

Stede Bonnet's gentleman background was unusual, but his career as a pirate was not. Hundreds of pirate ships lurked around the Spanish Main in the 1500s and 1600s, waiting to pick off Spanish treasure ships coming back laden with gold from the New World. Captain Kidd, Black Bart, Blackbeard, Calico Jack, Anne Bonney, and many other famous pirates came out of this age.

During most of this period, if one were to board a sailing ship and make one's way to North or South America, somewhere about halfway across the Atlantic Ocean one would cross a line that marked the end of the rule of law. After this, one was, in the phrase of the day, "beyond the line," a line that marked the law-bound from the lawless, a line between rules and anything goes, as Richard Dunn says so well in his classic book *Sugar and Slaves*.[1] This line was the result of an agreement not to agree. In 1559 the Spanish and French could not agree on a common policy toward the New World, for which they were both vying. So they established a treaty that explicitly stated where the rule of law was and was not in effect. "Frenchmen and Spaniards who crossed the 'line of amity,' who sailed west of the prime meridian in the mid-Atlantic or south of the Tropic of Cancer, were expected to take care of themselves."[2] (As Dunn reports, this "beyond the line" concept soon translated itself into a general flouting of European social customs and rules.) England, Portugal, Holland, Denmark, and other countries would soon join this policy in separate treaties. The result was a world where England, France, Spain, and other countries could be at peace on one side of the line, but at war on the other. At home around the Mediterranean, they would respect each other's ships, at least while not formally at war. But on the other side of the line, they would seize each other's ships, goods, and crews, or even sack entire cities without mercy.

This climate encouraged the production of pirates. Entire cities, such as Port Royal in Jamaica, were founded off the wealth of pirates and their commerce that flourished in this extralegal climate.

Further complicating things was "privateering," a practice where a nation authorized a private ship captain to seize the ships, goods, and crews of another nation, or its cities and towns, usually when at war with the nation. Such state-sponsored pirates were given "letters of marque," which entitled them to better treatment if captured, more similar to that of a prisoner of war than a common criminal. In modern parlance, it was "privatized" war. Letters of marque were so common they are even mentioned in the US Constitution. The distinction between privateers and pirates was fuzzy, though, for both nations and pirates, and sometimes fell by the wayside. Nations often convicted as pirates those calling themselves privateers, and pirates often tried to call themselves privateers, particularly when caught. Many pirates, such as Stede Bonnet, would go back and forth across this line between legal and illegal piracy. In 1718, Bonnet received a pardon from North Carolina governor Charles Eden and a letter of marque to go privateering against the Spanish. But Bonnet soon returned to illegal piracy and was eventually hanged. On the flip side, Sir Henry Morgan was knighted by England in 1674 after a long and violent career in the Caribbean that arguably was more as a pirate than a privateer.

Privateering, letters of marque, and similar legal devices are to warfare what giving government land and funding to private companies is to building a national rail system in the nineteenth century. They were an attempt by governments to do something on the cheap. The course of progress leads away from such things. Privateering largely ended with the signing of the Declaration of Paris Respecting Maritime Law in 1856 by France, Britain, and other countries in the wake of the Crimean War. The United States, believing it might still have use for privateering, did not sign the treaty, but then abandoned the practice anyway.

Piracy declined when it became more in the interests of the states to squelch it than allow it. As more legitimate trade expanded in the nineteenth century, as opposed to simply shipments of gold, nations withdrew their support for piracy. It was replaced with a web of laws that governs trade between nations and which has made the various eras of globalization possible. In 2009 pirates operating off the coast of Somalia made headlines, but such actions are now rare.

WHY MAILING A LETTER IS EASY

The Universal Postal Union is a product of the great nineteenth-century age of treaties, when the goalposts and sidelines of international trade and commerce were being pounded and painted into place. The people who complain about how useless and unnecessary government is probably don't think about the Universal Postal Union.

Before the Postal Union treaty, nations' postal services had individual bilateral treaties. Often they attempted to keep track of each other's mail, and to charge each other based on how many letters or packages were being sent and where they were going. It was a bookkeeping nightmare. The Universal Postal Union simplified all this. Like a lot of successful agreements, it involved everyone taking the risk that it would all work out, and the system would not be abused. Essentially, everyone agreed to deliver everyone else's mail for free. Some record of flow was kept, so that if, say, France was delivering ten times the amount of mail from the United States as vice versa, then some compensation would be made. But it was much simpler than the old system. The treaty was very successful, helping make possible the world economy that existed a century ago. Even after the invention and installation of the telegraph and telephone, regular mail was the foundation of most communication, and the world depended on it. So a postal treaty was not some obscure thing. These ministers were tinkering with the very gears of commerce.

I'll digress a bit from postal service and its evolution here, to comment on something they illustrate about systems, which is this: they aren't preordained. It is not preordained that we'll end up with Windows or Macintosh, with Intel or Motorola chips, GSM or CDMA cell phone standards, 8½-by-11-inch paper, screws that turn to the right, 110-volt or 220-volt electricity, alternating or direct current, Beta or VHS videotape, QWERTY or Dvorak keyboards, to name some of the many, many conflicting standards. One big factor is when government enters the picture. It can either eliminate these conflicts by setting a standard early—something the European Union did with cell phones—or it can come in later to end a destructive fight by picking a winner. But there's nothing to guarantee that the best standard will be set.

Which is why we should all thank British educator, tax reformer, and postal administrator Rowland Hill. It was Hill who invented the adhesive stamp and the practice of calculating postal rates by weight rather than distance. The change drastically simplified the British postal system and was one of a series of reforms that led to enormous increases in the volume of mail. Hill's book *Post Office Reform: Its Importance and Practicability* convinced postal services that distance had little to do with the costs of transporting a letter. This gradually resulted in eliminating charges based on distance, and the army of clerks and procedures necessary to implement them. Hill helped introduce a uniform rate of postage, which was prepaid. Hill's reforms led to the introduction of the "penny post," which allowed someone to mail a letter anywhere in England with an adhesive stamp for one penny for a half ounce. The cheapest price had been four pence and the average price six and a quarter pence. Britain, as the leader in industrialization, was also the leader in developing systems of communication. Hill's reforms were gradually adopted by countries around the world. They simplified the system and allowed it to expand tenfold. Hill did a lot of good for humanity through the boring field of postal mechanics.

The rise of state-supplied postal service can be compared to the emergence of the Internet today. It was a new and vital medium of national and international trade. It can also be compared to the emergence of public water systems in the nineteenth century, which replaced private ones. As with the Internet, the emergence of state postal systems made necessary further developments in international law. I've talked about the Universal Postal Union, and I'll now sketch out the immense body of international law that it became a part of, in comparison to which the postal treaty is as a drop to an ocean.

INTERNATIONAL LAW: ITS ORIGINS AND PRESENT-DAY ROLE

Not long after the start of his Cable News Network in 1980, as it expanded its reach around the globe, Ted Turner banned the term "foreign." From then on, correspondents and anchors would use the word "international." There would be no "foreign desk." There would be "international news." Foreign could conceivably have a jingoistic, xenophobic ring to it. International was polite, corporate, and neutral, if less earthy.

Something similar happened in international law two centuries ago. The term had always been "the law of nations," which conveyed quickly that the law that governed acts at sea or an act between nations was something formed by national governments. I like this term because it portrays the origin of such law in the term. Saying "international law" instead of "law of nations" reminds me of the word "infrastructure" replacing the term "public works." In each case, a vague bureaucratic term replaced a good, simple, descriptive one.

But Jeremy Bentham, the utilitarian philosopher and reformer with whom I often agree, disliked the term "law of nations" for various reasons and promoted the term "international." The term "international" fit better into his framework of utilitarianism. In a chain of logic difficult to follow, he saw the term "law of nations" fitting into an argument that such laws were grounded in "natural law," an argument put forth in the much-read and, by Bentham, much-ridiculed *Blackstone's Commentaries*.[3] This controversy two centuries ago about the raison d'être for international law points to a basic squishiness around international law, even as it becomes more and more important. Some esteemed jurists still argue that it essentially doesn't exist. But before I get into that debate, I'd like to sketch out a basic framework for you of what international law is.

I'd like to, but I warn you in advance that my description of this body of law has large gaps. It's an ocean full of turbulent waters and strange sea monsters, inlets and lagoons, that defy sorting out. The United Nations often figures in, but it is more of an international committee than a world government that one might place at the top of the pyramid. It is telling that at any given moment, most of us could not name a single piece of international law, save for something in the news then, like the Geneva Conventions, which produced the laws against torture. There are those ominous words that slide across a television screen about Interpol pursuing acts of DVD piracy. These more visible laws are just the tip of an iceberg. There are thousands and thousands of international laws, and they can overwhelm even an expert, as Mark Janis acknowledges in his excellent *An Introduction to International Law*.[4] But, here goes.

International law comes from two main sources: First, there are treaties and other specific rules agreed to by nations and usually ratified by a legislature. These are things like the Universal Postal Union, the SALT treaties, the Geneva Conventions, and the rules set by the World Trade Organization. This is written-down law, also called "conventional international law."

Second, there is the unwritten international law, the "customary practices" of nations themselves, which is an international version of common law. But these two bodies of international law, written and unwritten, that based on treaties and that based on custom, intersect and overlap each over. Furthermore, this is just one of several ways of dividing up and analyzing international law.

But let's start with the latter, the unwritten international law, or customary international law. It is a set of rules and practices that emerged over the ages and which has generally become law because courts enforce it. It is a conundrum conceptually, because no sovereign created it, but sovereigns enforce it. One particularly good example of this occurred when the American empire was in an expansionary phase.

In 1898, as a war with Spain over its colonial possession Cuba was just beginning, American warships seized two Spanish fishing boats plying their trade off Cuba. The fishermen had not done anything illegal yet, and in fact did not even know a war had begun. So the question was: did the United States act legally in seizing some fishing boats? The US Supreme Court, in a case known as *The Paquete Habana*, later ruled that the United States had violated something called "customary international law," because it was a long-standing precedent in war that fishing boats were exempted from seizure. So even though there was no written law forbidding the American seizure of the Spanish fishing boats, the Supreme Court ruled there was a precedent against it, and ordered the United States to pay restitution to the fishermen, which it did.

Said the court in the *Paquete Habana* case: "By an ancient usage among civilized nations, beginning centuries ago, and gradually ripening into a rule of international law, coast fishing vessels, pursuing their vocation of catching and bringing in fresh fish, have been recognized as exempt, with their cargoes and crews, from being captured as prize of war." Then the court "proved" the point by citing dozens of precedents over the centuries.[5]

WRITTEN INTERNATIONAL LAW

Written international law is based primarily on treaties, thousands of them. Some of them have in turn produced hundreds or thousands of treaty-based laws. Treaties are essentially contracts between nations. They derive their power from the states themselves. They go back many thousands of years.

"Treaties concluded between 1648 and 1919 fill 226 thick books, between 1920 and 1946 some 205 volumes, and between 1946 and 1978, 1,115 more tomes. The sheer quantity of treaties, more than 20,000, demonstrates their continuing utility in the course of international relations," Janis says.[6]

Some of these treaties create practices or institutions, which in turn take on a life of their own. "Virtually every human activity is to some degree the object of some treaty," says Janis. There are treaties that "assure international postal services, stabilize international monetary relations, set international standards for labor practices, as well as protect patents, fundamental rights, fisheries, diplomats, and women."[7] All these treaties created a need for a set of rules to govern them, and to work out what happens if someone violates them. In the past, this was done basically with a set of rules and practices that were called "the Law of Treaties," but were part of customary international law.

But after World War II, a group of jurists under the International Law Commission of the United Nations worked for thirty years to produce the Law of Treaties, or "Treaty on Treaties," officially called the Vienna Convention on the Law of Treaties. Adopted in 1969, it became an operative law in 1980 after the thirty-fifth nation signed on. The United States never ratified it, but the Treaty has such power that our nation customarily refers to it when looking for a precedent or set of rules to follow. This country's nonratification is an example of its ambivalence toward international law.

PUBLIC AND PRIVATE: THE LAWS OF MONEY AND THE LAWS OF STATECRAFT

You can also divide international law other ways. In addition to written and unwritten, you can separate it into public and private.

Public law is the laws between states regulating their conduct, such as whether it is legal to torture, or whether two nations are at war with each other. It's often what we think of when we think of international law.

Private law governs the conduct of business, such as whether a seller of computers can sell them in a particular nation, and what happens if they are stolen, and whether he needs to pay a tariff.

But the two spheres are often not so cleanly separated. And they can both emerge from written and unwritten international law.

When it comes to private international law, or laws regulating commerce and trade between private citizens of different countries, there is a reliance on a wide body of international law relating to commerce, going back many centuries. As in all avenues of the law, the sheer number and density of commercial international laws are staggering.

Private, or business, law goes back centuries to when traders in leaky wooden ships, transporting grain or treasure from one side of the Adriatic Sea to another, needed some sort of common set of rules to abide by and refer to. It was in the interest of both parties, whether they lived in Venice or Egypt, to have such a thing. Over time—in the Middle Ages, in fact—there developed the *lex mercatoria*, which means "the law merchant." It was essentially the common law of international trade, meaning a group of habits and customary procedures and codes of conduct that had been generally accepted. It often functioned in its initial centuries as a group of laws privately subscribed to, like those of a trade association, rather than of a nation or international treaty. The merchants had their own courts. In England, they were known as "pie powder courts," which were arbitration courts to resolve trade disputes.[8] The *lex mercatoria* developed in the Italian city-states in the twelfth century, and I suspect Venice had a role in creating it, given this commercial empire's influence. As history went on, this *lex mercatoria* was gradually replaced by a more formal set of rules, although the *lex mercatoria*, like common law in common law nations, was still referred to sometimes when decisions were made.

One way to make sense of international commercial law is to see it as an outgrowth of the internal laws governing trade *within* a nation, which were then extended, like linked hands, to create a body of international law. These are sets of rules such as the Uniform Commercial Code in the United States, the Sale of Goods Act in Great Britain, and the Code of Commerce in France. Although these codes are different, they exhibit many similarities and common principles. Their extension, with some mechanism for resolving differences, becomes a basis for international commercial law.

The instruments that function to extend these national rules are treaties like the United Nations Convention on Contracts for the International Sale of Goods, which was passed in 1980 in Vienna, and supervised by UNCITRAL, which is the United Nations Commission on International Trade Law. The US Senate unanimously approved this treaty in 1986. The Senate failed to ratify the predecessors of the 1980s agreement, which were written in 1964 and called the Uniform Law on International Sale of Goods and the Uniform Law on the Formation of Contracts for the International Sale of Goods. They were the product of more than thirty years of work, Janis says, by an organization with the acronym of UNIDROIT, dating back to the League of Nations.

It again strikes me how much we owe people who labor for lifetimes in obscure, but important, areas. The lawyers and diplomats drafting these treaties did not get rich, and were unlikely to be paid off by some big company hoping to profit from the treaty. Besides UNIDROIT and UNCITRAL, there are also the Hague Conference on Private International Law, the International Maritime Committee, and the International Chamber of Commerce. These and other bodies have worked to "codify international private law."[9]

The list goes on. There are the treaties and laws that allow ships to pass unmolested in international waters, or "friendship, commerce and navigation" treaties between nations. They date back centuries and include elements of the Jay Treaty of 1794 between Great Britain and the United States. But they are still used now, and the United States is party to many of them.[10]

All this is just a summary, and the sheer magnitude of international law, and its lack of clear hierarchical structure, overwhelm even established legal experts, says Janis.

"Within the broad ambit of the law of international trade are a legion of subjects too vast to be any more than merely counted here," Janis says. "Each constitutes a legal specialty of considerable complexity, importance, and employment. There are, for example, international securities law, international antitrust law, international tax law, and international investment law."[11]

All this shows that governments create international trade or stifle it through the laws they make or support. We haven't even begun to get into the World Trade Organization, the World Bank, or the International Monetary Fund, the three heavyweights. They are the most visible and disputed of international institutions governing and shaping trade, but they are not the most elemental.

The body of law being fashioned by the European Union is becoming "the most developed" in the world, says Janis. The laws governing trade within the EU, Janis reminds us, are transnational or supranational. From a positivist perspective, there is no sovereign to enforce these laws. They exist in the ether.

"European economic law has . . . become so effective that some have, probably mistakenly, come to question whether EEC [EU] law remains international law or has instead become a kind of European municipal law."[12]

I'll hit a few other high points.

There is a kind of private court system that enforces international private law. There are also private "arbitration boards" that enforce rules, much as was done in the Middle Ages with the *lex mercatoria*. Often it is agreed to in a contract that a dispute will be resolved by such and such private arbitration board. The biggest is the International Court of Arbitration, which is sponsored by the International Chamber of Commerce. Since its creation in 1922, it has decided thousands of cases. These private arbitration boards have friendly relations with states and are sometimes supported by them in various ways— which again raises the question of what is private and what is public. This array of institutions and rules shows that the reality of international commerce is far from the simplistic notions of "globalization" and a "flat world." The world is not flat. It is a dense forest of rules and regulations, and if the path sometimes appears to be free and easy, it is only because nations have formed and kept clear such paths.

PUBLIC INTERNATIONAL LAW

The last time I was in Holland, I took the train to the city of The Hague, and went and stared at the grand, vaguely Victorian brick building, known as the "Peace Palace," that houses the International Court of Justice. It is perhaps the premiere institution representing public international law, the flip side of private international law.

Public law is the laws governing the conduct between states by states. As with commercial law, there are institutions that enforce it in addition to the courts of nations. The International Court of Justice was formed in 1945 by a UN charter. This court hears relatively few cases every year. They mostly are disputes between nations. While some are high profile, many are not. Does Senegal have the obligation to extradite someone to Belgium under a treaty previously signed, for example, was a case in 2009.

Tellingly, the United States withdrew in 1986 from the treaty that created the International Court of Justice. The United States now only recognizes the court's jurisdiction when it chooses to. The United States has usually been more sympathetic to commercial international law than public international law, although it has at times been hostile to both. Those who fear the loss of sovereignty are more comfortable allowing foreign bodies to prosecute someone for copying a DVD illegally than for torturing someone.

Despite the US withdrawal from the treaty in 1986, much of the pressure for the International Court of Justice came from the United States, as well as Great Britain, two nations with a long tradition of having the law resolve disputes. An important precedent was contained in the Jay Treaty in 1794, when Great Britain and the United States, among other things, set up an arbitration method to resolve future disputes. Another important precedent was from 1872, when an ad hoc tribunal composed of judges from five nations decided that Great Britain had violated neutrality by building warships for the Confederacy, and ordered it to pay about $10 million to the United States. It did so. A copy of the receipt is still framed inside the prime minister's residence at 10 Downing Street in London.

The reach of Law extends even outside the earth's atmosphere. The Outer Space Treaty, formally known as the "Treaty on Principles Governing the Activities of States in the Exploration and Use of Outer Space, Including the Moon and Other Celestial Bodies," went into effect in 1967 and codifies conduct in the heavens. It is signed by most countries on earth, and among other things, prohibits countries from putting nuclear weapons in outer space or on the planets, and rules that no one nation can claim a planet or heavenly body as its own. We may snicker at the treaty's existence, but it may very well have helped prevent a land grab in the heavens, or may do so in the future.

THE MAN WHO WASN'T THERE, OR DOES INTERNATIONAL LAW EXIST?

There has been debate for several centuries as to whether international law, written or unwritten, public or private, exists at all. Scholars know that people and institutions follow international law, but are uncertain of its foundations.

"Why then—if international law is so historically legitimate and ethically relevant, so doctrinally legitimate and functionally necessary—do so many people (including lawyers, policy makers and scholars) believe it does not exist?" asked David J. Bederman in *The Spirit of International Law*.[13]

The conundrum of international law is that there exists no state to back it up. It is not "positive law," said the famous legal scholar John Austin, who came up with the theory of "legal positivism," writing in 1832. Austin, who was a fan of Jeremy Bentham, viewed law as a command, and to be valid, it is issued by a commander, that is, a sovereign state. That state can be a democracy or a dictatorship, but it is the presence of the state, the authority, that makes a wish a law.

"Laws proper, or properly so called, are commands; laws which are not commands, are laws improper or improperly so called," said Austin in the opening lines of his influential book, *The Province of Jurisprudence Determined*.[14]

Early on, international law derived its power from religious rules. If you broke the treaty you signed, God would get you. The religious overtone was, interestingly, reminiscent of conventional common law.[15]

The pope has played the role of international cop, or a supranational authority. In medieval times or in the Renaissance, you could turn to the pope if a party in your opinion was not living up to a contract. The pontiff, in turn, could excommunicate the offender, making it instantly okay to rob his ships without fear of punishment.

Natural law also pokes up its misshapen head. There is considerable sentiment over the centuries of people saying, basically, that the rules and laws governing trade or warfare are simply codifying what is "natural." I find this the refuge of, if not scoundrels, at least lazy thinkers.

Conservatives are more skeptical of international law, while leftists are more skeptical of domestic law. When it comes to global law, conservatives tend to say that "law is simply a mask for power, and in the end power prevails." When it comes to domestic law, the Left says that.[16]

With regular law there exists an authority, the Peoria police, the attorney general of Illinois, the FBI, just to name a few, who will make you follow the law if you do not.

But with international law, what authority exists? Who are the subjects of international law, and who is the master? Usually a nation-state enforces international law. A New York court can prosecute someone for violating an international law. In part because of this, there has been a lot of work put into defining what a nation-state is. Janis says that "within the ambit of international law, a state is understood to be composed of four essential elements: a defined territory, a permanent population, a government, and a capacity to conduct international relations."[17] There are also international courts, tribunals, and arbitration boards, as previously mentioned.

As I wander among this dense thicket of laws and institutions, I am reminded that we are, in many ways, like children. We believe ourselves acting independently when we mail a letter to that summer love in Paris. We have no idea that this simple act is made possible by years of work by long-dead men, laboring a century and a half ago. I am reminded of John Maynard Keynes's line that "Practical men, who believe themselves to be quite exempt from any intellectual influence, are usually the slaves of some defunct economist."[18]

My point in discussing all of this is to remind us all that there are rules, and that *we make the rules*! This isn't to say it would be easy to go out and change, say, the Universal Postal Union. But we can influence such treaties as easily as we can an American presidential race. It's clear that international law is here to stay. It would be good if we would recognize its existence and actively seek to manage it for the public good.

LOOKING FORWARD: MAKING BETTER MARKETS

MAKING BETTER MARKETS

Q—What is your definition of Design?
A—A plan for arranging elements in such a way as best to
accomplish a particular purpose.
CHARLES EAMES, DESIGNER OF THE EAMES CHAIR
AND MANY OTHER OBJECTS

IN THIS BOOK, I have endeavored to show that market economies don't just happen, they are made. They are designed.

If one accepts this analysis, then several implied prescriptions come to the fore. First of all, if we are designing markets, then we should do so *actively*. Their contours and shapes should not be left to judges and lawyers, or to lobbyists, or to regulators, but the public and the public's servants, their elected leaders, should be the fashioners, with expert advice, of course. The designing of our markets, in other words, should be an active part of the democratic political process.

Following the outline of this book, I see six or seven areas where there is room for improvements.

First of all, property rights themselves. The expression "rights" is problematic, seeming to be a designation for something that falls from the sky, rather than something that is a privilege or a social good. Which, of course, owning property is. Like it or not, God does not grant the right to own property. Governments do, those collective institutions. That being the case, the right to own property, being created by the collective, necessarily comes with responsibilities and limitations as well as privileges. Even if we retain the phrase "property rights," there should be more active debate about how property can be owned, what the limits of it are, how it can be passed from one generation to the next, what restrictions can be put on its sale, the extent to which one owner binds the hands of future owners, and so forth. While the courts may interpret the laws, they should not be the first in line in making them. The legislature should do that, backed by an informed public. Institutions such as the Lincoln Institute of Land Policy in Cambridge, Massachusetts, which studies and evaluates the different methods of "land tenure," would be of assistance here.

The role of judges and legislatures brings us to the second order of business, the common law. I cannot expect, and would not hope, that the great edifice of the common law, consisting of thousands upon thousands of precedents, could or would be thrown into the dustbin. But the legislatures, those instruments of the people, can assert themselves more forcefully over the common law, converting it into a servant rather than a master.

Let's move on to some of the other building blocks of modern markets, corporations and intellectual property.

Corporations, as I have shown in this book, are creations and instruments of the state. They are minirepublics, pieces of the state with special powers, broken off from the whole and given free will. I would not change this. Corporations are a wonderful invention that has helped create much wealth. They are instruments of creativity. But they should be our servants, not our masters. Ridiculous assertions that corporations are "persons" should simply be invalidated, difficult though this may be. Congress should do this. Such a declaration could be part of a National Companies Act, which set national standards and rules for the conduct and powers of corporations. A US National Companies Act would help set global standards, because the United States is so big a player here. For example, a National Companies Act could state that corporations created by other nations could not do business in the United States unless certain rules were followed. This would end the absurd habit of corporations seeking out places with lax incorporation rules, such as the Cayman Islands.

Much of the time corporations these days are producing not shoes, steel, or stationery, but bits and bytes, the language of digital media, as encoded in computer software, movies, television shows, music, and even words themselves, of which you the reader may be partaking in digital form at this very moment. This leads us to talk about intellectual property—patents, copyrights, and trademarks. On this subject, debate is actually going on, publicly, over how intellectual property should be fashioned. Judges and legislatures are debating whether one can patent genes, the building blocks of life. There are proposals to shift copyright protection toward methods that suit an age where thousands, if not millions, of copies of something can be distributed instantly and virtually without cost. Ways should be found that harness the power of such communications infrastructure, that give people more access to culture, while still reimbursing the creators of such content. The debates over the Google Books project, which has digitized millions of books, a good portion of all that have ever been written, illustrate this. Still, for the most part, the public components of these debates are like water made turbulent by large fish fighting deep underwater, with their fins just occasionally breaking water. We can do more. There should be more specific acknowledgment that patents, copyrights, and other forms of intellectual property are social goods that should change to suit the changing needs of the public. Copyrights, established by printers five hundred years ago, don't have to be the vehicle for compensating authors when words are transmitted digitally. Converting these social goods into inalienable and eternal "rights," society be damned, is a perversion.

From here I turn to the physical form of our world, our streets and the homes that sit upon them, our squares and plazas, as well as the trees and fields that surround them. As with laws and legal instruments that make markets possible, so, too, our physical environment did not just happen. Our cities and towns and the spaces between them are designed, most actively by the major instruments of transportation that government lays down. I would like to have a more active conversation about how our cities and neighborhoods are designed. I would like us to get away from prejudicial use of words like "subsidies," which pop up in transportation debates. As far as I can tell, transportation—roads, bridges, train lines, ports, airports, and the other related instruments— is subsidized everywhere and in every nation, just as education is. The reason is that countries with the best transportation and the best education tend to prosper. It makes sense to subsidize them. We should not debate *whether* to subsidize a road or a train line, but talk about what the effects will be, and whether they are worth it. It is our good luck on this earth to live in the physical world, being able to walk, stroll, ride, and drive in it. Fashioning this physical world, through a democratic process, is one of the great benefits of living in a free country.

The debates over education tend to turn on both how our children should be taught and what they should be taught. We talk about charter schools versus conventional neighborhood public schools, as well as creationism versus evolution, and that's all well and good in a democracy. But along with concern about test scores, I would like to see more recognition of the importance in education of forging us into a unified nation, with a common culture and language. I am carrying E. D. Hirsch's water here, and this may seem like a sideline to the central theme of this book. But the fact is market economies are more accessible and more equitable when there is a common culture and language, a lingua franca. As a nation we still benefit from having our citizens possess a common body of knowledge, encompassing our history, government, and literature, along with an accepted method of how to speak and write English, which should be the primary language. This will help not only our markets, but our democracy, function more fully. In not recognizing this, many liberals are at fault. Their view of the world resists all hierarchy, even one necessary to a more fully functioning and equitable nation.

After education, I turn to the great global arena in which so much of commerce functions today, where computers and phones designed in California are produced in China and then bought in Indonesia. Not since the late nineteenth century has global commerce been so intertwined. This state of affairs ended badly, with World War I. Here's hoping that some better future awaits the current world.

Our increasingly wired economies rest not only on underwater fiber optic cables, orbiting satellites, and global software, but on the political agreements that have made those possible, and encouraged them. A thick web of treaties and protocols, promulgated and overseen by the World Trade Organization and other bodies, makes it possible for contracts to be enforced between Spain and Brazil, for ships to arrive safely in one port or another, and for a call center in Mumbai to function effectively with an insurance company in Peoria. They even rest on still-functioning nineteenth-century agreements, like the Universal Postal Union. And these global protocols should be the subject of political discourse, as much as the next presidential election is. They should not be left to bureaucrats and business officials who craft them for private purposes, not public ones. The broad parameters and priorities can be decided on and set by the public.

Finally, we should recognize markets and capitalism for what they are, not objects bound by physics-like laws that need to be learned and used, but creations that can be experimented with and made into an infinite number of forms, for an infinite number of purposes. I have tried to show this with my chapter on cooperatives. Although I admire cooperatives, and think them worth emulating, I hold them up more as an example of the possibilities of how capitalism and its institutions can be experimented with, played with, to produce different results. We should recognize the extraordinary creativity that can be put into the design of markets. We can reshape our systems of copyrights, patents, property rights, corporations, and other tools, as well as invent new ones, to meet a variety of ends. Perhaps there should be a major offered in universities, a doctorate of markets, where the best and brightest could actively study the ways we could design our markets. Once upon a time, this would simply have been called "political economy." While the term still exists, it is more of a historical artifact. In a more enlightened world, it could serve as a banner to lead us forward into new choices, rather than just a descriptor of ones made.

MY OWN STORY: A CIRCUITOUS JOURNEY

WHEN I WAS A SOPHOMORE at Carnegie Mellon University in Pittsburgh in 1978, I sat on a grassy hillside on a sunny spring or fall day and protested the contemplated reinstatement of the draft, wearing a T-shirt that said "Uncle Sam Doesn't Want You—Libertarians Against the Draft." Yes, at that time, I was a reasonably devout Libertarian. I had gone through high school in Virginia Beach reading science fiction by Robert Heinlein and political philosophy by Ayn Rand and slowly being drawn into their beguiling universes. I saw the essential task in life and political philosophy as a sweeping away of structures, of encumbrances, of prohibitions. Why should government or anyone compel anyone else to do anything? Life should be governed by a series of voluntary exchanges between free individuals. To a sophomore in college, this was an incredibly appealing philosophy.

But I progressed. I gradually realized that life is all about structures. This desire to sweep away structures is not only unrealistic, it's not even sane. It misunderstands how things work. The capitalistic economy that people like Milton Friedman, Rand, and Alan Greenspan worship was built in part by voluntary exchanges by individuals, but only within structures that had been centuries in the making, most of them by government. The political philosophy of Libertarianism was at its core adolescent. It was the philosophy of a teenager who doesn't respect or see the work of others.

After college various circumstances and choices led me to become a journalist. For me, it was a wonderful profession to find, because parts of myself that did not fit in well with other professions, particularly the probing, seeking part, were actually a plus in journalism. I had by then, in my mid-twenties, tried on the roles of chef, musician, history teacher, Spanish teacher, political economist, massage therapist, and probably a few more, and this broad life experience was also good training for journalism. This life experience also included living in Spain for two years, which helped me see the United States from a more objective vantage point.

After graduate school at Columbia Journalism School, and after being hired by my hometown newspaper, *The Virginian-Pilot*, in Norfolk, I initially was a political reporter, and wanted to become a foreign correspondent. But I found myself drawn to urban planning and cities, and writing about community and what builds it. I was lucky that *The Virginian-Pilot* allowed me to focus on what interested me. The great thing about being a reporter is that you generally get out into the world and talk to people. Reporters tend to be less ideological than the politicians they write about because of this. They are faced with conflicting evidence all the time. On the other hand, many newspaper reporters tend to be less interested in ideas. They place the facts they find in conventional containers.

THE CITY AS MACHINE

Life to me breaks down into a series of moments. One for me was standing in a few inches of water in someone's yard in a suburban section of Virginia Beach. I was standing there because I was writing a story, if memory serves, about the failure of the city's storm water management system. Until that moment I hadn't realized cities had storm water systems. I suddenly visualized a series of pipes running underground, siphoning off water and disposing of it in the right places. Even a very spread-out city like Virginia Beach, a flat schmear of about 500,000 people, had such a system. Cities, I realized right then, are machines. They are not just organic accumulations of houses and businesses. A home was not a man and his castle; it was an addition to a mechanized system, on which it depended for its existence. For it wasn't just storm water management that a house and the family within it relied on. They relied on the roads to get to their home, and to work. They relied on an electrical system for light, on a sewage system to dispose of their waste. They relied on schools to teach their children, and fire departments and police to protect them. Without this larger system, I realized, this family was as helpless as a flower ripped from the soil and thrown onto concrete, condemned to shrivel and die.

These realizations led me for a while to being a sort of quasi–political philosopher at *The Virginian-Pilot*, in between covering Norfolk City Council meetings.

"[W]e depend on the most obvious manifestation of 'country'—the system of laws and institutions we call government—to make our lives work," I said in an essay that was displayed on the top of the Sunday commentary page on February 25, 1996.

> We owe its maintenance a debt. If we only take from it, we erode our safety and security and those of future generations. . . . By government, . . . I'm talking about a court system, laws that define acceptable behavior and police who enforce them, a money supply and a deed room at City Hall that keeps track of who owns what. These fundamentals, and their efficient and fair operations, support our lives, from the homes we own up to the functioning of the New York Stock Exchange. . . . These essentials do not run on automatic pilot.

> Many who came of age in the 1960s value personal growth through work, art, or spirituality—painting a great picture, discovering the self through meditation or getting the right mixture of home, work and family. To many of them, a devotion to country or government symbolizes only the blind devotion to the powers-that-be that led thousands of young men to travel to Vietnam and die for a cause of dubious worth or possibility. . . . Others in recent times glorify individual economic achievement—the rich man or woman who has created a computer company or successfully played the stock market. They believe if everyone worked hard to get rich all common problems would be solved by Adam Smith's invisible hand. To these devotees of the capitalist system, government only symbolizes intrusion into the "free market," which they fail to recognize does not operate without a functioning system of laws and institutions below it.

> I have a home, a job that pays me to think and write about stuff, and a system of businesses around me where I can spend what I earn. As I drive around town or enjoy a nice meal somewhere, it dawns on me that I owe an enormous debt to whomever constructed the society I live in. Any individual achievement or success on my part is only possible because I live in a society that has allowed me to compete with my ability to write a story, rather than my ability to fight or instill fear. I owe this system something in return.

As I read these words almost fifteen years later, I can see that I'm groping here, trying to figure out what is the exact relationship between the individual and the state. I'm still groping. This book is one result. Thinking about the nature of cities led me to write my first book, *How Cities Work: Suburbs, Sprawl, and the Roads Not Taken* (University of Texas Press, 2000), which had a specific chapter, called "The Master Hand," out of which this present book grew. The chapter was about how governments build both places and markets with their decisions.

One step on my intellectual journey was a Loeb Fellowship at Harvard University in 1999–2000, which I did before my book *How Cities Work: Suburbs, Sprawl, and the Roads Not Taken* came out, but after it was written. While there, I investigated my theory of markets, and found there were others thinking along the same lines. That gave me confidence. Over at the well-maintained Harvard Business School, with its green lawn and good food, I audited "The Economic Strategies of Nations," taught by Professor Bruce Scott. At the Kennedy School of Government, I audited "Varieties of Capitalism," taught by Professor Pepper Culpepper, which included a weeklong visit to the École Nationale D'Administration in Paris, the elite state school. At the Law School in the ornate old grey-stone H. R. Richardson Building, I audited "One Way or Many?," which was structured as a weekly debate between Roberto Unger, a law professor who promoted the idea of markets as constructed and experimental, and economist and professor Jeffrey Sachs, a promoter then of "the Washington consensus" of open markets as the path to prosperity for developing nations. Also at the Law School I audited "Perspectives in American Law," which led one through the fundamentals of the American legal system. All this was in addition to studying urban design and architecture within the Graduate School of Design, where the Loeb Fellowship was housed.

Since then, it's taken me more than a decade to get a book out about these ideas. It's taken so long because I struggled to find the right container for them. I opted for the approach of delving into the history of how the component parts of our society, which together make our economic life possible, have been constructed. If I could show people how markets are made, and learn more myself, I could help shift the national conversation from how markets should be regulated to how they should be designed. We can design markets to create a better, more just, and more prosperous society. Market economies are political institutions. And given this, it is appropriate and just that they serve the society that made them.

ACKNOWLEDGMENTS

As with any project that took so long to conceive and complete, countless people and institutions helped me. My biggest worry concerns the many and important ones I will forget to name. In advance, I apologize.

I first want to thank my longtime friend Robert Clark. This book could be described as the evolution of a conversation that began with him when we were undergraduates at Carnegie Mellon University more than thirty years ago.

My agent Jennifer Carlson of Dunow, Carlson & Lerner was patient and insightful in helping me shape the proposals that led to this book, as well as reviewing much of the final text.

I worked in and with several different libraries on this book. They include the Allen Room, Humanities and Social Sciences Library, New York City Public Library system, Fifth Avenue and 42nd Street, New York City. They also include the Brooklyn Public Library, not far from my home, and the libraries of the New Jersey Institute of Technology, where I have taught. I used the libraries of Harvard University. Most extensively, I used the many libraries of my alma mater Columbia University, where I attended the Graduate School of Journalism. I used Butler Library, the Business and Economics Library, the Law Library, and the Avery Architectural and Fine Arts Library.

Many people helped shape this book with their conversations, or in reviewing chapters. They include Mike Wallace, Bruce Scott, Robert Fishman, Gerald Frug, Harvey Jacobs, Robert Clark, and Rebecca Tushnet, among others.

My good friend Jim Crutchfield, an excellent lawyer, historian, and literary scholar, was very valuable with his suggestions about common law as well as assorted other subjects.

Lee Egerstrom, a former reporter for the St. Paul Pioneer Press and now a fellow at Minnesota 2020, was particularly helpful in sending me books and papers on cooperatives free of charge, and shepherding me all over Minneapolis and its peripheries.

Peter Dougherty, director of Princeton University Press, donated a boxful of books from his series, the Economic History of the Western World, after my old contact Larry Sabato from the University of Virginia introduced us.

Randy Swearer, who has been the patron of this book and my first,

How Cities Work, was invaluable in his constant reassurance and continued belief in the value of this project.

Jim Burr of the University of Texas Press has always been a pleasure to work with and had excellent editorial suggestions.

Lawrence Krubner contributed many notes and thoughts that helped the genesis of this project.

My old friends Andy and Caroline Vaaler put me up on my trip to study cooperatives in Minneapolis.

My colleagues at the Regional Plan Association in New York City, where I am a senior fellow, have been greatly supportive. I did much of the editing of the manuscript in my office there.

And finally I thank my wife Kristin Barlow, whose love and support were even more valuable than her excellent editorial skills.

INTRODUCTION

1. The quote about "one gigantic potted plant" is from my friend and colleague Charles McKinney, Principal Urban Designer for the city of New York.

2. Thanks to my good friend Robert Clark for this analogy.

3. Gerald Frug, telephone interview with author, March 20, 2008.

4. Richard Posner, "How I Became a Keynesian," *New Republic*, September 23, 2009, http://www.tnr.com/article/how-i-became-keynesian.

CHAPTER 1

1. Bruce Scott, *The Concept of Capitalism* (Heidelberg and New York: Springer Verlag, 2009).

2. Keith Roberts, *The Origins of Business, Money and Markets* (New York: Columbia University Press, 2011), p. 9.

3. Ibid., p. 66.

4. R. H. Coase, *The Firm, the Market, and the Law* (Chicago: University of Chicago Press, 1988), p. 9.

5. Max Weber, *General Economic History* (orig. 1927; New Brunswick, NJ: Transaction Publishers, 1995), p. 221.

6. Market Historical Commission, City of Seattle, "Pike Place Market Historical Commission: Revised Guidelines," http://pikeplacemarket.s3.amazonaws.com/PDFs/Applications/pikeplace_guidelines.pdf.

7. Nassim Nicholas Taleb, *The Black Swan: The Impact of the Highly Improbable*, 2nd ed. (New York: Random House, 2010), p. 184.

8. Eric D. Beinhocker, *The Origin of Wealth: Evolution, Complexity and the Radical Remaking of Economics* (Boston: Harvard Business School Press, 2006), pp. 32, 33, 39.

9. As it happens, my own undergraduate major from Carnegie Mellon University in Pittsburgh was in social science, with a concentration in "political economy." So the term does survive, although it is not widely used.

10. Michael Perelman, *The End of Economics* (Oxford: Taylor and Francis, 1996), p. 16.

11. Taleb, *Black Swan*, p. 184.

12. Lewis Mumford, "The Highway and the City," in *The Highway and the City* (New York: Harcourt, Brace & World, 1963), pp. 234–246. Title essay first published in 1958 in *The New Yorker*.

13. http://www.templeton.org/market.

14. Neil Postman, *Conscientious Objections: Stirring Up Trouble about Language, Technology and Education* (New York: Vintage, 1992), p. 93.

15. John Lanchester, "Outsmarted: High Finance vs. Human Nature," *The New Yorker*, June 1, 2009, p. 87.

16. John McMillan, *Reinventing the Bazaar: A Natural History of Markets* (New York: W. W. Norton, 2002), p. 8.

17. Lewis Mumford, *The City in History* (New York: Harcourt, Brace & World, 1961), p. 403.

18. Tony Judt, "Captive Minds," *New York Review of Books*, September 30, 2010, p. 8.

19. http://www.alternet.org/story/18147/free_market_debunked/.

20. Exchange taken from my class notes.

21. Sachs went on to write several well-regarded books about ending global poverty. He moved from Harvard to Columbia University, where he founded and leads the Earth Institute, a think tank dedicated to fighting big global problems from poverty to global warming. I attempted to interview Sachs about how and whether his thinking had changed since 1999, but we were unable to arrange a date for an interview.

CHAPTER 2

1. Harvey Jacobs, "U.S. Private Property Rights in International Perspective," in *Property Rights and Land Policies*, ed. Gregory K. Ingram and Yu-Hung Hong (Cambridge, MA: Lincoln Institute of Land Policy, 2009), p. 55.

2. Nicholas Mercuro and Warren J. Samuels, eds., *The Fundamental Interrelationships between Government and Property* (Stamford, CT: Jai Press, 1999), p. 3.

3. Michael Moran and Maurice Wright, "Introduction," in *The Market and the State*, ed. Moran and Wright (New York: St. Martin's Press, 1991), p. xii.

4. Mercuro and Samuels, *Fundamental Interrelationships*, p. 3.

5. Theodore F. T. Plucknett, *A Concise History of the Common Law* (Rochester, NY: Lawyers Co-Operative Publishing Company, 1929), p. 12.

6. Andro Linklater, *Measuring America: How an Untamed Wilderness Shaped the United States and Fulfilled the Promise of Democracy* (New York: Walker and Company, 2002).

7. Ibid., p. 8.

8. John McDonald, "The Economy of England at the Time of the Norman Conquest" (Santa Clara, CA: EH.net, Economic History Association, 2010), http://eh.net/encyclopedia/article/mcdonald.domesday.

9. Harvey Jacobs, from e-mail to author on June 9, 2009, following up on a telephone interview in January 2008. Jacobs holds a joint appointment as professor in the Department of Urban and Regional Planning and the Gaylord Nelson Institute for Environmental Studies at the University of Wisconsin–Madison.

10. Linklater, *Measuring America*, p. 11.

11. Bernard H. Siegan, *Property Rights: From Magna Carta to the Fourteenth Amendment* (New Brunswick, NJ: Social Philosophy and Policy Foundation and Transaction Publishers, 2001).

12. James W. Ely, *Guardian of Every Other Right: The Constitutional History of Property Rights* (New York: Oxford University Press, 1998), p. 10.

13. James Foreman-Peck, *A History of the World Economy: International Relations since 1850* (London: Harvester/Wheatsheaf, 1995), p. xiv.

14. Ely, *Guardian of Every Other Right*, p. 10.

15. Linklater, *Measuring America*, p. 47.

16. Ely, *Guardian of Every Other Right*, p. 10.

CHAPTER 3

1. Matthew Hale, *The History and Analysis of the Common Law of England* (Union, NJ: Law Book Exchange Ltd, 2000). Hale lived from 1609 to 1676.

2. Richard Hamm, "Introduction," in *Essays on English Law and the American Experience*, ed. Elizabeth A. Cawthon and David E. Narrett (University of Texas at Arlington, 1994), p. 4.

3. Peter Baker and Neil Lewis, "Sotomayor Vows 'Fidelity to the Law' as Hearings Start," *New York Times*, July 14, 2009.

4. Legal Information Institute, "Eggshell Skull Rule" (Cornell University Law School), http://topics.law.cornell.edu/wex/eggshell_skull_rule.

5. Theodore F. T. Plucknett, *A Concise History of the Common Law* (Rochester, NY: Lawyers Co-Operative Publishing Company, 1929), p. 4.

6. Ibid., Chapter 2.

7. G. R. C. Davis, trans., *Magna Carta*, rev. ed. (British Library, 1989), http://www.fordham.edu/halsall/source/magnacarta.html.

8. Bernard H. Siegan, *Property Rights: From Magna Carta to the Fourteenth Amendment* (New Brunswick, NJ: Social Philosophy and Policy Foundation and Transaction Publishers, 2001), Chapter 2.

9. Plucknett, *Concise History*, p. 24.

10. Ibid., p. 44.

11. Ibid., p. 49.

12. Ibid., p. 63.

13. Hamm, "Introduction," p. 4.

14. William Blackstone, *Commentaries on the Laws of England* (Avalon Project: Documents in Law, History and Diplomacy; Lillian Goldman Law Library, Yale Law School), http://avalon.law.yale.edu/subject_menus/blackstone.asp.

15. Howard Schweber, *The Creation of American Common Law, 1850–1880: Technology, Politics and the Construction of Citizenship* (New York: Cambridge University Press, 2004), p. 2. From review by Richard Dagger, *American Historical Review* 109, no. 5 (December 2004): 1583–1584, http://www.jstor.org/pss/10.1086/530995.

16. Oliver Wendell Holmes, *The Common Law* (orig. 1881; Boston: Back Bay Books, 1963), p. 5.

17. Ibid., pp. 2, 5, 3.

18. *Pollock v. Farmers Loan and Trust Company* (US Supreme Court, 1895), *ABA Journal* 39 (June 1953): 473.

19. Salem Witchcraft Trials, 1692, http://www.law.umkc.edu/faculty/projects/ftrials/salem/SALEM.HTM.

20. Plucknett, *Concise History*, p. 105.

21. Ibid.

22. Thomas Jefferson, *Notes on the State of Virginia* (orig. 1787; Richmond: J. W. Randolph, 1853), pp. 169–173.

CHAPTER 4

1. Bill Oemichen (president, Cooperative Network), interview with author at Minneapolis convention in November 2009.

2. Jan Eliassen, e-mail to author, January 10, 2009.

3. The Co-operative Group, website, http://www.co-operative.coop/aboutus/. See also http://en.wikipedia.org/wiki/The_Co-operative_Group.

4. Lee Egerstrom, *Make No Small Plans: A Cooperative Revival for Rural America* (Rochester, MN: Lone Oak Press, 1994), p. 101.

5. Coincidentally, I lived in the village of Oñate near the town of Mondragon in 1982–1983 while living in Spain as a young adult just out of college. Mondragon was just over a mountain. Even then I was hearing talk about the successful and fair form of business called a cooperative being done there. But I lacked the interest and skill to investigate further at the time.

6. Mondragon Annual Report 2010, http://www.mondragon-corporation.com/ CAS/Magnitudes-Econ%C3%B3micas/Informe-anual.aspx.

7. Lawrence Mishel, "CEO-to-Worker Pay Imbalance Grows" (Washington, DC: Economic Policy Institute, June 21, 2006), http://www.epi.org/economic_snapshots/ entry/webfeatures_snapshots_20060621/.

8. I toured Desjardins's Victorian house, now a museum, in Lévis, across the river from Quebec City. It was moving somehow to see the simple home.

9. http://www.landolakes.com/ourCompany/LandOLakesHistory.cfm.

10. Based on interview at convention with Todd Rosvold, director of Pulaski Chase Cooperative. "We keep the markets honest," Rosvold said.

11. Apple Computers, for example, has the ability to set prices for its products at a high profit level, because its products are unique. In contrast, Dell Computers has little ability to set its prices at high levels, because its products are not unique. Thus, it is said that Dell lacks "market power."

12. There are multiple sources documenting executive pay levels and disparities in total wealth. They include the AFL-CIO's "Executive Paywatch" (http://paywatch .org) and *Forbes Magazine*'s "CEO Compensation" report (http://www.forbes.com/ lists/2010/12/boss-10_CEO-Compensation_CompTotDisp.html).

13. https://www.chsinc.com/portal/server.pt/community/2investors/351.

14. Because the town owns the team, the team cannot move elsewhere at the drop of a hat. The owner can't extort a new stadium out of a city, because the owner *is* the city, essentially. (The exact mechanism is that a nonprofit company owns the team, and thousands of individual citizens own the nonprofit.) This unusual structure dates back to the team's early history before World War II, when some community leaders took ownership of the team when it was in danger of collapsing financially. The NFL now expressly prohibits community ownership of teams (the Packers are grandfathered) precisely because it would subordinate football to the interest of the communities, not the financial interests of the owners. Congress should require the NFL to do away with this prohibition in exchange for its current exemption from some antitrust rules.

15. Egerstrom, *Make No Small Plans*, p. 114.

16. Florence Fabricant, "Butter Bites Back," *New York Times*, March 22, 1995.

17. Egerstrom, *Make No Small Plans*, p. 35.

CHAPTER 5

1. Alex Marshall, trip to Park City, Utah, January 21, 2008.

2. Benjamin Craig, "History of the Sundance Film Festival," *Sundance: A Festival Virgin's Guide*, http://www.sundanceguide.net/basics/history/.

3. "Car Talk," Wikipedia, http://en.wikipedia.org/wiki/Car_Talk.

4. Floyd Abrams, *Speaking Freely: Trials of the First Amendment* (New York: Viking, 2005); extensive description of *Newsday* project in Chapter 5. Also relied on for this event was Roy J. Harris, *Pulitzer's Gold: Behind the Prize for Public Service Journalism* (Columbia: University of Missouri Press, 2008).

5. Dana Priest and William M. Arkin, "Top Secret America," *Washington Post*, July 19, 2010, http://projects.washingtonpost.com/top-secret-america/.

6. Mitch Waldrop, "DARPA and the Internet Revolution," http://www.darpa.mil/WorkArea/DownloadAsset.aspx?id=2554.

7. John Kay, *The Truth about Markets: Their Genius, Their Limits, Their Follies* (London: Allen Lane, 2003), p. 116.

8. The idea of the commons and the potential abuse of it gained traction with Garrett Hardin's famous article "The Tragedy of the Commons," *Science*, n.s., 162, no. 3859 (December 13, 1968): 1243–1248.

9. Bruce Scott, *The Concept of Capitalism* (Heidelberg and New York: Springer Verlag, 2009), p. 52.

CHAPTER 6

1. Taken from Tim O'Reilly and Richard Koman, "Code + Law: An Interview with Lawrence Lessig," in Web journal *O'Reilly P2P*, January 29, 2001, http://openp2p.com/pub/a/p2p/2001/01/30/lessig.html.

2. Christopher Hill, *The Century of Revolution* (orig. 1961; London and New York: Routledge Classics, 2002), pp. 31–32.

3. Ibid., p. 32.

4. Fritz Machlup, *An Economic Review of the Patent System*, Study of the Subcommittee on Patents, Trademarks, and Copyrights, Senate Committee on the Judiciary, 85th Cong., 2d Sess. (Washington, DC: U.S. Government Printing Office, 1958), p. 80.

5. John Julius Norwich, *A History of Venice* (New York: Vintage, 1989), p. 84.

6. Ibid., p. 102.

7. Vandana Shiva, *Protect or Plunder? Understanding Intellectual Property Rights* (London and New York: Zed Books, 2001), p. 15.

8. Machlup, *Economic Review*.

9. Luca Mola, *The Silk Industry of Renaissance Venice* (Baltimore: Johns Hopkins University Press, 2000), pp. 186–188. Includes a picture of the actual text taken from the Venetian Archives, written in Latin and old Venetian script.

10. Shiva, *Protect or Plunder?* The translation here is less extensive than the one in Luca Mola's *The Silk Industry of Renaissance Venice*, and the choices of words are different. But the meaning is essentially the same.

11. Mola, *Silk Industry*, p. 188.

12. Edith Penrose, *The Economics of the International Patent System* (Baltimore: Johns Hopkins University Press, 1951), p. 223.

13. Stephan R. Epstein and Maarten Roy Prak, eds., *Guilds, Innovation, and the European Economy, 1400–1800* (Cambridge: Cambridge University Press, 2008), p. 222.

14. U.S. Patent Statistics Chart, Calendar Years 1963–2010, http://www.uspto .gov/go/taf/us_stat.htm.

15. Shiva, *Protect or Plunder?*, p. 15.

16. Adrian Johns, *Piracy: The Intellectual Property Wars from Gutenberg to Gates* (Chicago: University of Chicago Press, 2009), p. 20.

17. Machlup, *Economic Review*.

18. Lawrence Krubner, e-mail exchange with author, January 24, 2005.

19. Thomas O. Jewett, "Thomas Jefferson: Father of Invention," *Early America Review* 3, no. 1 (Winter 2000), http://www.earlyamerica.com/review/winter2000/ jefferson.html.

20. Thomas Jefferson, Letter to Isaac McPherson, August 13, 1813, quoted in Victor Abramson, "The Patent System: Its Economic and Social Basis," study number 20, 85th Cong., 2d Sess., p. 1.

21. Gavin Kennedy, "Patents Are Monopolies?," *Adam Smith's Lost Legacy*, October 21, 2005, http://adamsmithslostlegacy.blogspot.com/2005/10/patents-are-monopolies.html.

22. Johns, *Piracy*, pp. 272–273.

23. Machlup, *Economic Review*, p. 22.

24. Ibid., p. 23.

25. Ibid., p. 29.

26. Fritz Machlup and Edith Penrose, "The Patent Controversy in the Nineteenth Century," *Journal of Economic History* 10, no. 1 (May 1950): 4.

27. Machlup, *Economic Review*; Machlup and Penrose, "Patent Controversy."

28. F. A. Hayek, *The Road to Serfdom*, ed. Bruce Caldwell (orig. 1944; Chicago: University of Chicago Press, 2007), p. 87.

29. Machlup, *Economic Review*.

30. Ralph Oman, "Foreword," in *Introduction to Intellectual Property Law*, ed. Donald Gregory, Charles Saber, and Jon Grossman (Washington, DC: Bureau of National Affairs, 1994), p. v.

31. James E. Bessen and Michael J. Meurer, *The Private and Social Cost of Patent Trolls*, September 19, 2011, Boston University School of Law, Law and Economics Research Paper No. 11-45, http://papers.ssrn.com/sol3/papers.cfm?abstract_id=1930272.

32. Tim Wu, *The Master Switch: The Rise and Fall of Information Empires* (New York: Knopf, 2011).

33. Laia Reventos, "Software Del Siglo XXI Patentado Con Leyes Del XIX," *El Pais*, November 10, 2009.

34. John Bowe, "The Music-Copyright Enforcers," *New York Times Magazine*, August 6, 2010, http://www.nytimes.com/2010/08/08/magazine/08music-t .html?scp=4&sq=%22copyrights%22%20%22times%20magazine%22&st=cse.

35. Lawrence Lessig, *The Future of Ideas* (New York: Vintage, 2002), p. 14.

36. http://www.aclu.org/2009/05/12/who-owns-your-genes.

37. William W. Fisher III, *Promises to Keep: Technology, Law and the Future of Enforcement* (Stanford, CA: Stanford University Press, 2004), p. 3.

CHAPTER 7

1. John Micklethwait and Adrian Wooldridge, *The Company: A Short History of a Revolutionary Idea* (New York: Modern Library, 2003).

2. W. S. Holdsworth, "English Corporation Law in the 16th and 17th Centuries," *Yale Law Journal* 31, no. 4 (February 1922): 382–407.

3. http://www.philosophy-index.com/hobbes/leviathan/29-of-weaken.php.

4. Micklethwait and Wooldridge, *The Company*, p. 34.

5. Ibid., p. xvi.

6. Fernand Braudel, *Capitalism and Material Life, 1400–1800* (New York: Harper & Row, 1973), p. 402.

7. Micklethwait and Wooldridge, *The Company*, pp. 16–33.

8. Ibid.

9. Ibid., p. 44.

10. Ibid., p. 46.

11. David A. Moss, *When All Else Fails: Government as the Ultimate Risk Manager* (Cambridge, MA: Harvard University Press, 2002), pp. 53–54.

12. Ibid.

13. Thom Hartmann, *Unequal Protection: How Corporations Became "People"— and How You Can Fight Back*, 2nd ed. (San Francisco: Berrett-Koehler Publishers, 2010), p. 114.

14. Ibid., pp. 24, 114.

15. Ibid., p. 28.

16. *Citizens United v. Federal Election Commission*, text of decision, http://www.scotusblog.com/wp-content/uploads/2010/01/citizens-opinion.pdf.

17. President Grover Cleveland, State of the Union Address, December 3, 1888, http://www.infoplease.com/t/hist/state-of-the-union/100.html.

18. Edwin Burrows and Mike Wallace, *Gotham: A History of New York City to 1998* (New York: Oxford University Press, 1999), p. 354.

19. Gerald Frug, "The City as a Legal Concept," *Harvard Law Review* 93, no. 6 (April 1980): 1113.

CHAPTER 8

1. John W. Brabner-Smith, "Federal Incorporation of Business," *Virginia Law Review* 24, no. 2 (December 1937): 159.

2. Ibid.

3. Jonathan Charkham, *Keeping Good Company: A Study of Corporate Governance in Five Countries* (Oxford: Clarendon Press, 1994), pp. 1–2.

4. Ibid., p. 1.

5. John Micklethwait and Adrian Wooldridge, *The Company: A Short History of a Revolutionary Idea* (New York: Modern Library, 2003), p. 182.

6. Charkham, *Keeping Good Company*, p. 7.

7. "International Labor Comparisons. Country at a Glance: Germany," Bureau of Labor Statistics, United States Department of Labor, http://www.bls.gov/fls/country/germany.htm.

8. Charkham, *Keeping Good Company*, p. 134.

9. Daniel Costello, "Executive Pay: A Special Report. The Drought Is Over (at Least for C.E.O.'s)," *New York Times*, April 9, 2011, http://www.nytimes.com/2011/04/10/business/10comp.html.

10. Kenji Hall, "No Outcry about CEO Pay in Japan," *Bloomberg Businessweek*, February 10, 2009, http://www.businessweek.com/globalbiz/content/feb2009/gb20090210_949408.htm.

11. Maximilian C. Karacz, "A Market for Incorporations in Germany: American Competitive Federalism as a Viable Model for the Largest Economy in the EU?," *Harvard ILJ Online* 49 (November 30, 2008): 83, http://www.harvardilj.org/wp-content/uploads/2011/02/HILJ-Online_49_Karacz.pdf.

12. Mark J. Roe, "Delaware's Competition," Harvard Law School, Olin Center, October 30, 2002, p. 12, http://www.law.harvard.edu/programs/corp_gov/papers/Roe_Paper.pdf.

13. Melvin I. Urofsky, "Proposed Federal Incorporation in the Progressive Era," *American Journal of Legal History* 26, no. 2 (April 1982): 160–183.

CHAPTER 9

1. David Leonhardt, "Club Wagner," *New York Times*, July 7, 2009, http://economix.blogs.nytimes.com/2009/07/07/club-wagner/.

2. David Brooks and Gail Collins, "Taylor Swift and America's Future," *New York Times*, September 16, 2009, http://opinionator.blogs.nytimes.com/2009/09/16/taylor-swift-and-americas-future/.

3. http://www.usgovernmentspending.com/us_20th_century_chart.html.

4. Alan Altshuler, "Infrastructure Investment," *Journal of Policy Analysis and Management* 8, no. 3 (Summer 1989): 505–508, http://www.jstor.org/stable/3324941.

5. "Infrastructure: History of the Term," Museum of Learning, http://www.museumstuff.com/learn/topics/infrastructure::sub::History_Of_The_Term.

6. Herbert Muschamp, "Art/Architecture; Public Spirit, Private Money and a New New Deal," *New York Times*, March 24, 2002, http://www.nytimes.com/2002/03/24/arts/art-architecture-public-spirit-private-money-and-a-new-new-deal.html.

7. Alex Marshall, *Beneath the Metropolis* (New York: Carroll and Graf, 2006), p. 28.

8. David P. Jordan, *Transforming Paris: The Life and Labors of Baron Haussmann* (New York: Free Press, 1995).

9. Marshall, *Beneath the Metropolis*, p. 85.

10. Richard Trench and Ellis Hillman, *London under London: A Subterranean Guide* (London: J. Murray, 1993), Chapter 4.

11. J. C. Wylie, *The Wastes of Civilization* (London: Faber and Faber, 1959), quoted in Trench and Hillman, *London under London*.

12. John Kay, *The Truth about Markets: Their Genius, Their Limits, Their Follies* (London: Allen Lane, 2003), p. 87.

13. Zachary Schrag, interview with author in New York City, December 2003.

14. Andro Linklater, *Measuring America: How an Untamed Wilderness Shaped the United States and Fulfilled the Promise of Democracy* (New York: Walker and Company, 2002), pp. 195–196.

CHAPTER 10

1. Keith Roberts, *The Origins of Business, Money and Markets* (New York: Columbia University Press, 2011).

2. H. W. Burton, *The History of Norfolk, Virginia* (Norfolk: Norfolk Virginian, 1877), p. 3.

3. Robert Lang, interview with author by telephone, Spring 2005.

4. Lewis Mumford, *The Highway and the City* (New York: Harcourt, Brace & World, 1963), p. 234.

5. Jonathan Barnett, *Redesigning Cities: Principles, Practice, Implementation* (Chicago: Planners Press, 2003), pp. 52–54.

6. Carol Sheriff, *The Artificial River: The Erie Canal and the Paradox of Progress, 1817–1862* (New York: Hill & Wang, 1996).

7. Thomas Catan, "Spain's Bullet Train Changes Nation—And Fast," *Wall Street Journal*, April 20, 2009, http://online.wsj.com/article/SB124018395386633143.html.

CHAPTER 11

1. "The Earliest Railroads," *New York Times*, July 29, 1890.

2. Thomas Jefferson, "First Inaugural Address," *The Papers of Thomas Jefferson*, Princeton University, http://www.princeton.edu/~tjpapers/inaugural/inednote.html; quotation from http://www.princeton.edu/~tjpapers/inaugural/infinal.html.

3. Brian Hayes, *Infrastructure: A Field Guide to the Industrial Landscape* (New York: Norton, 2005), p. 391.

4. John Micklethwait and Adrian Wooldridge, *The Company: A Short History of a Revolutionary Idea* (New York: Modern Library, 2003), p. 60.

5. Paul Johnson, *A History of the American People* (New York: HarperCollins, 1997), p. 248.

6. Ibid., p. 353.

7. Charles Perrow, *Organizing America: Wealth, Power, and the Origins of Corporate Capitalism* (Princeton, NJ: Princeton University Press, 2002), p. 111.

8. Wolfgang Schivelbusch, *The Railway Journey* (Berkeley: University of California Press, 1986), p. 92.

9. Richard White, *Railroaded: The Transcontinentals and the Making of Modern America* (New York: Norton, 2011), p. 22.

10. James W. Ely Jr., "Abraham Lincoln as a Railroad Attorney" (Indianapolis: Indiana Historical Society, 2005), http://www.indianahistory.org/our-services/books-publications/railroad-symposia-essays-1/Abe%20Lincoln%20as%20a%20Railroad%20Attorney.pdf.

11. Johnson, *A History of the American People*, p. 353.

12. Ibid., p. 354.

13. Perrow, *Organizing America*, p. 104.

14. In his discussion of nineteenth-century railroads, White states and then elabo-

rates on the thesis of this book, which is that governments construct markets. He says: "The question is not whether governments shape markets; it is how they shape markets. . . . A wild capitalism is as much an oxymoron as wild agriculture. Markets are cultivated. They can be cultivated in many different ways with many different possible results" (pp. xxv, xxvi).

15. Michael Perelman, *Railroading Economics: The Creation of the Free Market Mythology* (New York: Monthly Review Press, 2006), p. 10.

16. Perrow, *Organizing America*, p. 120.

17. Ibid., p. 121.

18. Ibid., p. 109.

19. Ibid.

20. Ibid., p. 106.

21. Frank Dobbin, *Forging Industrial Policy: The United States, Britain and France in the Railway Age* (New York: Cambridge University Press, 1994), p. 109.

CHAPTER 12

1. Bruce E. Seely, *Building the American Highway System: Engineers as Policy Makers* (Philadelphia: Temple University Press, 1987).

2. Earl Swift, *The Big Roads: The Untold Story of the Engineers, Visionaries, and Trailblazers Who Created the American Superhighways* (Boston: Houghton Mifflin Harcourt, 2011), Chapter 1.

3. Earl Swift, e-mail exchange with author from July 2011.

4. Seely, *Building the American Highway System.*

5. Ibid., p. 62.

6. "Highway Statistics 2008," Federal Highway Administration, http://www.fh wa.dot.gov/policyinformation/statistics/2008/.

7. Steve Hawley, "TxDOT: No Road Pays for Itself," *Houston Tomorrow*, December 2, 2009, http://www.houstontomorrow.org/livability/story/txdot-no-road-pays-for-itself/.

CHAPTER 13

1. Figures from NYMTC (the New York Metropolitan Transportation Council) show that in 2008, 405,000 passengers got on and off trains at Penn Station, up from 178,000 in 1963. This figure does not include the 150,000 who board subway trains at the station.

2. Research and Innovative Technology Administration, Bureau of Transportation Statistics, http://www.TranStats.bts.gov/Data_Elements.aspx?Data=1.

3. Jill Jonnes, *Conquering Gotham: A Gilded Age Epic: The Construction of Penn Station and Its Tunnels* (New York: Viking, 2007).

CHAPTER 14

1. Jared Diamond, "The Curse of QWERTY: O Typewriter? Quit Your Torture!," *Discover Magazine*, April 1997, http://discovermagazine.com/1997/apr/thecurseof qwerty1099.

2. Ibid.

3. The well-known economist Joseph Schumpeter seemed to be referring to a version of path dependence when he said, in his *The Theory of Economic Development*, "All knowledge and habit once acquired become as firmly rooted in ourselves as a railway embankment in the earth" (orig. 1934; New Brunswick, NJ: Transaction Books, 1983, p. 84).

4. S. J. Liebowitz and Stephen E. Margolis, "The Fable of the Keys," *Journal of Law and Economics* 33 (April 1990), http://www.utdallas.edu/~liebowit/keys1.html.

5. Ibid.

6. Independent Institute, "The Lighthouse Logo," http://www.independent.org/aboutus/lighthouse.asp.

7. Wolfgang Schivelbusch, *The Railway Journey* (Berkeley: University of California Press, 1986), pp. 93–117.

8. Ibid., p. 108.

9. John R. Stilgoe, *Metropolitan Corridor: Railroads and the American Scene* (New Haven, CT: Yale University Press, 1983), p. 55.

10. Telephone interview with author, October 1998.

11. http://en.wikipedia.org/wiki/Wang_Laboratories.

CHAPTER 15

1. New York City Police Museum, 100 Old Slip, New York City, visit by author in October 2010.

2. New South Wales Police Museum, http://www.south-wales.police.uk.

3. "Sir Robert Peel," *History of the Metropolitan Police*, Metropolitan Police Service, http://www.met.police.uk/history/peel.htm.

4. New York City Police Museum, visit by author.

5. International Centre for Prison Studies, University of Essex, http://www.prisonstudies.org/info/worldbrief/wpb_country.php?country=190.

CHAPTER 16

1. Romolo Augusto Staccioli, *The Roads of the Romans* (Los Angeles: J. Paul Getty Museum, 2003), p. 10.

2. John Mills, *A Critical History of Economics* (New York: Palgrave Macmillan, 2002), p. 47.

3. Max Weber, *General Economic History* (orig. 1927; New Brunswick, NJ: Transaction Publishers, 1995), p. 236.

4. James Buchan, *Frozen Desire* (New York: Farrar, Straus & Giroux, 1997), p. 77.

5. Barack Obama, *The Audacity of Hope* (New York: Three Rivers Press, 2006), p. 86.

6. Thomas Hobbes, *Of Man, Being the First Part of Leviathan*, Vol. 34, Part 5, Harvard Classics (New York: P. F. Collier & Son, 1909–1914; Bartleby.com, 2001), http://www.bartleby.com/34/5/.

7. John Locke, *Second Treatise on Government*, Chapters 5 and 2, http://www.constitution.org/jl/2ndtr05.htm, http://www.constitution.org/jl/2ndtr02.htm.

8. John Micklethwait and Adrian Wooldridge, *The Company: A Short History of a Revolutionary Idea* (New York: Modern Library, 2003), p. 177.

9. John Locke, *Second Treatise on Government*, Chapter 7, Section 85, http://www.constitution.org/jl/2ndtr07.htm.

10. Richard Adelstein, "The Origins of Property and the Powers of Government," in *The Fundamental Interrelationships between Government and Property*, ed. Nicholas Mercuro and Warren J. Samuels (Stamford, CT: Jai Press, 1999), p. 26.

11. Theodore F. T. Plucknett, *A Concise History of the Common Law* (Rochester, NY: Lawyers Co-Operative Publishing Company, 1929), p. 63.

12. Barack Obama, "Obama's Nobel Remarks," *New York Times*, December 10, 2009, http://www.nytimes.com/2009/12/11/world/europe/11prexy.text.html.

CHAPTER 17

1. Stuart Noble, *A History of American Education* (Westport, CT: Greenwood Press, 1954), p. 122.

2. "Thaddeus Stevens," Pennsylvania Historical & Museum Commission, http://www.portal.state.pa.us/portal/server.pt/community/people/4277/stevens,_thaddeus/443778.

3. Noble, *History of American Education*, p. 168.

4. Chris A. De Young and Richard Wynn, *American Education* (orig. 1942; New York: McGraw-Hill, 1968), p. 156.

5. With his "speller," Webster would decisively break with Dilworth on matters linguistic. For example, he, controversially, said that words ending in *sion* or *tion*, like *explosion* or *salvation*, had only one syllable at the end, not two.

6. From Noah Webster, "On Education," *American Magazine*, 1787, as quoted in E. Jennifer Monaghan, *A Common Heritage: Noah Webster's Blue-Back Speller* (Hamden, CT: Archon Books, 1983).

7. David Simpson, *The Politics of American English, 1776–1850* (New York: Oxford University Press, 1986), p. 2.

8. Ibid., p. 30.

9. E. D. Hirsch, *Cultural Literacy: What Every American Needs to Know* (New York: Vintage Books, 1988), p. 112.

10. Jocelyn Proulx, from unpublished memoir in possession of author.

11. Eugen Weber, *My France: Politics, Culture, Myth* (Cambridge, MA: Harvard University Press, 1991), p. 93.

12. Hirsch, *Cultural Literacy*, p. 105.

13. Ibid., pp. 105–106.

14. Ibid., p. 93.

15. Deborah Madison, "School Lunch Abroad: Another Way to Eat," Culinate.com, September 6, 2007, http://www.culinate.com/columns/deborah/french_school_lunch.

CHAPTER 18

1. Roger Gocking, *The History of Ghana* (Westport, CT: Greenwood Press, 2005), p. 279. See also "A Survey of the Third World," *Economist*, September 23, 1989. Ac-

cording to the article, Ghana in 1957 had a per capita income of $490 compared to $91 for South Korea, in 1980 American dollars.

2. Douglas North, Nobel Prize acceptance speech, December 9, 1993.

3. Bruce Cumings, *Korea's Place in the Sun: A Modern History* (New York: Norton, 1998), p. 300.

4. Ibid., p. 314.

5. Ibid., p. 302.

6. Ibid., p. 305.

7. Ibid., p. 310.

8. Ibid., p. 316.

9. World Bank, *The East Asian Miracle: Economic Growth and Public Policy* (New York: Oxford University Press, 1993), p. 5.

10. Thomas Friedman, *The World Is Flat* (New York: Farrar, Straus and Giroux, 2005).

11. Cumings, *Korea's Place*, p. 328.

12. Daniel Waley, *The Italian City-Republics* (New York: McGraw-Hill, 1969), p. 96, as quoted in unpublished manuscript by Bruce Scott.

13. Neil Sheehan, *A Fiery Peace in a Cold War: Bernard Schriever and the Ultimate Weapon* (New York: Vintage, 2010), p. 172.

14. Jon Jeter, "A Smoother Road to Free Markets," *Washington Post*, January 21, 2004.

15. Joseph E. Stiglitz, *Globalization and Its Discontents* (New York: Norton, 2002), p. 12.

16. John B. Judis, "Trade Secrets: The Real Problem with NAFTA," *New Republic*, April 9, 2008.

CHAPTER 19

1. Richard Dunn, *Sugar and Slaves* (Chapel Hill: University of North Carolina Press, 1972).

2. Ibid., p. 11.

3. M. W. Janis, "Jeremy Bentham and the Fashioning of 'International Law,'" *American Journal of International Law* 78 (1984): 405–418.

4. Mark W. Janis, *An Introduction to International Law* (Boston: Little, Brown and Company, 1988), p. 121.

5. Ibid., p. 50.

6. Ibid., p. 11.

7. Ibid., pp. 12–13.

8. Ibid., p. 283.

9. Ibid., Chapter 8.

10. Ibid., p. 52.

11. Ibid., p. 212.

12. Ibid., p. 214.

13. David J. Bederman, *The Spirit of International Law* (Athens and London: University of Georgia Press, 2002), p. 1.

14. John Austin, *The Province of Jurisprudence Determined* (orig. 1832; Amherst, NY: Prometheus Books, 2000), p. 1.

15. Janis, *An Introduction to International Law*, p. 66.

16. Harold Hongju Koh, "The 1994 Roscoe Pound Lecture: Transnational Legal Process," *Nebraska Law Review* 75 (1996): 192.

17. Janis, *An Introduction to International Law*, p. 121.

18. John Maynard Keynes, *The General Theory of Employment, Interest and Money* (orig. 1936; Houndmills, Basingstoke, Hampshire; New York: Palgrave Macmillan, 2007), p. 383.

Abrams, Floyd. *Speaking Freely: Trials of the First Amendment.* New York: Viking, 2005.

Abramson, Victor. "The Patent System: Its Economic and Social Basis." Study number 20 from *Proposals for Improving the Patent System: Study of the Subcommittee on Patents, Trademarks and Copyrights of the Committee on the Judiciary, United States Senate.* Washington, DC: U.S. Government Printing Office, 1956.

Adelstein, Richard. "The Origins of Property and the Powers of Government." In *The Fundamental Interrelationships between Government and Property,* ed. Nicholas Mercuro and Warren J. Samuels. Stamford, CT: Jai Press, 1999.

Aitken, Hugh G. *The State and Economic Growth.* New York: Social Science Research Council, 1959.

Albert, Michel. *Capitalism vs. Capitalism: How America's Obsession with Individualism and Short-term Profit Has Led It to the Brink of Collapse.* orig. 1991; London: Whurr, 1993.

Alperovitz, Gar. *America beyond Capitalism: Reclaiming Our Wealth, Our Liberty, and Our Democracy.* Hoboken, NJ: Wiley, 2005.

———. "Another World Is Possible." *Mother Jones,* January/February 2006.

———. "A Rich Country Can Be More Generous." *Philadelphia Inquirer,* March 27, 2005.

Altshuler, Alan. "Infrastructure Investment." *Journal of Policy Analysis and Management* 8, no. 3 (Summer 1989): 505–508.

Arthur, W. Brian, Steven N. Durlauf, and David A. Lane. *The Economy as an Evolving Complex System II.* Santa Fe, NM: Santa Fe Institute, 1997.

Austin, John. *The Province of Jurisprudence Determined.* orig. 1832; Amherst, NY: Prometheus Books, 2000.

Avebe corporate website. http://www.avebe.com/Aboutus/Cooperative/tabid/81/Default.aspx.

Baker, Peter, and Neil Lewis. "Sotomayor Vows 'Fidelity to the Law' as Hearings Start." *New York Times,* July 14, 2009.

Barber, Benjamin R. "A Failure of Democracy, Not Capitalism." *New York Times,* July 29, 2002.

Barber, Dan, chef and owner, Blue Hill Restaurant at Stone Barns. Undated interview with author about food system done in person at Stone Barns in Pocantico Hills, New York.

Beatty, Jack. *Colossus: How the Corporation Changed America.* New York: Broadway Books, 2001.

Beaud, Michel. *History of Capitalism, 1500–2000.* Translated by Tom Dickman and Anny Lefebvre. New York: Monthly Review Press, c2001.

Bederman, David J. *The Spirit of International Law.* Athens and London: University of Georgia Press, 2002.

Beinhocker, Eric D. *The Origin of Wealth: Evolution, Complexity and the Radical Remaking of Economics.* Boston: Harvard Business School Press, 2006.

Benko, Robert. *Protecting Intellectual Property Rights*. Washington, DC: American Enterprise Institute, 1987.

Bick, Julie. "Book Lovers Ask, What's Seattle's Secret?" *New York Times*, March 9, 2008.

Blackstone, Sir William. *Commentaries on the Laws of England*. Avalon Project: Documents in Law, History and Diplomacy; Lillian Goldman Law Library, Yale Law School. http://avalon.law.yale.edu/subject_menus/blackstone.asp.

Blau, Judith R. *Social Contracts and Economic Markets*. New York: Plenum Press, 1993.

Bowe, John. "The Music-Copyright Enforcers." *New York Times Magazine*, August 6, 2010. http://www.nytimes.com/2010/08/08/magazine/08music-t.html?scp=4&sq=%22copyrights%22%20%22times%20magazine%22&st=cse.

Boynton, Robert S. "The Tyranny of Copyright?" *New York Times Magazine*, January 25, 2004.

Brabner-Smith, John W. "Federal Incorporation of Business." *Virginia Law Review* 24, no. 2 (December 1937).

Branscomb, Anne. *Who Owns Information?* New York: Basic Books, 1994.

Braudel, Fernand. *Capitalism and Material Life, 1400–1800*. Translated by Miriam Kochan. orig. 1967; New York: Harper & Row, 1973.

Brooks, David. "Questions for Doctor Retail." *New York Times*, February 28, 2008.

Brooks, David, and Gail Collins. "Taylor Swift and America's Future." *New York Times*, September 16, 2009. http://opinionator.blogs.nytimes.com/2009/09/16/taylor-swift-and-americas-future/.

Brown, Bruce. *The History of the Corporation, Volume 1*. Sumas, WA: BF Communications Inc., 2003.

Brown, Eliot. "Related, Vornado Spend $47 M. and Counting on Moynihan Station." *New York Observer*, February 26, 2008. http://www.observer.com/2008/related-vornado-spend-47-m-and-counting-moynihan-station.

Bryson, Bill. *Made in America*. London: Secker & Warburg, 1994.

Buchan, James. *Frozen Desire*. New York: Farrar, Straus & Giroux, 1997.

Burton, H. W. *The History of Norfolk, Virginia*. Norfolk: Norfolk Virginian, 1877.

Cameron, Rondo. *A Concise Economic History of the World*. New York: Oxford University Press, 1997.

"Car Talk." Wikipedia. http://en.wikipedia.org/wiki/Car_Talk.

Catan, Thomas. "Spain's Bullet Train Changes Nation—and Fast." *Wall Street Journal*, April 20, 2009. http://online.wsj.com/article/SB124018395386633143.html.

Charkham, Jonathan. *Keeping Good Company: A Study of Corporate Governance in Five Countries*. Oxford: Clarendon Press, 1994.

Cipolla, Carlo M. *Between Two Cultures: An Introduction to Economic History*. New York: Norton, 1988.

———. *The Economic Decline of Empires*. London: Methuen, 1970.

Citizens United v. Federal Election Commission, text of decision. http://www.scotusblog.com/wp-content/uploads/2010/01/citizens-opinion.pdf.

Clark, Barry. *Political Economy: A Comparative Approach*. Westport, CT: Praeger, 1998.

Cleveland, President Grover. State of the Union Address, December 3, 1888. http://www.infoplease.com/t/hist/state-of-the-union/100.html.

Clough, Shepard B., and Richard T. Rapp. *European Economic History: The Economic Development of Western Civilization*. New York: McGraw-Hill, 1975.

Coase, R. H. *The Firm, the Market, and the Law*. Chicago: University of Chicago Press, 1988.

Conklin, David W. *Comparative Economic Systems*. Cambridge, UK, and New York: Cambridge University Press, 1991.

Co-operative Group. Website, http://www.co-operative.coop/aboutus/, and http://en.wikipedia.org/wiki/The_Co-operative_Group.

Costello, Daniel. "Executive Pay: A Special Report. The Drought Is Over (at Least for C.E.O.'s)." *New York Times*, April 9, 2011. http://www.nytimes.com/2011/04/10/business/10comp.html.

Craig, Benjamin. "History of the Sundance Film Festival." *Sundance: A Festival Virgin's Guide*. http://www.sundanceguide.net/basics/history/.

Creighton, Andrew. "The Emergence of Incorporation as a Legal Form of Organization." PhD diss., Stanford University, 1990.

Cumings, Bruce. *Korea's Place in the Sun: A Modern History*. New York: Norton, 1998.

Dagger, Richard. Review of Howard Schweber, *The Creation of American Common Law, 1850–1880: Technology, Politics, and the Construction of Citizenship*. *American Historical Review* 109, no. 5 (December 2004): 1583–1584. http://www.jstor.org/pss/10.1086/530995.

Davis, G. R. C., trans. *Magna Carta*. Rev. ed. British Library, 1989. http://www.fordham.edu/halsall/source/magnacarta.html.

Davis, John P. *Corporations: A Study of the Origin and Development of Great Business Combinations and of Their Relation to the Authority of the State*. New York: G. P. Putnam's, 1905.

De Young, Chris A., and Richard Wynn. *American Education*. orig. 1942; New York: McGraw-Hill, 1968.

Diamond, Jared. "The Curse of QWERTY: O Typewriter? Quit Your Torture!" *Discover Magazine*, April 1997. http://discovermagazine.com/1997/apr/thecurseofqwerty1099.

Dobbin, Frank. *Forging Industrial Policy: The United States, Britain and France in the Railway Age*. New York: Cambridge University Press, 1994.

Dowd, Douglas. *Capitalism and Its Economics: A Critical History*. London; Sterling, VA: Pluto Press, 2004.

Dreyfuss, Rochelle (Pauline Newman professor of law at New York University). Undated interview with author by telephone.

Dunn, Richard. *Sugar and Slaves*. Chapel Hill: University of North Carolina Press, 1972.

"The Earliest Railroads." *New York Times*, July 29, 1890.

Economist. Special section on Korea. September 27–October 3, 2008.

Egerstrom, Lee (fellow, Minnesota 2020, Minneapolis; former agricultural reporter for the *St. Paul Pioneer Press*). Interviews with author.

———. *Make No Small Plans: A Cooperative Revival for Rural America*. Rochester, MN: Lone Oak Press, 1994.

Eliassen, Jan. E-mail to author, January 10, 2009.

———. Telephone interview with author, January 10, 2009.

Ely, James W., Jr. "Abraham Lincoln as a Railroad Attorney." Indianapolis: Indiana Historical Society, 2005. http://www.indianahistory.org/our-services/books-publications/railroad-symposia-essays-1/Abe%20Lincoln%20as%20a%20Railroad%20Attorney.pdf.

———. *Guardian of Every Other Right: The Constitutional History of Property Rights.* New York: Oxford University Press, 1998.

———. "The Marshall Court and Property Rights: A Reappraisal." *John Marshall Law Review* 33 (Summer 2000): 1023–1061.

Emerson, Ralph Waldo. *The Complete Works of Ralph Waldo Emerson: Nature Addresses and Lectures.* n.p.: Nabu Press, 2010.

Epstein, Stephan R. "Property Rights to Technical Knowledge in Premodern Europe, 1300–1800." *American Economic Review* 94 (2): 382–387.

Epstein, Stephan R., and Maarten Roy Prak, eds. *Guilds, Innovation, and the European Economy, 1400–1800.* Cambridge: Cambridge University Press, 2008.

Fabricant, Florence. "Butter Bites Back." *New York Times,* March 22, 1995.

Fisher, William W., III. *Promises to Keep: Technology, Law and the Future of Enforcement.* Stanford, CA: Stanford University Press, 2004.

Flyvbjerg, Bent, Nils Bruzelius, and Werner Rothengatter. *Megaprojects and Risk: An Anatomy of Ambition.* Cambridge, UK, and New York: Cambridge University Press, 2003.

Foreman-Peck, James. *A History of the World Economy: International Relations since 1850.* London: Harvester/Wheatsheaf, 1995.

Foroohar, Rana. "Why China Works." *Newsweek,* January 19, 2009.

Frank, Thomas. *One Market under God.* New York: Anchor Books, Random House, 2000.

Frentrop, Paul Marie Louis. *A History of Corporate Governance: 1602–2002.* Brussels: Deminor, 2003.

Frey, Bruno S., and Alois Stutzer. *Happiness and Economics: How the Economy and Institutions Affect Well-being.* Princeton, NJ: Princeton University Press, 2002.

Freyfogle, Eric. *On Private Property: Finding Common Ground on the Ownership of Land.* Boston: Beacon Press, 2007.

Friedman, Thomas. *The World Is Flat.* New York: Farrar, Straus and Giroux, 2005.

Frug, Gerald. "The City as a Legal Concept." *Harvard Law Review* 93, no. 6 (April 1980): 1062–1138.

———. Several interviews and e-mail exchanges with author, 2007–2009.

Gocking, Roger. *The History of Ghana.* Westport, CT: Greenwood Press, 2005.

Gordon, Jennifer. "Workers without Borders." *New York Times,* March 10, 2009.

Gordon, John Steele. *A Thread across the Ocean: The Heroic Story of the Transatlantic Cable.* New York: Perennial, 2003.

Grandy, Christopher. "New Jersey Corporate Chartermongering: 1875–1929." *Journal of Economic History* 49, no. 3 (September 1989): 677–692, http://www.jstor.org/pss/2122510.

Gregory, Donald, Charles Saber, and Jon Grossman. *Introduction to Intellectual Property Law.* Washington, DC: Bureau of National Affairs, 1994.

Gudeman, Stephen. *The Anthropology of Economy*. Oxford: Blackwell Publishers, 2001.

Hale, Matthew. *The History and Analysis of the Common Law of England*. Union, NJ: Law Book Exchange Ltd, 2000.

Hall, Kenji. "No Outcry about CEO Pay in Japan." *Bloomberg Businessweek*, February 10, 2009. http://www.businessweek.com/globalbiz/content/feb2009/gb20090210_949408.htm.

Hamm, Richard. "Introduction." In *Essays on English Law and the American Experience*, ed. Elizabeth A. Cawthon and David E. Narrett. University of Texas at Arlington, 1994.

Hardin, Garrett. "The Tragedy of the Commons." *Science*, n.s., 162, no. 3859 (December 13, 1968): 1243–1248.

Harris, Roy J. *Pulitzer's Gold: Behind the Prize for Public Service Journalism*. Columbia: University of Missouri Press, 2008.

Hartmann, Thom. "Free Market Debunked." AlterNet, March 17, 2004. http://www.alternet.org/story/18147/.

———. *Unequal Protection: How Corporations Became "People"—and How You Can Fight Back*. 2nd ed. San Francisco: Berrett-Koehler Publishers, 2010.

Hartz, Louis. *Economic Policy and Democratic Thought: Pennsylvania, 1776-1860*. Cambridge, MA: Harvard University Press, 1948.

Hawley, Steve. "TxDOT: No Road Pays for Itself." *Houston Tomorrow*, December 2, 2009. http://www.houstontomorrow.org/livability/story/txdot-no-road-pays-for-itself/.

Hayek, F. A. *The Road to Serfdom: Texts and Documents, the Definitive Edition*. Edited by Bruce Caldwell. orig. 1944; Chicago: University of Chicago Press, 2007.

Hayes, Brian. *Infrastructure: A Field Guide to the Industrial Landscape*. New York: Norton 2005.

"Highway Statistics 2008." Federal Highway Administration. http://www.fhwa.dot.gov/policyinformation/statistics/2008/.

Hill, Christopher. *The Century of Revolution*. orig. 1961; London and New York: Routledge Classics, 2002.

Hirsch, E. D. *Cultural Literacy: What Every American Needs to Know*. New York: Vintage Books, 1988.

Hirshleifer, Jack. *The Dark Side of the Force*. Cambridge, UK, and New York: Cambridge University Press, 2001.

Hobbes, Thomas. *Of Man, Being the First Part of Leviathan*. Vol. 34, Part 5, Harvard Classics. New York: P. F. Collier & Son, 1909–1914; Bartleby.com, 2001, http://www.bartleby.com/34/5/.

Hodgson, Geoffrey. *Evolution and Institutions: On Evolutionary Economics and the Evolution of Economics*. Cheltenham, UK: Edward Elgar Publishing, 1999.

Holdsworth, W. S. "English Corporation Law in the 16th and 17th Centuries." *Yale Law Journal* 31, no. 4 (February 1922): 382–407.

Holmes, Oliver Wendell. *The Common Law*. orig. 1881; Boston: Back Bay Books, 1963.

Horwitz, Morton J. *The Transformation of American Law, 1780-1860*. Cambridge, MA: Harvard University Press, 1977.

Howe, John. *Language and Political Meaning in Revolutionary America*. Amherst: University of Massachusetts Press, 2004.

Independent Institute. "The Lighthouse Logo." http://www.independent.org/about us/lighthouse.asp.

"Infrastructure: History of the Term." Museum of Learning. http://www.museum stuff.com/learn/topics/infrastructure::sub::History_Of_The_Term.

International Centre for Prison Studies, University of Essex. "Country: United States of America." http://www.prisonstudies.org/info/worldbrief/wpb_coun try.php?country=190.

"International Labor Comparisons. Country at a Glance: Germany." Bureau of Labor Statistics, United States Department of Labor. http://www.bls.gov/fls/country/germany.htm.

Jacobs, Harvey. "U.S. Private Property Rights in International Perspective." In *Property Rights and Land Policies*, ed. Gregory K. Ingram and Yu-Hung Hong. Cambridge, MA: Lincoln Institute of Land Policy, 2009.

Jaffe, Adam, and Josh Lerner. *Innovation and Its Discontents: How Our Broken Patent System Is Endangering Innovation and Progress, and What to Do about It*. Princeton, NJ: Princeton University Press, 2004.

Janis, M. W. "Jeremy Bentham and the Fashioning of 'International Law.'" *American Journal of International Law* 78 (1984): 405–418.

Janis, Mark W. *An Introduction to International Law*. Boston: Little, Brown and Company, 1988.

Jauhar, Sandeep. "Many Doctors, Many Tests, No Rhyme or Reason." *New York Times*, March 11, 2008.

Jefferson, Thomas. "First Inaugural Address." *The Papers of Thomas Jefferson*. Princeton University. http://www.princeton.edu/~tjpapers/inaugural/inednote .html.

———. Letter to Isaac McPherson, August 13, 1813. *The Writings of Thomas Jefferson*. Quoted in Abramson, p. 1.

———. *Notes on the State of Virginia*. orig. 1787; Richmond: J. W. Randolph, 1853.

Jeter, Jon. "A Smoother Road to Free Markets: Chile's Success Makes the Case for State Involvement in Economy." *Washington Post*, January 21, 2004.

Jewett, Thomas O. "Thomas Jefferson: Father of Invention." *Early America Review* 3, no. 1 (Winter 2000), http://www.earlyamerica.com/review/winter2000/jeffer son.html.

Johns, Adrian. *Piracy: The Intellectual Property Wars from Gutenberg to Gates*. Chicago: University of Chicago Press, 2009.

Johnson, Paul. *A History of the American People*. New York: HarperCollins, 1997.

John Templeton Foundation. "Does the Free Market Corrode Moral Character?" http://www.templeton.org/market.

Jonnes, Jill. *Conquering Gotham: A Gilded Age Epic: The Construction of Penn Station and Its Tunnels*. New York: Viking, 2007.

Jordan, David P. *Transforming Paris: The Life and Labors of Baron Haussmann*. New York: Free Press, 1995.

Judis, John B. "A Man for All Seasons." *New Republic*, February 4, 2009. http://www .tnr.com/politics/story.html?id=b5f61f74-dde6-43ea-a433-9febof752c3b.

————. "Trade Secrets: The Real Problem with NAFTA." *New Republic*, April 9, 2008.

Judt, Tony. "Captive Minds." *New York Review of Books*, September 30, 2010.

————. "The Wrecking Ball of Innovation." *New York Review of Books* 54, no. 19 (December 6, 2007), http://www.nybooks.com/articles/20853.

Karacz, Maximilian C. "A Market for Incorporations in Germany: American Competitive Federalism as a Viable Model for the Largest Economy in the EU?" *Harvard ILJ Online* 49 (November 30, 2008): 83–94, http://www.harvardilj.org/wp-content/uploads/2011/02/HILJ-Online_49_Karacz.pdf.

Katz, Stanley N. "Thomas Jefferson and the Right to Property in Revolutionary America." *Journal of Law and Economics* 19 no. 3 (October 1976): 467–488.

Kay, John. *The Truth about Markets: Their Genius, Their Limits, Their Follies.* London: Allen Lane, 2003.

Keegan, John. *A History of Warfare.* New York: Alfred A. Knopf, 1993.

Kennedy, David. "The Disciplines of International Law and Policy." *Leiden Journal of International Law* 12, no. 1 (1999): 9–133.

Kennedy, Gavin. "Patents Are Monopolies?" *Adam Smith's Lost Legacy*, October 21, 2005. http://adamsmithslostlegacy.blogspot.com/2005/10/patents-are-monopolies.html.

Keynes, John Maynard. *The General Theory of Employment, Interest and Money.* orig. 1936; Houndmills, Basingstoke, Hampshire; New York: Palgrave Macmillan, 2007.

Kierkegaard, Søren, and Alexander Dru. *The Soul of Kierkegaard: Selections from His Journal.* Mineola, NY: Dover Publications, 2003.

Kindleberger, Charles P. *Historical Economics: Art or Science?* New York: Harvester Wheatsheaf, 1990.

Krubner, Lawrence. Numerous conversations and e-mail exchanges with author, 2000–2009.

Lanchester, John. "Outsmarted: High Finance vs. Human Nature." *New Yorker*, June 1, 2009.

Land of Lakes Corporation website. http://www.landolakes.com/ourCompany/LandOLakesHistory.cfm.

Landsburg, Steven E. "What to Expect When You're Free Trading." *New York Times*, January 16, 2008.

Lang, Robert. Interview with author by telephone, Spring 2005.

Layard, Richard. *Happiness: Lessons from a New Science.* New York: Penguin, 2005.

Legal Information Institute. "Eggshell Skull Rule." Cornell University Law School. http://topics.law.cornell.edu/wex/eggshell_skull_rule.

Leonhardt, David. "Club Wagner." *New York Times*, July 7, 2009. http://economix.blogs.nytimes.com/2009/07/07/club-wagner/.

Lessig, Lawrence. *The Future of Ideas.* New York: Vintage Books, 2002.

LeVine, Steve. "IBM May Not Be the Patent King after All." *Business Week*, January 13, 2010. http://www.businessweek.com/magazine/content/10_04/b4416405 1608050.htm.

Liebowitz, S. J., and Stephen E. Margolis. "The Fable of the Keys." *Journal of Law and Economics* 33 (April 1990). http://www.utdallas.edu/~liebowit/keys1.html.

Linklater, Andro. *Measuring America: How an Untamed Wilderness Shaped the United States and Fulfilled the Promise of Democracy.* New York: Walker and Company, 2002.

Liptak, Adam. "Inmate Count in US Dwarfs Other Nations." *New York Times,* April 23, 2008.

Locke, John. *Second Treatise on Government.* http://www.constitution.org/jl/2ndtreat.htm. First published 1689.

McCloskey, Deirdre (professor, University of Illinois at Chicago). Undated telephone interview with author about markets.

McDonald, John. "The Economy of England at the Time of the Norman Conquest." Santa Clara, CA: EH.net, Economic History Association, 2010. http://eh.net/encyclopedia/article/mcdonald.domesday.

Machlup, Fritz. *An Economic Review of the Patent System.* Study of the Subcommittee on Patents, Trademarks, and Copyrights, Senate Committee on the Judiciary, 85th Cong., 2d Sess. Washington, DC: U.S. Government Printing Office, 1958.

Machlup, Fritz, and Edith Penrose. "The Patent Controversy in the Nineteenth Century." *Journal of Economic History* 10, no. 1 (May 1950): 1–29.

Madison, Deborah. "School Lunch Abroad: Another Way to Eat." Culinate.com, September 6, 2007. http://www.culinate.com/columns/deborah/french_school_lunch.

Madrick, Jeff. "Regardless of the Progress of a Few, Many Nations Still Face Economic Despair." *New York Times,* August 7, 2003.

Market Historical Commission, City of Seattle. "Pike Place Market Historical Commission: Revised Guidelines." http://pikeplacemarket.s3.amazonaws.com/PDFs/Applications/pikeplace_guidelines.pdf.

Marshall, Alex. "America Should Hear Kennedy's Words Again." *The Virginian-Pilot,* February 25, 1996. Commentary page.

———. *Beneath the Metropolis.* New York: Carroll and Graf, 2006.

———. *How Cities Work: Suburbs, Sprawl, and the Roads Not Taken.* Austin: University of Texas Press, 2000.

Mercuro, Nicholas, and Warren J. Samuels, eds. *The Fundamental Interrelationships between Government and Property.* Stamford, CT: Jai Press, 1999.

Micklethwait, John, and Adrian Wooldridge. *The Company: A Short History of a Revolutionary Idea.* New York: Modern Library, 2003.

Mills, John. *A Critical History of Economics.* New York: Palgrave Macmillan, 2002.

Mishel, Lawrence. "CEO-to-Worker Pay Imbalance Grows." Washington, DC: Economic Policy Institute, June 21, 2006. http://www.epi.org/economic_snapshots/entry/webfeatures_snapshots_20060621/.

Mola, Luca. *The Silk Industry of Renaissance Venice.* Baltimore: Johns Hopkins University Press, 2000.

Monaghan, E. Jennifer. *A Common Heritage: Noah Webster's Blue-Back Speller.* Hamden, CT: Archon Books, 1983.

Mondragon Annual Report 2010. http://www.mondragon-corporation.com/CAS/Magnitudes-Econ%C3%B3micas/Informe-anual.aspx.

Monkkonen, Eric H. *America Becomes Urban: The Development of U.S. Cities & Towns, 1780–1980.* Berkeley: University of California Press, 1988.

Monroe, Arthur Eli. *Early Economic Thought: Selections from Economic Literature Prior to Adam Smith*. Cambridge, MA: Harvard University Press, 1948.

Moran, Michael, and Maurice Wright, eds. *The Market and the State*. New York: St. Martin's Press, 1991.

Moss, David A. E-mail exchanges with author, April 6, 2004.

———. *When All Else Fails: Government as the Ultimate Risk Manager*. Cambridge, MA: Harvard University Press, 2002.

Mumford, Lewis. *The City in History*. New York: Harcourt, Brace & World, 1961.

———. *The Highway and the City*. New York: Harcourt, Brace & World, 1963.

Muschamp, Herbert. "Art/Architecture; Public Spirit, Private Money and a New New Deal." *New York Times*, March 24, 2002. http://www.nytimes.com/2002/03/24/arts/art-architecture-public-spirit-private-money-and-a-new-new-deal.html.

Neuhart, John, Charles Eames, Ray Eames, and Marilyn Neuhart. *Eames Design: The Work of the Office of Charles and Ray Eames*. New York: H. N. Abrams 1989.

Neumeyer, Fredrik. "Compulsory Licensing of Patents under Some Non-American Systems." Study number 19 from *Proposals for Improving the Patent System: Study of the Subcommittee on Patents, Trademarks and Copyrights of the Committee on the Judiciary, United States Senate*. Washington, DC: U.S. Government Printing Office, 1956.

New South Wales Police Museum. http://www.south-wales.police.uk.

New York City Police Museum. 100 Old Slip, New York City. Visit by author in October 2010.

Nietzsche, Friedrich. *Beyond Good and Evil*. http://www.authorama.com/beyond-good-and-evil-1.html.

Noble, Stuart. *A History of American Education*. Westport, CT: Greenwood Press, 1954.

North, D. C. *Understanding the Process of Economic Change*. Princeton, NJ: Princeton University Press, 2005.

North, D. C., and R. P. Thomas. *The Rise of the Western World: A New Economic History*. Cambridge: Cambridge University Press, 1973.

Norwich, John Julius. *A History of Venice*. New York: Vintage, 1989.

Norwood, Christopher. *About Paterson: The Making and Unmaking of an American City*. New York: Saturday Review Press, 1974.

Nourissier, François. *The French*. Translated by Adrienne Foulke. London: Readers Union, 1971.

Obama, Barack. *The Audacity of Hope*. New York: Three Rivers Press, 2006.

———. "Obama's Nobel Remarks." *New York Times*, December 10, 2009. http://www.nytimes.com/2009/12/11/world/europe/11prexy.text.html.

Oemichen, Bill (president, Cooperative Network). Interview with author at convention in Minneapolis, November 2009.

O'Reilly, Tim, and Richard Koman. "Code + Law: An Interview with Lawrence Lessig." *O'Reilly P2P*, January 29, 2001. http://openp2p.com/pub/a/p2p/2001/01/30/lessig.html.

Penrose, Edith. *The Economics of the International Patent System*. Baltimore: Johns Hopkins University Press, 1951.

Perelman, Michael. *The End of Economics*. Oxford: Taylor and Francis, 1996.

———. *Railroading Economics: The Creation of the Free Market Mythology*. New York: Monthly Review Press, 2006.

———. *Steal This Idea: Intellectual Property Rights and the Corporate Confiscation of Creativity*. New York: Palgrave, 2002.

Perrow, Charles. *Complex Organizations: A Critical Essay*. Glenview, IL: Scott, Foresman and Company, 1979.

———. *Organizing America: Wealth, Power, and the Origins of Corporate Capitalism*. Princeton, NJ: Princeton University Press, 2002.

Plucknett, Theodore F. T. *A Concise History of the Common Law*. Rochester, NY: Lawyers Co-Operative Publishing Company, 1929.

Pollock v. Farmers Loan and Trust Company (US Supreme Court, 1895). *ABA Journal* 39 (June 1953).

Posner, Richard. "How I Became a Keynesian." *New Republic*, September 23, 2009. http://www.tnr.com/article/how-i-became-keynesian.

Post, Robert C. *Physics, Patents, and Politics: A Biography of Charles Grafton Page*. New York: Science History Publications, 1976.

Priest, Dana, and William M. Arkin. "Top Secret America." *Washington Post*, July 19, 2010. http://projects.washingtonpost.com/top-secret-america/.

Proulx, Jocelyn. Unpublished memoir sent to author.

Prychitko, David L. *Markets, Planning and Democracy*. Cheltenham, UK: Edward Elgar Publishing Limited, 2002.

Ravitch, Diane. *The Great School Wars: A History of the New York City Public Schools*. New York: Basic Books, 1988.

Reidy, Chris. "Pepsi to Help Ocean Spray Get on More Store Shelves." *Boston Globe*, July 14, 2006.

Research and Innovative Technology Administration. Bureau of Transportation Statistics. http://www.TranStats.bts.gov/Data_Elements.aspx?Data=1.

Reventos, Laia. "Software Del Siglo XXI Patentado Con Leyes Del XIX." *El Pais*, November 10, 2009.

Roberts, Keith. *The Origins of Business, Money and Markets*. New York: Columbia University Press, 2011.

Roe, Mark J. "Delaware's Competition." Harvard Law School, Olin Center, October 30, 2002. http://www.law.harvard.edu/programs/corp_gov/papers/Roe_Paper.pdf.

Rosvold, Todd (director, Pulaski Chase Cooperative). Interview with author at convention in November 2009.

Salem Witchcraft Trials, 1692. http://www.law.umkc.edu/faculty/projects/ftrials/salem/SALEM.HTM.

Salutin, Rick. Column in *Globe and Mail* (Toronto), August 25, 2006.

Schivelbusch, Wolfgang. *The Railway Journey*. Berkeley: University of California Press, 1986.

Schrag, Zachary. Interview with author in New York City, December 2003.

Schumpeter, Joseph. *The Theory of Economic Development*. orig. 1934; New Brunswick, NJ: Transaction Books, 1983.

Schwartz, John. "Justices Hear Patent Case on Protecting the Abstract." *New York Times*, November 10, 2009.

Schweber, Howard. *The Creation of American Common Law, 1850–1880: Tech-*

nology, Politics and the Construction of Citizenship. New York: Cambridge University Press, 2004.

Scott, Bruce. *The Concept of Capitalism*. Heidelberg and New York: Springer Verlag, 2009.

Seely, Bruce E. *Building the American Highway System: Engineers as Policy Makers*. Philadelphia: Temple University Press, 1987.

Sengupta, Somini. "As Indian Growth Soars, Child Hunger Persists." *New York Times*, March 13, 2009.

Sheehan, Neil. *A Fiery Peace in a Cold War: Bernard Schriever and the Ultimate Weapon*. New York: Vintage, 2010.

Sheriff, Carol. *The Artificial River: The Erie Canal and the Paradox of Progress, 1817–1862*. New York: Hill & Wang, 1996.

Shiva, Vandana. *Protect or Plunder? Understanding Intellectual Property Rights*. London and New York: Zed Books, 2001.

Siegan, Bernard H. *Property Rights: From Magna Carta to the Fourteenth Amendment*. New Brunswick, NJ: Social Philosophy and Policy Foundation and Transaction Publishers, 2001.

Simpson, David. *The Politics of American English, 1776–1850*. New York: Oxford University Press, 1986.

"Sir Robert Peel." *History of the Metropolitan Police*. Metropolitan Police Service. http://www.met.police.uk/history/peel.htm.

Slaughter, Anne-Marie (dean, Princeton Law School). E-mail exchange with author, February 2008.

Staccioli, Romolo Augusto. *The Roads of the Romans*. Los Angeles: J. Paul Getty Museum, 2003.

Stiglitz, Joseph E. *Globalization and Its Discontents*. New York: Norton, 2002.

———. "Markets, Climate and Katrina." *TomPaine.com*, September 19, 2005. http://www.tompaine.com/print/markets_climate_and_katrina.php.

Stiles, T. J. *The First Tycoon: The Epic Life of Cornelius Vanderbilt*. New York: Knopf, 2009.

"A Survey of the Third World." *Economist*, September 23, 1989.

Swift, Earl. *The Big Roads: The Untold Story of the Engineers, Visionaries, and Trailblazers Who Created the American Superhighways*. Boston: Houghton Mifflin Harcourt, 2011.

———. E-mail exchange with author from July 2011.

Taleb, Nassim Nicholas. *The Black Swan: The Impact of the Highly Improbable*. 2nd ed. New York: Random House, 2010.

"Thaddeus Stevens." Pennsylvania Historical & Museum Commission. http://www.portal.state.pa.us/portal/server.pt/community/people/4277/stevens,_thaddeus/443778.

Trench, Richard, and Ellis Hillman. *London under London: A Subterranean Guide*. London: J. Murray, 1993.

Tushnet, Rebecca. Undated interview with author about patent law.

Uldbjerg, Lee (Land O'Lakes executive and board member of Minnesota Cooperatives). Telephone interview with author, January 29, 2009.

Unger, Roberto Mangabeira. *False Necessity—Anti-Necessitarian Social Theory in the Service of Radical Democracy*. Rev. ed. London: Verso 2004.

————. Interview in with author his office at Harvard Law School, April 13, 2007.

US Government Spending as Percentage of GDP. http://www.usgovernmentspend ing.com/us_20th_century_chart.html.

U.S. Patent and Trademark Office, U.S. Patent Statistics Chart, Calendar Years 1963–2010. http://www.uspto.gov/go/taf/us_stat.htm.

Urofsky, Melvin I. "Proposed Federal Incorporation in the Progressive Era." *American Journal of Legal History* 26, no. 2 (April 1982): 160–183.

Vaughan, Floyd. *United States Patent System: Legal and Economic Conflicts in American Patent History.* Norman: University of Oklahoma Press, 1956.

Waldrop, Mitch. "DARPA and the Internet Revolution." http://www.darpa.mil/ WorkArea/DownloadAsset.aspx?id=2554.

Waley, Daniel. *The Italian City-Republics.* New York: McGraw-Hill, 1969.

"Wang Laboratories." Wikipedia. http://en.wikipedia.org/wiki/Wang_Laboratories.

Weber, Eugen. *My France: Politics, Culture, Myth.* Cambridge, MA: Harvard University Press, 1991.

Weber, Max. *General Economic History.* orig. 1927; New Brunswick, NJ: Transaction Publishers, 1995.

Wilson, Arlene. "The GATT and the WTO: An Overview." Washington, DC: Congressional Research Service, Library of Congress, 1995. http://digital.library.unt .edu/govdocs/crs/permalink/meta-crs-227.

World Bank. *The East Asian Miracle: Economic Growth and Public Policy.* New York: Oxford University Press, 1993.

Wylie, J. C. *The Wastes of Civilization.* London: Faber and Faber, 1959.

Yu-Hung Hong (senior fellow, Lincoln Land Institute). Telephone interview with author about property rights, January 29, 2008.

Zakaria, Fareed. *The Future of Freedom: Illiberal Democracy at Home and Abroad.* New York: Norton, 2003.

**Surprising design of market
economies / by Alex Marshall.**

**HB171 .M333 2012
Gen Stx**

DATE DUE